Youth
and the

Canadian

Criminal

Justice

System

Shahid Alvi
University of St. Thomas

anderson publishing co.
2035 Reading Road
Cincinnati, OH 45202
800-582-7295

EDITOR Ellen S. Boyne
ASSISTANT EDITOR Sharon L. Boyles
ACQUISITIONS EDITOR Michael C. Braswell

Cover digital composition and design: Tin Box Studio, Inc.
Cover photo credit: © Klaus Lahnstein/Tony Stone Images

Photo credits—
p. x   Mike Ridewood/Associated Press CP
p. 40   David Lazarowych/CP CGYH
p. 74   Karsten Thielker/Associated Press AP
p. 120 Daniel Hulshizer/Associated Press AP
p. 146 Chuck Robinson/Associated Press AP

Youth and the Canadian Criminal Justice System

Copyright © 2000
       Anderson Publishing Co.
       2035 Reading Rd.
       Cincinnati, OH 45202

    Phone 800.582.7295 or 513.421.4142
  Web Site www.andersonpublishing.com

Library of Congress Cataloging-in-Publication Data

Alvi, Shahid.
    Youth and the Canadian criminal justice system / Shahid Alvi.
       p.   cm.
    Includes bibliographical references and index.
    ISBN 0-87084-891-7 (pbk.)
    1. Juvenile delinquency--Canada. 2. Juvenile delinquents--Canada. 3. Juvenile corrections--Canada.
    4. Juvenile justice, Administration of--Canada I. Title.
    HV9108.A58   1999
    364.36'0971--dc21   99-43544
                                           CIP

Statistics Canada information is used with the permission of the Minister of Industry, as Minister responsible for Statistics Canada. Information on the availability of the wide range of data from Statistics Canada can be obtained from Statistics Canada's Regional Offices, its World Wide Web site at http://www.statcan.ca and its toll-free access number 1-800-263-1136.

Dedication

For my wonderful parents, Zaheer and Gaiti Alvi.

Acknowledgments

I would like to thank Michael Braswell and Susan Braswell at Anderson Publishing Co. for their interest in publishing this book. Special thanks go to my editor, Ellen Boyne, who matched consummate professionalism with extraordinary patience.

This book benefited from the input of many individuals. Special thanks go to Walter DeKeseredy for his many helpful suggestions before and during the writing process. Portions of this book were written as I was teaching a course on criminal justice and youth crime at Carleton University. Shelley-Anne Steinburg, Jennifer Tufts, and Cathy Graham were outstanding students in that class who provided me with excellent feedback on various chapters and kept me honest in the classroom.

I also had the great pleasure and benefit of working with Susan Richter, who provided extensive and meticulous research support, particularly in panicked moments. Thanks, Sue.

Finally, and most importantly, I would like to thank my family, Pamela, Megan, and Erin, for their love and support. And yes, girls, we can go to the park now.

Table of Contents

Mourners arrive to pay tribute to Jason Lang, who was shot dead at an Alberta high school. A 14-year-old boy was charged with the murder. Dramatic and unusual incidents such as this grab media attention and contribute to the myth that youth crime in Canada has increased and is out of control.

Chapter One

Youth Crime in Context

Frank and Jocelyn Toope murdered by three boys 13 to 15 (Montreal Gazette, April 1, 1995)

Teenage boy convicted of killing Ryan Garrioch (Calgary Herald, February 2, 1995: B1)

Three 14-year-old girls charged with the murder of Kulwarn Dhiman (Montreal Gazette, July 12, 1995: A10)

Five teens accused of beating murder of Trygue Magnusson, "The Gentle Giant." (The Globe and Mail, July 17, 1995: A4)

Teenager Jody Larson is stabbed to death by group of teens over an insulting remark (Montreal Gazette, April 2, 1995: D7)

Six teens accused in beating death of transient James Baldwin (Montreal Gazette, May 1, 1995: A9)

An adolescent girl is charged in the drive-by shooting death of Joseph Spence (Winnipeg Free Press, August 26, 1995: A16)

Ishmael Spence, 15, stabbed to death in the subway. A 15-year-old boy is charged with the murder (Toronto Star, January 14, 1996: A14)

A 16-year-old girl is convicted in the stabbing death of Brian Harris Baylen (Toronto Star, January 30, 1995: A18)

Seven teens accused in torture killing of Sylvain Leduc (Montreal Gazette, October 28, 1995: A13) (from Canada, National Longitudinal Survey of Children and Youth, 1996: 134)

INTRODUCTION

Headlines like the ones at the beginning of this chapter add fuel to the perception that many of today's youth are out of control. Such public panic over the problem of youth crime seems to be driving political interest in reforming the *Young Offenders Act* (YOA) (Schissel, 1997). Many people assume that the only way to deal with the apparent "epidemic" of youth crime is to get tougher on young offenders by imposing longer and stiffer sentences, transferring more youths to adult court, publicly disclosing the names of young offenders, lowering the age at which young people should come under the auspices of the Act, fining the parents of children who have run afoul of the law, and even repealing the law altogether (Bala, 1996).

The "get tough on youth crime" and anti-YOA rhetoric that dominates current public and political discourse is somewhat ironic, because at one time the YOA was widely regarded as ushering in a new era of juvenile justice. It was thought that the Act's emphasis on due process, accountability and alternatives to processing in the traditional criminal justice system signaled a more humane and progressive approach to youth in conflict with the law. The new Act, which came into force in 1984, was seen as a significant improvement over its predecessor, the Juvenile Delinquents Act of 1908 (JDA), which was criticized by many as being too lenient, arbitrary, and paternalistic. As the Canadian criminal justice system moves into a new century, however, differences between the two Acts that were once apparently clear have become murky and the subject of considerable controversy. It appears as if no one can really agree on the nature and causes of youth crime, and what is to be done about it.

This book takes a sociological stance on key debates about the causes and consequences of youth crime in Canada. Throughout this text, I have attempted to link these controversies to their socioeconomic, cultural, and political contexts. In many ways, the book raises as many questions as it answers, because much of what we think we know about youth crime continues to be open to theoretical and empirical debate. For example, consider whether there are simple answers to questions such as:

- How much youth crime is there?
- What kinds of youth are most likely to offend?
- Is youth crime really out of control?
- Are youth becoming more violent?
- Should we get tougher on young offenders?
- Are the causes of youth crime to be linked to bad parenting, or poverty, or impulsiveness?
- Is the Young Offenders Act too lenient?

Answering such questions requires an understanding of the characteristics of youth crime, some evaluation of the usefulness of theories that attempt to explain youth crime, and an assessment of the effectiveness of public responses to crime. To assume that such tasks can be approached without examining the societal context in which youth live is to neglect a central truth of human life: people are shaped by the social conditions in which they live and the people they encounter in those contexts. In this chapter we will concentrate on the social and legal context in which youth exist. We will also explore some basic definitions of youth and crime and the role of the media in our perceptions of the so-called youth crime problem. We will begin by examining the social and economic environment that conditions the status of Canadian youth.

THE STATUS OF CANADIAN YOUTH

People do not exist in a vacuum. Our social environment *conditions* our behaviour by setting limits on our life chances. Put differently, not everyone is born into the same social circumstances, and this inequality of condition sets the boundaries within which people make their lives. If we are to understand the status and behaviour, "good or bad," of Canada's youth, we must take account of their social circumstances. This section provides an overview of some key economic and social factors affecting young people's lives.

Youth, Families, and the Economy

As this book emphasizes sociological approaches to understanding youth crime, we will focus on social-structural issues such as unemployment and poverty, the parts they play in conditioning young people's lives and their implications for youth crime. However, the sociological approach advocated here does not only consider such macro level forces; we must also pay attention to the role of smaller social groups such as families and subcultures in both creating and containing youth crime. What, then, is modern family and economic life like for Canada's youth?

In this book, we take a perspective on the family that emphasizes its functions—what families do for their members. According to the Vanier Institute of the Family (1994: 10), these functions are:

- Physical maintenance and care of group members
- Addition of new members through procreation or adoption
- Socialization of children

- Social control of members

- Production, consumption, and distribution of goods and services, and

- Affective nurturance—love

The ability of families to perform most of these functions depends greatly on the economic resources they hold. Given a long-standing interest in sociology in the relationship between economic conditions and crime (Becker, 1968; Bonger, 1916; Britt, 1994; Cohen, 1981; Cohen, Kluegel, and Land, 1981; MacLean, 1986), in this section, we concentrate on the experiences of children and their families in relation to today's economy.

Children are poor because their families are poor. When families are economically disadvantaged, their children face reduced opportunities to participate in "legitimate" everyday life. Canada has witnessed steadily escalating levels of poverty for many children (see Table 1.1), due in part to the difficulties faced by many single parents and continuing economic instability in the country. Economic instability not only creates under- and unemployment; it has also forced many people to work at two or more jobs, and to work harder and faster, for less pay, and diminished or nonexistent benefits. Thus, while some people are "treading water," economically speaking, many others end up falling through the cracks of the economic system, creating higher rates of family stress, poverty, disenfranchisement, resentment, and bitterness.

Table 1.1
Incidence of Child Poverty by Province, Canada, 1990-1996

	Year						
	1990	1991	1992	1993	1994	1995	1996
Province	Incidence (%)						
Atlantic Provinces	8.3	19.9	19.9	20.6	20.1	23.1	21.2
Newfoundland	20.8	20.6	26.8	21.8	23.4	26.2	20.2
PEI	14	15.6	12.7	11.4	13.3	14.2	18.5
Nova Scotia	16.8	20.6	19.4	23.4	20.5	21.5	23.5
New Brunswick	18.6	19.2	15.9	18	18.3	24.4	19.8
Québec	19.5	20.4	19.3	21.4	19.8	22.6	22
Ontario	14.8	17.3	16.3	20.8	18.1	19.1	20.3
Prairie Provinces	21.1	22.4	24.3	22.7	20.4	22.1	22.3
Manitoba	24	30.9	24.2	26.1	22.8	23.2	26.6
Saskatchewan	21.8	22.4	24	24.8	22.9	21.8	22.3
Alberta	19.8	19.2	24.5	20.6	18.5	21.7	20.7
British Columbia	17.6	14.4	19.3	21.5	21.2	20.8	20.2
Canada	17.8	18.9	19.2	21.3	19.5	21	21.1

Source: Prepared by the Centre for International Statistics at the Canadian Council on Social Development, using data from Statistics Canada, Cat. 13-569-XPB. Reprinted with permission.

Note: Children under 18 years of age. Based on Statistics Canada's Low-income Cut-offs, 1992 base.

If children's parents are having difficulty finding and keeping meaningful, well-paying work, the same can be said for young people of working age. According to the Canadian Council for Policy Alternatives, "labour market conditions for Canada's young people are the worst since the Great Depression." Between 1984 and 1994, the real median income of young people fell by 23 percent, and the unemployment rate among youths aged 15 to 24 has consistently been double the rates for adults (Rehnby and McBride, 1997). Between 1989 and 1996, the proportion of 16-year-olds who had never had a job increased from 26 to 58 percent (Canadian Council on Social Development, 1999). At the same time, the average young person in Canada earned less in 1997 than in the 1980s, reflecting a shift in the nature of work toward low-paying, part-time jobs as food servers and store clerks (Canadian Council on Social Development, 1997). Further, the participation of young people in the labour market has dropped by more than 10 percent in the 1990s, and the gap between the youth and overall employment rates continues to grow.

Market-oriented societies increasingly require technical skills and expertise, yet young people are being forced into a "prolonged state of social marginality" (Petersen and Mortimer, 1994). In effect, although employment during adolescence could provide significant experiences for growth into later work roles, as well as a sense of belonging to the conventional social order, for some time now Canadian society has been unable to provide many youths with meaningful work experiences.

Ironically, though youth unemployment is high, Canadian society places tremendous pressure on youths to consume goods and services that they may not be able to afford. As Caston (1998) points out, along with the family and schools, advertising is one of the most important agents of socialization in our society, and thus fosters:

> . . . a market orientation by depicting consumption as an end in itself and as a measure of social status and human value. Whether it is hawking overpriced designer jeans and underwear, prescription drugs, credit cards, or any one of tens of thousands of other products and services, advertising's messages to us are "be a consumer," "spend it now," "live for today," "your worth is measured by the name brands you buy." (1998: 248)

Families also look very different than they did four decades ago. The main family form between the early 1900s and the 1950s was what is sometimes called the "traditional nuclear" family, consisting of a mother at home, a working father and usually two or more children. As we shall see, although some people want to return to the days when this family was seen as the norm, it would be wrong to suggest that such family structures are in any sense "normal," given that change is constant, and that the life of a tradition is relatively short. For example, today, nearly one-quarter of families are blended (consisting of parents, children and other relatives from different families, usually brought together through remarriage), extended (made up of parents and their children as well as other relatives such as aunts, uncles or grandparents all living under the same roof), or consist of single parents with children (see Table 1.2).

Table 1.2
Distribution of Children Aged 0 to 11 by Family Type, 1994-1995

Family Type	Percent
Both biological parents	78.7
One biological and one step-parent	4.3
Other two-parent families	1.2
Children with a single female parent	14.6
Children with a single male parent	1.1
Children not with a parent	Less than 1

Source: Adapted from Canada, National Longitudinal Survey of Children and Youth, 1996:29

In addition, nearly one-half (45 percent) of all two-parent families in Canada have two incomes (Canadian Council on Social Development, 1997). Yet, despite the fact that two people are working in these family units, most have very little economic security compared to the families of 20 years ago because real incomes (income in constant dollars) have remained constant since the mid-1980s (see Table 1.3). In other words, many families require two working parents to maintain the standard of living they would have enjoyed nearly 20 years ago.

Other factors have contributed to changes in the nature of families. Divorce rates have risen dramatically in Canada since the country liberalized its divorce laws in the 1960s. This is not to say that divorced parents are any less likely to provide a loving, nurturing environment in which children can grow up. However, divorce does have some important implications for family life. For instance, research in both Canada and the United States has consistently shown that women fare far worse economically than men after divorce and that, in fact, the economic status of males after divorce actually improves (Finnie, 1993; Smock, 1993, 1994). Thus, the experience of divorce is economically gendered. Another consequence of the unequal experience of divorce is that many single-parent, female-headed families experience high rates of poverty (Casper, McLanahan, and Garfinkel, 1994). In fact, 97 percent of single-parent families in which the mother is unemployed are classified as low-income in Canada (Canadian Centre for Justice Statistics, 1998: 57). This means

Table 1.3
Average Incomes of Families in Canada, 1951-1995 (In 1995 Dollars)

Year	Income	Year	Income
1951	22,401.00	1980	55,061.00
1954	25,701.00	1981	54,214.00
1957	27,552.00	1982	52,869.00
1959	28,334.00	1983	52,304.00
1961	29,748.00	1984	52,135.00
1965	33,987.00	1985	53,472.00
1967	36,823.00	1986	54,462.00
1969	39,756.00	1987	55,153.00
1971	43,437.00	1988	56,366.00
1972	45,200.00	1989	58,024.00
1973	47,231.00	1990	57,133.00
1974	49,668.00	1991	55,771.00
1975	50,208.00	1992	55,465.00
1976	53,434.00	1993	54,325.00
1977	52,340.00	1994	55,342.00
1978	53,583.00	1995	55,247.00
1979	53,989.00		

Source: Statistics Canada, Income Distributions by Size in Canada, 1995.

that both the children and female parents in such families are disadvantaged compared to most dual-income or two-parent families. Indeed, according to Eshlemen (1997: 241):

> Single parent families are characterized by a high rate of poverty, a high percentage of minority representation, more dependents, relatively low education, and a high rate of mobility . . . psychologically, single parents are more depressed, are more anxious, have poorer self images, and are less satisfied with their lives.

Recent data from an ongoing national survey of young people in Canada indicate that many children from poor, single-mother families suffer a range of problems, many of which are linked to deviant behaviour (see Table 1.4). The important point here is that while such problems occur in high- *and* low-income families, it is the most disadvantaged families that seem to experience them the most. This does *not* mean however, that criminal or deviant behaviour is a property of the "lower classes" as some commentators seem to think (see DeKeseredy and Schwartz, 1996 for an elaboration and critique of this argument).

Table 1.4
Rates of Problems for Children From Single-Mother Families Compared with Those of Children From Two-Parent Families, by Income

| Type of problem | Rates of problems by income (%) | | | |
| | Low Income | | Not Low income | |
	Single Mother	Two parent	Single mother	Two parent
Hyperactivity	16.7	9.6	13.7	9.6
Conduct Disorder	19.2	9.2	13.2	7.9
Emotional Disorder	16.7	8.6	11.6	7.3
One or more behaviour problems	33.5	21.0	27.9	18.3
Repeated a grade	12.5	7.9	9.1	4.1
Social impairment	7.4	4.6	3.8	2.1
One or more total problems[a]	43.5	28.9	35.8	22.6

Source: Adapted from Canada, National Longitudinal Survey of Children and Youth, 1996: 88.

[a] Data available for 6-to 11-year-old children only. All other variables use data from 4- to 11-year-old children.

It might seem obvious that children are adversely affected by divorce. However, there is some controversy over this view. It is true that divorce has negative economic and social consequences for children. For instance, as Eshleman (1997) points out, adolescents from divorced homes are less likely to graduate from high school, they have a lower probability of ever marrying, and have greater chances of getting divorced themselves. In addition, there is some evidence to suggest that children from such homes are more likely to commit crime, and to experience problems in relating to peers (Wells and Rankin, 1991). What is uncertain is the extent to which such problems actually come from the relationships between family members *during* the marriage. It may be, then, that parental conflict, abuse, or persistent economic stress may actually be the factors that influence children in negative ways, and not the actual strain of divorce and separation itself.

Regardless of the implications of such debates, it is clear that many Canadian youths are today more likely to grow up in single-parent, female-headed homes than their predecessors a generation ago. These family circumstances place them at some risk of experiencing poverty and a host of other social pathologies, including criminality. To be sure, there are also young people in Canada who do not experience such deprivation, and whose paths to higher social and economic status seem less littered with obstacles. As we shall see, however, although criminal behaviour cuts across income levels, poor youth are significantly more "at risk" of encountering the criminal justice process (Bartollas, 1997).

Education

As numerous studies have pointed out, the young person's experience of school is an important factor in understanding youth crime (Bartollas, 1997). According to the Canadian Centre for Justice Statistics, "lack of attachment to school is a significant risk factor in youth crime," primarily because such individuals are more likely to experience underemployment or unemployment, and are more likely to become involved with high-risk behaviours such as regular alcohol or drug use. About one in five (18 percent) of youths between ages 18 and 20 left school without graduating in 1991 for a variety of reasons, including boredom, the perception that school rules are too stringent, associating with peers who attach little value to education, and (for many teenage girls) pregnancy (1998: 58).

However, most Canadian children go to school, do reasonably well there, and go on to attend institutions of higher education. In 1994, there were 5.5 million students in elementary and high schools—almost 100 percent enrollment. Canada also has one of the highest enrollments in post-secondary institutions among industrialized countries. In 1994, there were 1.5 million students (53 percent of youths aged 18 to 24) enrolled in colleges, technical institutes, or universities on a part-time or full-time basis. Still, the education system is changing. Consider the following facts from the Canadian Council on Social Development (1996).

- Recent provincial cutbacks mean that many parents of elementary and secondary school students must now pay user fees for activities that were previously free, including cultural and sporting activities and special services such as speech therapy.

- At the post-secondary level, tuition fees are rising; 50 percent of post-secondary students require government loans to finance their education.

- Funding for kindergarten programs is being cut across Canada. Fewer children have access to high-quality preschool programs.

These data illustrate the changing nature of the Canadian educational system. They are important because of the positive association between education and the type of job one can expect to hold in adulthood. In addition, however, it is clear that poorer children are the ones who will most be affected by some of the recent shifts described above. For instance, we know that poverty negatively affects family functioning and children's school results. Data from the 1994 National Longitudinal Survey of Children and Youth indicates "that rates of family dysfunction and parental depression are higher in poor families than in more afflu-ent families, and that poor children do not have the same scholastic and verbal skills entering school as their non-poor peers." (Canadian Coun-cil on Social Development, 1997: 1).

Summary

A young person's position in the social and economic world affects all aspects of his or life. A central idea in sociological criminology has been the idea that the social and economic environment affects both why crimes occur and how we react to them (Cohen, 1980; Sutherland, 1947). Moreover, common sense suggests that factors such as depriva-tion, poor school performance and family dysfunction are related to youth crime. As we will see later in this book, however, the exact rela-tionship between a person's standing in the social world and their propensity to commit crime is both complex and controversial. Rather than providing an assessment of this relationship, this section has pro-vided an overview of some important socioeconomic aspects of the world in which youth live. In doing so, we have shown that a significant number of Canadian youth live in relatively disadvantaged and uncer-tain conditions. We now turn to an examination of problems surround-ing definitions of young people and crime itself.

THINKING CRITICALLY ABOUT "YOUTH" AND "YOUTH CRIME"

Defining what constitutes a young offender seems on the surface to be a relatively simple task. Most of us believe that there is nothing inher-ently difficult about defining what it is to be "young," and what it means to "offend," and that therefore, a young offender is simply a person between the ages of 12 and 17 who has broken a law. This is precisely how young offenders are defined when we use conventional *legalistic def-initions* of youth crime. Box 1.1 provides a list of such official definitions because these are the ones we will work with in this book. However, the definitions are not necessarily straightforward. In fact, if you spend a bit of time contemplating the meaning of the words "youth" and "crime," you may well begin to question whether there are any solid yardsticks we can use to answer the question "what is a young offender?"

Think of the implications of the word "young" for a moment. Though I am approaching what some call "middle age," a friend of mine is fond of consoling me by asking "how old would you be if you didn't know how old you are?" His question prompts us to ask whether being young is a matter of how old we *think* we ought to act (you're as young as you feel) or whether it is simply a case of somehow objectively deciding that people who are say, under 18, are to be defined as "young." Indeed, the issue of defining the "young person" is intimately related to the expectations we have of youth, and the consequences they may face when they do not meet these expectations. Given that expectations tend to change over time, it is not surprising, then, that the concepts of "childhood," "adolescence" and "young persons" have meant different things at different times (Caputo and Goldenberg, 1986; Currie, 1986).

Box 1.1

Legalistic Definitions of Youth Crime: Criminal Code and Federal Statute Offences

Criminal Code Offences

Violent Offences: homicide, assault, sexual assault, and robbery. Violent offences involve the use or threatened use of violence against a person. Robbery is considered a violent offence because unlike other theft offences, it involves the use or threat of violence. Assault can be *common assault,* considered to be the "least serious" of assaults, including such acts as pushing, slapping, punching, and face-to-face verbal threats; and *major assault,* which includes "more serious" forms of assault such as assault with a weapon or causing bodily harm, and *aggravated assault*, which includes acts that wound, maim, disfigure, or endanger the life of someone.

Property Offences: include break and enter theft of goods over $5000 or under $5000, possession of stolen property and fraud. Property offences involve unlawful acts to gain property, but do not involve the use or threat of violence against a person.

Other Criminal Code Offences: include prostitution, weapons offences, and failure to appear in court.

Other Federal Statutes

Drug Offences: include offences for the possession, trafficking, importation, and production of illegal drugs. The relevant federal status are the *Controlled Drugs and Substances Act* (which came into force in May 1997), and previous legislation, the *Narcotic Control Act* and the *Food and Drugs Act.*

Young Offenders Act: *The Young Offenders Act* (YOA) is primarily concerned with the process for dealing with youths accused of crime. Youths can, however, be charged under the act, usually for failing to comply with court orders.

Other federal statutes: include all other federal statutes, such as the *Income Tax Act* and the *Immigration Act.* When not presented separately, drug and YOA offences are included with other federal statutes.

Source: Adapted from Canadian Centre for Justice Statistics, 1998: 21.

There are important legal issues associated with the definition of youth. Think about the consequences of recent proposals to change the minimum age for which youth should be tried under the YOA from 12 to 10. At what age can we reasonably expect that young people will understand the consequences of their actions? To what extent can youth be said to understand their legal rights and obligations? At what point can we reasonably compare the knowledge and "morality" of a young person to that of an adult? Clearly, these are not easy questions (Peterson-Badali, Abramovitch, and Duda, 1997). In fact, according to Morse (1998), it is unlikely that the social and behavioural sciences or even "common sense" can provide us with a clear idea of what differentiates between adult and youth responsibility.

Similarly, consider the question, "what is an offence?" Is an offence *only* something that occurs when one breaks the law? You may think that this is the obvious answer, but in fact, this issue has been hotly debated by many criminologists who argue that although certain acts (such as verbal and psychological abuse, or corporate wrongdoing) are not strictly against the law, they do cause harm and should be viewed as criminal acts (Elias, 1986; Schwendinger and Schwendinger, 1975).

The same logic also works the other way. For instance, some students of crime maintain that several violations of the criminal code *should not* be treated as crimes because they do not victimize anyone but the perpetrator. A good example of such an act is the possession or use of cannabis, a drug that is illegal in Canada despite much evidence that it is essentially harmless in comparison to the huge damage caused by alcohol or tobacco, both of which are restricted for youth but legal. Thus, although certain acts are violations of the Canadian Criminal Code, whether these acts should be included in the Code is open to debate.

Hence, the concept of "young offender" is contentious. This is an important point because, as we shall see later in this chapter, definitions of youth and crime have changed over the past 100 years. As commentators such as Schissel (1993) have argued, the ways in which we have treated youths in conflict with the law have generally depended on our perspectives on the nature and value of youth in our society. For instance, about 100 years ago, Canada was a developing country that needed cheap labour to help move the nation from an agricultural to industrial economic base. Our view of youths at that time was that they, among other groups, could be counted on to provide the labour needed to build such an economy.

Therefore, it was necessary to make youths work. As the economy developed and new skills were required, it was important to educate youths so they could take their place in the economy. When youths were not at work or at school, they were considered to be "disrespecting" the norms and values of society at that time. It is not surprising, then, that there were laws prohibiting vagrancy and idleness that were used to channel young people into particular behaviours deemed acceptable and "normal" to the public.

The concepts of "youth" and "criminal behaviour" have never been written in stone and have shifted according to different social norms. This is significant, because it is in the notion of *norm violation* that we can find a provisional answer to the questions of what is a youth and what is a crime. As Trojanowicz (1978) points out, the answers to such questions depend upon the norms or *social criteria* by which deviant behaviour can be identified. Norms are not eternal, nor do we necessarily always agree on what they should be. Norms change to reflect economic, social, cultural and political realities in society. Accordingly, what may have been seen as "normal" behaviour 25 years ago might well be perceived as "deviant" today and vice versa. Common sense would suggest, then, that the law must reflect shifting norms and cannot be a self-contained, fixed system. As the jurist Oliver Wendall Holmes pointed out more than a century ago, "the life of the law has not been logic, it has been experience" (Brockman and Rose, 1996:7).

Regardless of which side we take in discussions about the appropriate age of a youth or the types of crime that should be considered harmful, one thing is clear; definitions of a young offender are "social constructions," subject to different interpretations of the role of youth in society and the social conditions that shape those interpretations.

If these definitions are a matter of interpretation, then the same can be said for answers to the question of what is to be done about youth crime. The debate over solutions to the problem of youth crime is covered more extensively in Chapter Five, but most ideas on what to do about it are centered on one of two central assumptions about the causes of crime. First, there is the idea that crime is a *social process*, which builds on the basic idea that the experiences of youth in Canada do not occur in a social, legal, political or economic vacuum. Criminal acts and our responses to crime are embedded in a social and economic context, and therefore we cannot understand crime without some knowledge of these broader social conditions and processes.

Second, there are those who take the position that crime is a *property of the individual*. For these thinkers, crime is a "personal choice," in which case the social response to crime should reflect the idea that those who have made the wrong choice only have themselves to blame, and must take personal responsibility for their actions. For others in this camp, crime is a function of biological or psychological problems, which means that the solution entails "treating" the individual.

In Chapter Three, we will examine a number of theories falling within these two general categories of thought on the causes of youth crime. It must be remembered that academics and practitioners remain deeply divided over the causes of crime. Indeed, though criminology has made important advances in the past 100 years, there remains much work to be done in determining the causes and correlates of criminal behaviour. In the meantime, of course, society must respond to youth crime in some way—there must be criminal justice policy, and one would hope that our policy responses would reflect what we *do* know about criminal behaviour among youths. Having examined some of the more important aspects of the social and economic environment in which youths live, we now turn to an examination of the legal context.

THINKING CRITICALLY ABOUT CRIMINAL JUSTICE POLICY

When I was an undergraduate student, I once made a comment in a criminology class to the effect that punishment would be more effective if we created stiffer sentences for offenders. I really had no clue about the data on punishment and the problems of defining "effectiveness" (probably because I had not read the required readings for that week), but I made the comment anyway. My professor proceeded to discuss the findings of numerous studies showing that, in fact, punishment, as we have used it in the criminal justice system in Canada and elsewhere, does not work very well at all. He concluded his lecture by sarcastically remarking that perhaps one should "never let a little data spoil a good theory." His point was that despite ample evidence regarding what works and what does not work with respect to crime, we continue to implement criminal justice policies reflecting "false" knowledge. We are often uncomfortable when the facts seem to challenge what we think we know about crime and so we soldier on with our misconceptions.

Despite people's reluctance to accept the facts about crime, we might assume that people in our society are somewhat rational. If this is the case, then coordinated, effective, and responsible criminal justice policies *should* reflect the current state of knowledge about the issues they purport to concern. However, as much of this book points out, what we know and what we do about criminal behaviour are often at odds. There is no simple, linear relationship between theory and empirical evidence about the causes of crime, what works in dealing with crime, and the criminal justice policies created by the state.

Where Does Law Come From? Two Models

We can better understand the troubled relationship between research on crime and criminal justice policy by briefly considering two different perspectives on the sources of criminal justice policy and law in modern societies. The first model is the *value consensus approach*. Proponents of this theory claim that although many groups in society compete with one another for the attention of state administrators and managers, in general most people agree that certain acts are nearly universally condemnable (crimes *mala in se*, or wrong in themselves), or are wrong because they have been prohibited by law (crimes *mala prohibita*). The value consensus approach contends that in a liberal democracy like Canada, no one group has any more power than another to have their views heard and implemented by governments of the day. In effect, the state is seen as a "neutral arbitrator" that democratically mediates competing claims regarding what ought to be done about youth crime or any other issue. For these theorists, the state reflects the collective interests of the majority.

The second model assumes the viewpoint of *conflict theorists* who maintain that many groups in society enjoy greater power and hence greater capacity than others to have their views and goals implemented by the state. This group of theorists argues that Canada (and most other nations) do not have a "level playing field" in which all members of society have equal say in how things get done. They point to the fact that men have more power than women, for example, and that the very wealthy have more power than the middle class or poor. Accordingly, they suggest that such power imbalances often lead to policies that disproportionately reflect the goals, objectives, and beliefs of those who hold the upper hand. They further point out that the basic idea of unequal power relationships helps us to understand why certain criminal justice policies receive more attention than others, despite the existence of evidence that calls such policies into question. For instance, we may have plenty of evidence to support the idea that building more youth detention centres, sending delinquent youths to boot camps, or toughening sentencing provisions in the Young Offenders Act will *not* reduce the youth crime rate. However, such strategies are often *politically* attractive for politicians who aspire to reelection or who wish to support the goals and objectives of the powerful. At the same time, by taking a "tough" stand on crime, policymakers can create the illusion of responsiveness to public demand by preying on the public's deep-seated fear of the specter of "young, out-of-control, urban, toughs." In this way, then, the conflict theorists suggest that crime control policies are often implemented regardless of the evidence.

The extent to which either of these two perspectives is correct is a matter of empirical evidence, and cannot be discussed in detail here. Nevertheless, recent scholarship strongly suggests that although policy should reflect the realities of crime, in Canada current public perceptions of crime reflect mild hysteria over a "violent youth crime epidemic" despite any real evidence that such an epidemic exists (Jenson and Howard, 1998). In Chapter Two we will explore in more detail what we know about levels of youth crime. In the next section we will examine a central reason for why many Canadians have come to believe that youth crime is out of control: the media.

YOUTH CRIME, THE MEDIA, AND OTHER "MYTH MAKERS"

Many groups play an important role in constructing the public's understanding of youth crime. For instance, governments, law enforcement officials, reform groups, political parties, and the media all engage in making images of young offenders, the nature of the criminal acts they commit, and the responses to these acts.

Of all these actors, however, the media is by far the most powerful and influential. Indeed, some commentators argue that public perceptions of the criminal justice system are coloured by the media (Kappeler, Blumberg, and Potter, 1996). Some maintain that the media is the *main* source of false public perceptions regarding crime and the functions of the criminal justice system. It is not unusual to see stories in newspapers, magazines, television, and radio proclaiming that "youth crime is out of control," that "youth are increasingly violent," or that "we are far too soft on youth crime" (see Box 1.2).

Despite the fact that headlines and "news nuggets" like these are often unclear, biased, or factually incorrect, they have very real consequences. For example, many have argued that sensational and oversimplified portrayals of crime in the media contribute to increased fear of crime, desensitization to real-life violence, and aggressive behaviour. Thus, although the fear of youth crime may be completely unjustified, it is certainly the case that fear can drive political agendas to "get tough on crime" by strengthening legislation, increasing policing, or tinkering with various other elements of the criminal justice system. Moreover, notwithstanding that there are some important problems with official statistics on crime, it seems clear that crime rates have gone down. Nevertheless, according to a poll conducted by the Angus Reid Group in 1994, one-third of Canadians "identified fear of victimization and worries about personal property as some of the most pressing community concerns"(Justice Canada, 1998: 1).

To understand why the media is so important to our perceptions of youth crime we must accept that the media itself does not exist in a vacuum. Indeed, media accounts are often the only source of information on crime available to the public, and as a result, the media often determines what news events are considered to be significant (Hall et al., 1978). Those responsible for writing news stories in various types of media are neither neutral nor necessarily interested in telling the public "the facts" about youth crime, or in presenting balanced accounts. They are more interested in selling newspapers and radio and television advertising (Bohm, 1986; Tunnell, 1992a).

Box 1.2

'Tougher' Youth Crime Law Needed

Gordon Kent
Edmonton Journal
June 19, 1997
Journal Staff Writer

EDMONTON—The blind fury sparked by Barb Danelesko's murder three years ago has cooled, but people are still angry at the Young Offenders Act, says one of her neighbours. "It's struck a chord with every citizen," said Caroline Balisky. "We want to be safe, we want our kids to be safe . . . that has been taken away from us." She helped put together a petition calling for tougher sentences in youth court and naming of serious offenders, after Danelesko was stabbed to death during a 1994 break-in by two 16-year-old boys and one 15-year-old boy.

Balisky and her husband Kim took the 64,000-name petition to Ottawa in 1995 and lobbied MPs to change the law. More than 4,000 people also attended a rally in Edmonton. Although the Young Offenders Act has since been amended, she isn't satisfied. Young murderers can still get out of prison on parole too soon—within seven years—and the act doesn't stop even minor criminals, she said. "I think overall it needs to be tougher because I think that would be a deterrent," said Balisky, who is no longer publicly involved in the issue. "Without a deterrent, they start with stealing the car or stealing the chocolate bar and go on to bigger things."

In April, the Commons justice committee recommended amending the act, including allowing children as young as 10 to face court in some circumstances and letting judges order the naming of some offenders.

Pierre Gratton, spokesperson for Justice Minister Anne McLellan, said from Ottawa the minister is studying what action she might take on the issue. "It is clear the Young Offenders Act is a priority. It's something she's looking at closely."

But Edmonton lawyer Jim Robb cringes at the emphasis many people place on harsher sentences. Canada already has the world's second-highest rate of incarceration for young offenders, behind the United States, despite evidence that it doesn't solve anything. "There is a huge perception out there that the act is soft, which isn't true . . . it's almost an unquenchable thirst—it's just one of those hot buttons."

Robb, senior counsel in the Legal Aid Youth Office, doesn't see any benefit to the repeated amendments made to tighten the Young Offenders Act since its introduction in 1984. He wants more emphasis on dealing with the causes of crime. Such programs as anger management courses and drug and alcohol treatment are successful in keeping young offenders from breaking the law again, he said. But money for these programs is drying up, meaning Edmonton street kids have to wait 18 months for sex-abuse counselling, he said. "When you have a kid who has been on cocaine since they were 10 or 11 and there has been no intervention at all . . . I would fall over dead if I didn't see the kid in youth court."

Source: *Edmonton Journal* (June 19, 1997). Reprinted with permission.

Thus, to increase the chances that potential consumers will watch, listen to, or read news stories, the media are driven to create sensationalized accounts of youth crime. Although there are not many Canadian studies of the media and crime, those that have been conducted have shown overwhelmingly that media accounts of youth crime vastly exaggerate both the nature and scope of the problem. Sprott (1996), for example, sampled three major Toronto newspapers for stories of youth crime and found that 94 percent of youth crime stories involved violent offences. However, less than one-fourth of youth court cases in Ontario actually involved violence. As we shall see in Chapter Two, the vast majority of crimes committed by youths are nonviolent.

To summarize, public perceptions of youth crime are in large part driven by media accounts that sensationalize and often exaggerate both the nature and amount of crimes committed by youths. Often, such accounts advance themes like "youth crime is out of control," or paint pictures of "increasingly violent youth offenders," despite the fact that the accuracy of these statements is highly debatable. Moreover, historically, youths have been punished via the criminal justice system for a range of behaviours quite outside of violent offences. To understand the extent to which societal reaction to youth crime is related to changing perceptions of the role of children in society, we must employ a historical perspective. In the next section, then, we examine changing perceptions of youth in Canada, as well as the objectives of the two most important pieces of legislation directed at youth crime in Canada: the *Juvenile Delinquents Act* (1908) and the *Young Offenders Act* (1984).

JUVENILE DELINQUENCY, YOUNG OFFENDERS, AND BEYOND: FROM THE JDA TO THE YOA TO THE YCJA

Just as young people are affected by the social and economic conditions in which they live, so too are they affected by the laws and criminal justice policies that exist at any given time. Put differently, the ways in which we act both informally (in everyday life) and formally (legally) toward laws and policies at any given time depends greatly on the norms, values, and political and economic conditions that exist at that time. This section provides an overview of justice for Canadian youths by providing a historical analysis of both the context and content of the Juvenile Delinquents Act (1908) and the Young Offenders Act (1984). It does so by addressing the following questions:

- What has been the changing role of youths in Canada during this century?

- How have we responded, as a society, to our perceptions of the role of youths?

- What are the key principles by which we can understand the changing nature of criminal justice policy for youths?

Youth Crime and the Creation of the Juvenile Delinquents Act

The children of the earliest Canadian pioneers were considered assets. They were treasured and valued by their parents and the community, and were even indulged. However, their situation changed with the gradual influx of immigrant European children between the late seventeenth and nineteenth centuries. These often parentless children came to fulfill the function of serving the rich or providing cheap labour as field workers or for an emerging class of industrializing entrepreneurs. As many of them were also considered to be "homeless waifs" or "street urchins" or were thought to be from questionable backgrounds, they tended to be blamed for the majority of youth deviance in this era (Schissel, 1993: 8-9; West, 1984). In effect, the children receiving the bulk of attention from the criminal justice system tended to be the poor and neglected. They were viewed as "problem children" (Currie, 1986).

Still, the majority of youth were relatively law-abiding, a somewhat surprising fact given that the primarily rural and loosely governed society of the day presented many opportunities for deviance. Youth crime in the pioneer days of Canada consisted of a wide range of mostly minor behaviours consisting of "violations of local ordinances, nuisance offences, vandalism, petty theft, and breaches of the moral laws" (Carrigan, 1998: 25). Some of these behaviours, which most of us would most certainly consider to be minor today, are called *status offences* because they are offences for which an adult would not be liable if he or she were to commit them. In other words, they are offences because it is the status of "youth" that matters.

Nevertheless, those youths who did commit crimes and were caught by authorities were often punished severely. It was not unusual for youths caught violating some moral or formal law to be whipped, incarcerated in work houses, detained in jail indefinitely, held in custody until their parents paid a fine, or even hanged. In addition, children could be punished even if they were considered to have the *potential* of committing a crime (Schissel, 1993).

The range of punishments that a young person might be subjected to indicates the extent to which the justice system of this time was disorganized and operated very much according to the whims of individual judges. More broadly, though, the early history of juvenile crime and punishment in Canada indicates that children were viewed as little more than "adults in training" (Carrigan, 1998). They were assumed to have the same levels of understanding of right and wrong as an adult, were tried according to the same principles of law existing in the adult courts, and were frequently incarcerated with adults.

Interestingly, the behaviour of young people in conflict with the law was also seen to emanate from the failure of their parents and families. During this era, Canadians saw a transformation of the family unit that reflected the rapidly urbanizing and industrial nature of their society. Families became smaller, more mobile and, according to some commentators, they internally mirrored the exploitative relationships characterizing capitalist economies (Alvi, 1986; Barrett and McIntosh, 1982; Currie, 1986). They began to be seen as central to the socialization and control of children who would have to take their place in a society that was no longer agricultural and rural and in which close kinship ties were eroding.

In addition, because the economy required trained and skilled labourers, compulsory schooling also came to be seen as a major player in the "proper" development and socialization of children. It is in this era, then, that adolescence came to be viewed as a period of "innocence" in which the child would delay entrance into the labour market by receiving compulsory education in the context of a nurturing family environment (Currie, 1986). A "child saving movement" composed largely of middle-class women argued that the justice system of the past could not preserve this state of innocence because it assumed that children's behaviour and adults' behaviour were essentially the same. Only children under age seven were considered to be incapable of understanding right from wrong. While those between the ages of seven and 14 could sometimes raise a defence of *doli inapax* (incapacity to do wrong), essentially, criminal liability began at the age of seven (Bala, 1997).

Developments in criminology, psychiatry, and psychology were also important in transforming Canada's approach to young offenders. *Positivist* criminology, which emphasized the role of social factors in causing crime, began to be preferred over the arguments that had previously been advanced in the field of classical criminology (we will make these distinctions clearer in Chapter Three). Thus, while classical criminology saw crime as a consequence of "bad decisionmaking," positivist criminologists argued that social-structural factors were to blame.

Accordingly, people came to believe that if a child committed a crime, responsibility for the child's condition should be laid on the family unit (more specifically, mothers) and the school. Many felt that it was the "lower-class" family that tended to fail; thus, any reform of the justice system for children should provide alternatives that fit more closely with an emerging "middle-class" ideal of the family. Essentially, the idea was that youth should be accorded special treatment. New legislation was needed to deal with these new perspectives on the role and nature of youth.

The first formal legislation enacted to address the new perspective on youth was titled *An Act for the More Speedy Trial and Punishment of Juvenile Offenders* (1857). Its general intent was to accelerate the trial process for juvenile delinquents and to reduce the probability of a lengthy term in jail before trial. A juvenile delinquent was defined as a person under the age of 16 who had committed an offence. Sentencing consisted of either imprisonment in a common jail or correctional house, either with or without hard labour for no longer than three months, or a fine not to exceed five pounds [British sterling]. In addition, the accused could be ordered to restore any stolen property or pay the equivalent compensation (Gagnon, 1984: 21-22).

In 1869, Québec was the first province to add a new sentencing provision that reflected the newfound emphasis on correction through proper schooling. In addition to the three-month sentence, Québec changed its legislation to abolish hard labour while including a mandatory two- to five-year term in a certified Reformatory School after a jail sentence had been served.

According to Gagnon (1984), by 1894, the following principles regarding juvenile delinquents had become entrenched:

- They were to be kept separate from adult offenders at all stages of the criminal justice process

- Instead of imprisonment, juvenile delinquents were to be sent to certified industrial schools, a children's aid society, or a home for neglected children, where they could be "taught to lead useful lives."

By 1908, the passage of the *Act Respecting Juvenile Delinquents* (which later became the *Juvenile Delinquents Act*) represented a solidified philosophy of aid and protection for juvenile delinquents that located the causes of delinquency in the child's environment and maintained that the solution to youth crime was to have the state take the place of the (incompetent) parent. In effect, it was assumed that if parents could not do the job of controlling and properly socializing their children, the state would have to intervene as a "kindly parent"—a principle referred to as *parens patriae*.[1]

The outcome of this philosophy was that judges were directed to treat children not as criminals but as "misdirected and misguided" children requiring "aid, encouragement, help and assistance" (Juvenile Delinquents Act, s. 38). The following points summarize the key principles of the Act (Alvi, 1986).

1. A juvenile delinquent was defined as "any child who violates a Provision of the Criminal Code, federal or provincial statute, municipal ordinance or by-law, or who is guilty of 'sexual immorality' or of similar vice, or who is liable for any other reason to be committed to an industrial school or reformatory"(s. 21).

2. The proceedings were to be as informal as possible and "consistent with a due regard for a proper administration of justice" (s. 17.1).

3. A child adjudged to be a juvenile delinquent would be subject to one or more of the following dispositions (outcomes):

   a. Suspension of the disposition

   b. Adjournment of the hearing or disposition of the case for any definite or indefinite period

   c. A fine not to exceed $25

   d. Commission of the child to the custody of a probation officer or any other suitable person

   e. The child could be allowed to remain at home, subject to the visitation of a probation officer, with the child having to report to the probation officer or court as often as required

   f. The child could be placed in a suitable family home as a foster home, subject to the friendly supervision of a probation officer and the further order of the court

   g. The court could impose further or other conditions as may be deemed advisable

   h. The child could be committed to the care of any children's aid society which must be approved by the legislature of the province and approved by the Lieutenant Governor in council, or, any municipality in which there is no children's aid society, to the care of the Superintendent if there is one, or;

   i. The child could be committed to an industrial school, duly approved by the Lieutenant Governor in council (s. 20).

4. The legislation was based on a commitment to the therapeutic treatment of the juvenile delinquent, as illustrated by the following quotation: "where a child is adjudged to have committed a delinquency, he shall be dealt with not as an offender, but as one in a condition of delinquency, and therefore requiring help and guidance and proper supervision." The emphasis was on treatment provided by professional social workers who were to aid families perceived to be lacking in supervisory skills.

In many ways, the Juvenile Delinquents Act represented a fundamental shift away from prior approaches to juvenile justice that tended to view youthful and adult behaviour as the same. However, although there was now a formal Act in place to address the uniqueness of the young person, much of its humanitarian potential was undermined by the fact that it consisted of vague language, lacked a guarantee of due process, still included a very wide range of "status" offences, and still allowed judges to invoke an extraordinarily wide range of dispositions (West, 1984).

More specifically, problems with the Juvenile Delinquents Act included the following (Bala, 1997):

1.   Due process, such as the right to legal representation, tended to be inconsistently applied in different jurisdictions.

2.   Gender bias: Female adolescents, but not males, tended to be arrested for the vague offence of "sexual immorality" and, typically, these girls came from socially disadvantaged backgrounds.

3.   Class bias: Middle-class children could be released to their parents, whereas immigrant and working-class children received more severe punishment.

4.   In the 1980s, it was discovered that many children had been abused while they were inmates in reformatory schools.

5.   Arbitrariness: There was a great deal of provincial variation with respect to age limits, access to legal services, and respect for legal rights, as well as in the use of diversion and custodial sentencing.

6.   The act seemed inadequate to meet new concerns around questions such as: Should the interests of the child be the *only* principle governing youth crime? Or, why should the system be based on rehabilitation and not some other principle such as punishment and deterrence? The latter was particularly important in light of the apparent "failure" of rehabilitation programs.

7.   Criminal justice officials such as police and judges had very broad powers to interpret the notion of "in the best interests of the child." This resulted in biased and inconsistent decision making.

During the first half of the 1900s, then, the Juvenile Delinquents Act provided the legal framework for youth in conflict with the law. But by the 1960s, enough questions and issues arose to warrant reconsideration of the legislation (Hylton, 1994). Eventually, this dissatisfaction resulted in the development and implementation of new legislation—the Young Offenders Act.

The Young Offenders Act

It took nearly 75 years before the Juvenile Delinquents Act was replaced by a new set of principles for dealing with youth crime. These were contained within the Young Offenders Act. We have seen that much of the impetus for change was related to dissatisfaction with both basic principles and implementation of the Act. However, we must also consider the role of changing perceptions and realities of youth in the context of a changing Canadian culture and political economy.

For the most part, the Juvenile Delinquents Act remained in force with few major complaints until the 1960s. This is not surprising, given that this decade stands out as one of unprecedented social and cultural change. Although it is difficult to say that such large-scale changes were *responsible* for shifting attitudes and policies toward young offenders, we would be remiss in completely dismissing their influence (Corrado and Markwart, 1992).

To capture the tenor of the times in one word, we would probably be safe in calling this a "liberal" era. Attitudes toward war, for example shifted away from a hawkish, "get tough with everyone" approach toward a more conciliatory, peacemaking tone, as the Vietnam war sensitized many to the problematic nature of foreign policy and the ultimately destructive nature of war. Bob Dylan, John Lennon, and other folk and rock musicians sang songs about peace, love, and achieving higher consciousness through the use of drugs such as LSD, mescaline, and marijuana. An attitude of "free love" seemed to be sweeping the public's sexual consciousness, as many young people attempted to break free from "traditional" social norms and customs.

Indeed, we could also characterize this era as one that compelled many people to seek out new freedoms, experiment with alternative lifestyles, and turn attention to those less fortunate in society. In short, the 1960s spawned new concerns about the importance of equality in all facets of life (including law) but, at the same time, it provided people with a framework that would permit them to re-examine notions like "immorality," "class," and "race." Importantly, while many people were calling "traditional" social values into question, it was the youth who were at the center of change. Indeed, commentators such as Bala (1997) have argued that the Young Offenders Act was the expression of "anti-youth sentiment," and that today's youths are less likely to respect adult conventions of dress, taste, style, and attitudes; are more individualistic; and are less likely to show respect for authority. Accordingly, there appears to be a longing for a return to "basic values," whatever these may be, and an impetus toward conformity (see Box 1.3 for an example).

Box 1.3

Ontario: Where Everyone Looks the Same?

Wendy McCann

Ottawa Citizen on-line TORONTO (CP)—Ontario students may soon be wearing uniforms, or at least be forced to conform to a dress code. Education Minister Dave Johnson said Tuesday the province is considering enforcing a dress code because it believes students learn better without the distractions of fashion.

"Not just the uniform itself but the atmosphere that's engendered with the uniform, the discipline, the general air that it brings to a school in many cases, yes, does make an environment that's more conducive to learning," Johnson told a group of public school students at a west-end Toronto school.

"If students are dressed in a sloppy manner, that kind of habit and dress may flow over into their learning habits and make it difficult to conduct proper teaching."

Parents, teachers and students will debate the merits of school uniforms during consultations with Ontario's Education Ministry on the wider issue of a new province-wide code of conduct.

Ontario Premier Mike Harris said this week he believes students, who are growing up on the likes of TV's Beavis and Butthead, need to be taught respect.

Along with a tougher Young Offenders Act for teenaged criminals, Harris is urging parents and teachers to teach children that there are consequences to their actions.

Harris suggested students who swear at a teacher would get suspended. Students who hit a teacher would get expelled.

The new rules for student behaviour will also deal with smoking on school grounds, vandalism, theft, assault, and weapons.

Johnson is also urging schools to adopt an attendance policy that will see volunteers telephone parents of children who do not arrive at school.

The policy is intended to ensure that students who are on their way to school arrive safely.

Source: © The Canadian Press, 1999.

Economic change was also important in creating the conditions for the transformation of juvenile justice. The 1960s were very prosperous; as many people enjoyed greater comforts and job security, they seemed more willing to look at those less fortunate than themselves. In Canada, these changing attitudes manifested themselves in several major social policy changes. For instance, socialized health care (which came to be called Medicare) began to be implemented in the early 1960s, and was a national program by the early 1970s. The federal Unemployment Insurance Act was reformed in 1955 and 1971, and the Canada Pension Plan Act was introduced in 1966. The ideas underpinning each of these important programs related to a philosophy of equality and help for those who had "fallen through the cracks" of an economic system whose fruits most people enjoyed. It was within the context of this emerging "liberal" ideology that Canadian policymakers began to question the relevance of the Juvenile Delinquents Act (JDA).

Finally, the Canadian Charter of Rights and Freedoms, implemented in 1982, provided much impetus for a new framework for interpreting the rights and responsibilities of Canadians. Among other freedoms, it guaranteed a host of legal rights, including equal treatment under the law, the right to legal counsel, and the right not to be subjected to cruel and unusual punishment. Given these new rights, it is likely that the JDA could not have withstood legal challenges under the Charter (Hylton, 1994).

After much extended debate over the problems with the Juvenile Delinquents Act discussed in the preceding section, the Federal Committee on Juvenile Delinquency in Canada concluded in 1965 that the legislation had to be changed. Three separate bills followed the decision to replace the JDA, and in 1984, the Young Offenders Act became law. The general principles of the act are set out in Table 1.5.

Table 1.5
The Young Offenders Act Declaration of Principle

Section 3
3. (1) It is hereby recognized and declared that
(a) crime prevention is essential to the long-term protection of society and requires addressing the underlying causes of crime by young persons and developing multi-disciplinary approaches to identifying and effectively responding to children and young persons at risk of committing offending behaviour in the future;
(a.1) while young persons should not in all instances be held accountable in the same manner or suffer the same consequences for their behaviour as adults, young persons who commit offences should nonetheless bear responsibility for their contraventions;
(b) society must, although it has the responsibility to take reasonable measures to prevent criminal conduct by young persons, be afforded the necessary protection from illegal behaviour;
(c) young persons who commit offences require supervision, discipline and control, but, because of their state of dependency and level of development and maturity, they also have special needs and require guidance and assistance;
(c.1) the protection of society, which is a primary objective of the criminal law applicable to youth, is best served by rehabilitation, wherever possible, of young persons who commit offences, and rehabilitation is best achieved by addressing the needs and circumstances of a young person that are relevant to the young person's offending behaviour;

Tabe 1.5, *continued*

(d) where it is not inconsistent with the protection of society, taking no measures or taking measures other than judicial proceedings under this Act should be considered for dealing with young persons who have committed offences;

(e) young persons have rights and freedoms in their own right, including those stated in the Canadian Charter of Rights and Freedoms or in the Canadian Bill of Rights, and in particular a right to be heard in the course of, and to participate in, the processes that lead to decisions that affect them, and young persons should have special guarantees of their rights and freedoms;

(f) in the application of this Act, the rights and freedoms of young persons include a right to the least possible interference with freedom that is consistent with the protection of society, having regard to the needs of young persons and the interests of their families;

(g) young persons have the right, in every instance where they have rights or freedoms that may be affected by this Act, to be informed as to what those rights and freedoms are; and

(h) parents have responsibility for the care and supervision of their children, and, for that reason, young persons should be removed from parental supervision either partly or entirely only when measures that provide for continuing parental supervision are inappropriate.

The Young Offenders Act was a "hybrid" of the Juvenile Delinquents Act and a new set of principles emphasizing the rights of society to protection from crime; the rights of accused young persons to fair, equitable, and consistent justice; and the notion that young people should be held accountable for their actions, although not in the same way as adults. In keeping with the Act's emphasis on the efficient and equitable administration of justice, McGuire (1997: 189) reminds us that:

> The Young Offenders Act provides instruction for criminal procedure and administration of dispositions relating to young persons. It is an offender management tool, not a crime prevention tool.

Thus, the Act stresses that a young person in conflict with the law is a criminal (albeit a "special kind" of criminal) and not a misguided child. At least on paper, the Young Offenders Act keeps the welfare approach to youth crime found in the Juvenile Delinquents Act, but also emphasizes law and order in a manner in keeping with the principle of "rights."

As well as the focus on the efficient and egalitarian administration of justice, the act includes an important section that allows individuals in conflict with the law to avoid the stigmatizing and potentially harmful effects of processing in the criminal justice system. Section 4, titled

"Alternative Measures," maintains that whenever possible, young offenders should be diverted from the criminal justice system, as long as such diversion is consistent with the principle of protection of society (see Table 1.6). Youths participating in diversion programs might engage in a variety of activities such as reconciliation and restitution to the victim, performing services for the victim, an apology, or service to the community. In addition, the provinces vary in their approach to the types of offences considered to be eligible for alternative measures. Some consider all offences while others exclude the more "serious" crimes such as murder and manslaughter.

The assumption behind alternative measures is that when young people go through the process of arrest, detention, court, and sentencing, the very act of being labeled a "young offender" greatly contributes to those individuals *seeing* themselves as young offenders. This theoretical approach to criminality will be explored in Chapter Three, but the main point to be made here is that alternative measures exist to divert "suitable" individuals away from the criminal justice system so that they do not see themselves as criminals and thus become criminals. In short, Section 4 provides the resources to divert young offenders from the criminal justice system while ensuring that the young offender accepts responsibility for the actions that are the basis of their offences.

Another important aspect of alternative measures is the emphasis on community delivery of programs (Wardell, 1986). While it could be argued that this strategy is designed to have the community more involved with children, it could also be suggested that community emphasis places the burden on the public to deal with the transgressions of youths. Indeed, an important shortcoming of the alternative measures section may be that it relies on the community—whoever that may be—to determine the level and kind of restitution that a young person should offer. This means that the community will have to look for the appropriate resources to make these dispositions happen, but communities often do not have access to such resources. On the other hand, governments may wish to pursue alternative measures in this way because it is inexpensive. Some, such as Wardell (1986), suggest that cost control is the real reason behind government commitment to the principle of "non-intervention."

There are other criticisms of this section of the act. For instance, some people maintain that using alternative measures is only slightly different than actually charging, processing, and incarcerating young offenders. This argument, called "net-widening," suggests that placing youth in a diversion program merely substitutes one form of social control for another (Matthews, 1979). Others, particularly those who subscribe to the "law, order and justice" ideal that underpins the Young Offenders Act, argue that placing youth in a diversion program does not permit "real" justice to be done.

Table 1.6
The Young Offenders Act, Alternative Measures

Section 4

4. (1) Alternative measures may be used to deal with a young person alleged to have committed an offence instead of judicial proceedings under this Act only if:

(a) the measures are part of a program of alternative measures authorized by the Attorney General or his delegate or authorized by a person, or a person within a class of persons, designated by the Lieutenant Governor in Council of a province;

(b) the person who is considering whether to use such measures is satisfied that they would be appropriate, having regard to the needs of the young person and the interests of society;

(c) the young person, having been informed of the alternative measures, fully and freely consents to participate therein;

(d) the young person has, before consenting to participate in the alternative measures, been advised of his right to be represented by counsel and been given a reasonable opportunity to consult with counsel;

(e) the young person accepts responsibility for the act or omission that forms the basis of the offence that he is alleged to have committed;

(f) there is, in the opinion of the Attorney General or his agent, sufficient evidence to proceed with the prosecution of the offence; and

(g) the prosecution of the offence is not in any way barred at law.

Restriction On Use

(2) Alternative measures shall not be used to deal with a young person alleged to have committed an offence if the young person

(a) denies his participation or involvement in the commission of the offence; or

(b) expresses his wish to have any charge against him dealt with by the youth court.

Admissions not admissible in evidence

(3) No admission, confession or statement accepting responsibility for a given act or omission made by a young person alleged to have committed an offence as a condition of his being dealt with by alternative measures shall be admissible in evidence against him in any civil or criminal proceedings.

No bar to proceedings

(4) The use of alternative measures in respect of a young person alleged to have committed an offence is not a bar to proceedings against him under this Act, but

(a) where the youth court is satisfied on a balance of probabilities that the young person has totally complied with the terms and conditions of the alternative measures, the youth court shall dismiss any charge against him; and

Table 1.6, *continued*

> (b) where the youth court is satisfied on a balance of probabilities that the young person has partially complied with the terms and conditions of the alternative measures, the youth court may dismiss any charge against him if, in the opinion of the court, the prosecution of the charge would, having regard to the circumstances, be unfair, and the youth court may consider the young person's performance with respect to the alternative measures before making a disposition under this Act.
>
> Laying of information, etc.
>
> (5) Subject to subsection (4), nothing in this section shall be construed to prevent any person from laying an information, obtaining the issue or confirmation of any process or proceeding with the prosecution of any offence in accordance with law.

Due to space limitations, the sociological orientation of this book, and our strategy of focusing on key aspects of the legislation, other aspects of the Young Offenders Act will not be discussed in detail in this chapter. The key aspects of the Act are covered in the declaration of principle. Issues such as protection of privacy, record-keeping, or procedural issues can be explored by researching the Act in libraries or through the Internet.

Amendments to the YOA:
The Pending Youth Criminal Justice Act

We have seen that laws are fluid. Certainly, the Young Offenders Act is no exception. A number of reforms have been proposed since the Act became law. Table 1.7 provides an overview of the major shifts in young offender legislation that have occurred since the implementation of the Young Offenders Act. These amendments are aimed at what the federal government has termed the Federal Youth Justice Strategy, which underpins the desire of the federal government to replace the YOA with new legislation. In a document titled *A Strategy for the Renewal of Youth Justice* (1998), the government outlines three shortcomings of the act, as follows:

> First, not enough is done to prevent troubled youth from entering a life of crime. Second, the system must improve the way it deals with the most serious, violent youth: not just in terms of sentencing but also in ensuring that these youth are provided with the intensive, long-term rehabilitation that is in their and society's interest. Third, the system relies too heavily on custody as a response to the vast majority of non-violent youth

when alternative, community-based approaches can do a better a job of instilling social values such as responsibility and accountability, helping to right wrongs and ensuring that valuable resources are targeted where they are most needed.

The results of this overall perception of the weaknesses of the Young Offenders Act resulted in a number of recommendations, which, at the time of this writing, have not been implemented (see Box 1.4). Briefly, they involve:

- **Technical and procedural revisions to the Act**

  The act has been regarded as somewhat technically and procedurally deficient. For example, it can sometimes take years to "bump" young offenders to adult court. Moreover, the length of time between the commission of an offence and sentencing is often far too long. Hence, one set of recommendations states that the act should be revised to make processing more efficient and timely, and that criminal justice officials should be given the power to exercise more discretion.

- **Prevention and "meaningful" alternatives**

  It has been argued that the way to deal with the root causes of delinquency is through community-based crime prevention that addresses "the social conditions" associated with these causes. In effect, this represents an attempt (on paper, at least) to strengthen the effectiveness of and re-emphasize the potential of alternative measures, while at the same time focusing on the lack of social and economic resources facing many of today's youth.

- **Meaningful consequences for youth crime**

  A perception that the Act does not address an alleged increase in violent crime, or deal effectively with repeat young offenders, has prompted an emphasis on "firm measures." Generally, this strategy seems to be in keeping with recent amendments that increased the length of sentences for murder. Moreover, it reinforces the idea that society should send a strong message to those who commit the most dangerous offences, and that young people need to be held accountable and responsible for their actions. In this way, it is presumed that other young people will be deterred from committing crimes. Another expression of this "deterrence" strategy is found in a proposal for the publication of the names of young offenders who receive an adult sentence or who commit serious crimes (i.e., murder, attempted murder, manslaughter, aggravated sexual assault and any offence that forms part of a pattern of serious violent offences).

- **Rehabilitation and reintegration**

  Based on the idea that the vast majority of young offenders can become law-abiding citizens, the Youth Justice Strategy emphasizes rehabilitation and reintegration of the young offender.

- **Increased participation**

  Finally, the Youth Justice Strategy document calls for increased participation in the youth criminal justice system from parents, victims, and the community. Although the Young Offenders Act already makes provisions for parental rights, there has been some discussion about the need to make parents more accountable and responsible for their children. In addition, it has been argued that the role of victims of youth crime needs to be enhanced, particularly with respect to the crime's impact, compensation issues, and the benefits youths might accrue by confronting the harms they have caused. Lastly, there have been calls for more community participation, especially with respect to the role of Youth Justice Committees, that would coordinate and deliver services to youths in conflict with the law under Section 4 of the Act.

There continues to be considerable debate about how the Young Offenders Act should be amended. As an alternative to the amendments suggested by the federal government, for example, Jack Ramsay, of the Reform Party of Canada M.P. for Crowfoot, Alberta, has proposed an act to amend the Young Offenders Act. This proposal recommends transferring to adult court older offenders who commit violent offences, limiting the application of alternative measures, designating certain young offenders as "dangerous offenders," establishing public safety as a dominant consideration in the application of the law respecting young offenders, and removing privacy provisions.

Regardless of the stated attempt to preserve key elements of the Young Offenders Act, it appears that proposed amendments to the Act have been designed to address alleged increases in violent crime and public concern over the perceived shortcomings of the act, including the perception that sentences are too lenient (Canadian Centre for Justice Statistics, 1998:10). More broadly, amendments to the Young Offenders Act since 1995 appear to be continuing a trend away from the welfare model evident in the Juvenile Delinquents Act, toward an emphasis on the rights of society (McGuire, 1997).

Table 1.7
Amendments to the Young Offenders Act, 1986 to 1998

Year	Amendments
1986	• Technical amendments to custody placements
1992	• Increased maximum sentence from 3 to 5 years for murder • Clarified rules for transferring youth to adult court
1995 Bill C. 19	• Increased maximum sentence to 10 years for murder • Created presumption of transfer for 16- and 17-year-olds charged with serious violent offences to adult court • Allowed victim impact statements in court • Supported information sharing among youth justice professionals
1996 (August) Federal-Provincial-Territorial Task Force on Youth Justice Report	• Review of the YOA • Report referred to Standing Committee on Justice and Legal Affairs for consideration
1997 (April) Standing Committee on Justice and Legal Affairs Youth Justice Review Report	• Review of the Youth Justice System • 14 recommendations
1997 (August) Meeting of First Ministers	• With exception of Québec, called for meaningful amendments to the YOA. • Committed to improving preventive and rehabilitative programs for young offenders
1997 (December) Federal-Provincial-Territorial Meetings of Ministers Responsible for Justice	• Proposed amendments to the YOA
1998 (May) Federal Youth Justice Strategy Announced	See above

Source: Adapted from Dell, 1998.

As of this writing, the federal government has tabled a new Youth Criminal Justice Act that will replace the Young Offenders Act and that takes into account many of the reforms outlined in Box 1.4. The extent to which these proposed reforms will become law remains to be seen, but several features are noteworthy, including the potential of punishing parents for repeated offences by their children, the chance that Québec will be allowed to opt out of the legislation because they favour a more "lenient" approach to youth justice, and permitting the publication of the names of young offenders over the age of 14 who receive adult sentences (see Box 1.5).

Box 1.4

Youth Crime Law is History: New Legislation Will Be Tougher on Violent Young Offenders

Stephen Bindman and Jim Bronskill
Tuesday 28 April 1998
Ottawa Citizen

The federal government plans to replace the much-maligned Young Offenders Act to signal a new approach to dealing with youth crime, the *Citizen* has learned.

Justice Minister Anne McLellan's long-awaited strategy for "renewal of youth justice" will include tougher penalties for a small number of violent and repeat offenders.

The package, to be unveiled in the next few weeks, will permit the naming of some young offenders convicted of serious crimes and will allow for the transfer to adult court of more youths charged with violent offences.

Ms. McLellan has repeatedly said there are no "simplistic approaches" to the problem of youth crime, and her package will combine measures to ensure the protection of society through crime prevention and enhanced rehabilitation of young offenders.

New legislation to replace the 14-year-old Young Offenders Act will not be tabled until the fall, after another round of consultations.

The Liberals plan to introduce a significant number of changes to the existing act and believe it will be easier to craft an entirely new law than add piecemeal amendments.

But because the act has been the subject of so much criticism, they also want to signal to Canadians that an entirely new legal regime is in place. The new law would, however, preserve many of the key parts of the old act that have been seen to be working.

Ms. McLellan's plan, which has already cleared a key cabinet committee, must still be approved by the full cabinet later this week and further changes are still possible.

The package will retain a separate justice system for young offenders. Some critics have suggested the maximum age in the law be lowered from 17, but no change is contemplated.

Among the changes being considered:

- Improved sentencing options to require youths to account for their crimes, learn about the damage they caused and make reparations to the victim and community.

- More alternatives to the formal court system for youths accused of minor criminal behaviour.

- Some young offenders could be named after they are convicted of serious crimes, although in some cases judges would have the discretion to ban publication.

Box 1.4, *continued*

- A new category of offences that would require some youths to convince a judge they should remain in the youth system. Currently, 16- and 17-year-olds charged with murder, attempted murder, manslaughter and aggravated sexual assault are presumed to face trial in adult court, and the package would add young persons who demonstrate a pattern of serious, violent crimes. Some 14- and 15-year-olds would also be presumed to face adult court.

The youth reforms will come in a detailed response to last year's report by the Commons justice committee, which conducted cross-country hearings and heard from more than 300 witnesses.

The package will be the first major initiative for the justice minister from Alberta, who must attempt to reconcile Reform calls for the toughening of the law with traditional Liberal values.

In recent speeches, Ms. McLellan has said the current youth law works for about 85 per cent of young offenders, those who are charged with property crimes and are not repeat offenders.

But she said the act's credibility has suffered because of how it is perceived to respond to violent crime.

"We must now confront the reality that the key piece of federal legislation dealing with young offenders is viewed as having little or no legitimacy," she said earlier this month. "For some, the youth justice system has sadly come to symbolize the failure of our criminal justice system to reflect the values of those it was meant to serve."

The justice minister said changes to the youth law are not the solution to the problem, and her proposals will reflect that view.

Early intervention for children at risk, prevention programs and other approaches involving families, communities, teachers and social workers are the most effective way to deal with youth crime, she has said.

"Despite what some might say, reforming our youth justice system to better reflect Canadians' concern does not mean putting kids in jail."

Source: *Ottawa Citizen* (April 28, 1998). Reprinted with permission.

Box 1.5

Provinces Will Be Able to Opt Out of Youth Law: Ottawa's Nod to Quebec

Janice Tibbetts
Southam News Monday, March 08, 1999

The federal government will allow provinces to opt out of some of the toughest measures contained in its new Youth Criminal Justice Act, a concession specifically designed to allow Quebec to maintain its more lenient approach to youth crime.

The act, which is to be tabled Thursday, will take some decision-making power away from judges and give it to provincial prosecutors, permitting them to

Box 1.5, *continued*

decide, case-by-case, whether to seek adult sentences for the most serious crimes and whether to allow young offenders' names to be published.

Provinces will also have the option to decide if they, rather than judges, will determine where a youth will serve prison time.

Ottawa decided to add the flexibility after some provinces, led by Quebec, balked at the prospect of tougher provisions, worried they would stigmatize young offenders.

Other provinces, such as Ontario, want a more severe approach to youth crime.

The long-promised legislation, to be introduced by Anne McLellan, the Justice Minister, will replace the 15-year-old Young Offenders Act, and will draw a much clearer line between violent and non-violent crime.

The new act, which will continue to apply to young offenders aged 12 to 17, will crack down on the most violent crimes and find alternatives to jail for lesser crimes such as petty theft and vandalism.

The choice of opting out of some of the tougher components was added after Ms. McLellan was faced with differing opinions when she met with provincial justice ministers last fall to present them with a blueprint of her plan.

Quebec, which jails young offenders far less frequently than other provinces, has long favoured a youth justice system that focuses on other means of punishment, such as community restitution programs.

The Liberal government has been under pressure for years to overhaul the Young Offenders Act, which has been criticized as being too lenient.

The changes will be based on a youth justice strategy Ms. McLellan announced last spring.

Other elements include:

- Children as young as 14, instead of the current 16, will be tried as adults if they have killed, committed aggravated sexual assault, or fit into a new category of repeat violent offender. That means they could serve a 25-year sentence for first-degree murder, instead of the current 10-year maximum for young offenders, and carry a life-long criminal record. Provincial Crown attorneys will have the choice not to seek the stiffer sentence.

- The publication of names of young offenders convicted of serious crimes unless a judge or provincial governments decide otherwise.

- Provinces can collect legal fees from young offenders or their parents when they are able to pay, instead of the current practice of the province paying the tab.

- Freeing the secret files of young offenders from lock and key for victims, schools, and police to see.

- Supervising young offenders after they are released from jail and providing mandatory halfway programs, instead of the current practice of allowing them to walk away with no strings attached.

Box 1.5, *continued*

- Creation of community-based programs that could include some sort of reparation to the victim or community service.

- A new special sentence for the most serious young offenders who suffer from severe psychological problems.

- In most serious cases, parents can be liable to two years' imprisonment if children in their care re-offend, an increase from the current maximum penalty of six months in jail and/or a $2,000 fine.

- Laws will be loosened so that voluntary confessions to police will be more admissible in court.

Ms. McLellan was expected to introduce her bill last September, but it was delayed because of provincial squabbling over what should be in the act.

Some provinces are still angry over Ms. McLellan's refusal to include a proposal to lower the minimum age of a young offender to 10 from the current 12.

Another element of Ms. McLellan's reforms will be to change the federal funding formula to give more money to provinces that take the community-based approach, including Quebec, B.C., Manitoba, and Alberta. The current formula favours provinces that put more emphasis on incarcerating young offenders.

The additional funding will come out of $206-million that Paul Martin, the Finance Minister, set aside over the next three years for the young offenders overhaul. Most of the money will be transfers to the provinces because they are responsible for administering youth justice.

Source: National Post Online. Page URL: *http://www.nationalpost.com/home.asp?f=990308/2350280*

SUMMARY

This chapter provides a context for understanding youths in conflict with the law. We began by showing that the social position of youths in Canada has changed over the past 100 years. In particular, many youths are the victims of deepening social and economic inequalities. We also examined some issues around the questions of what is a youth and what is an offence. We saw that these are complex issues, not easily resolved by reference to so-called "objective laws" or "universal truths." Additionally, we saw that understanding the notions of "youth" and "crime" requires recognition that these concepts have been subject to shifting definitions over time, which in turn reflect shifting social conditions.

We also examined the argument that the media and other "myth makers" have extraordinary power to construct images of youth in conflict with the law. These images, more often than not, tend to portray such individuals in highly stereotypical ways, for instance, as "crazed drug induced youth," "out of control," disrespecting authority, and committing violent crime. Above all, by creating the imagery of young offenders as pathological, or personally deficient, descriptions of "who is the young offender" tend to reflect the assumption that crime is a personal choice, not a societal issue.

We have also considered the legal context. The historical summary of key legislation supporting societal responses to youth crime in Canada illustrates the changing nature of perceptions of youth in general, as well as the contemporary emphasis on the rights of society and individual responsibility. The history of youth crime legislation in Canada reflects a gradual shift away from the attitude that children are no different than adults, through a period where children were seen as in need of protection and welfare, to a current situation that attempts to balance the rights of society with those of the young offender while recognizing, in principle, that the root causes of much crime are social. Increasingly, however, youth crime legislation seems to reflect the perception that individuals should be held responsible for their actions, and that parents should be punished for the misdeeds of youths. Put another way, the focus of policies to curb youth crime seems to be increasingly on families and individuals rather than society as a whole.

In the consensus model of law discussed earlier, law reflects the interests of the majority. We can presume from looking at recent developments that the majority believes that youth crime is enough of a problem to warrant harsher, more exacting penalties. This begs the question: Who are these youth and what crimes are they really committing? In the next chapter we turn our attention to the issue of determining the characteristics of young offenders and the nature and amount of youth crime in Canada.

NOTES

[1] Actually, the term *parens patriae* translates to "father of the country" or "parent of the state," but the term essentially means that the state should act as a wise, kind, but stern father.

DISCUSSION QUESTIONS AND PROBLEM-SOLVING SCENARIOS

1. Write a short essay comparing two different attitudes toward young people, and speculate as to the possible consequences of these differing attitudes.

2. To what extent do proposed amendments to the Young Offenders Act reflect the attitude that crime is a matter of personal choice?

3. Hold a debate with your classmates in which one side takes the position that the Young Offenders Act should emphasize the rights of victims while the other takes the position that it should focus on rehabilitation of youth in conflict with the law.

SUGGESTED READINGS

Bala, N. (1997). *Young Offenders Law*. Concord, ON: Irwin Law.

Carrigan, D.O. (1998). *Juvenile Delinquency in Canada: A History*. Concord, ON: Irwin.

Schissel, B. (1997). *Blaming Children: Youth Crime, Moral Panics and the Politics of Hate*. Halifax: Fernwood.

A teenage prostitute stands on a street corner in Calgary. Prostitution is one offence for which females are charged at greater rates than males. While there are a variety of factors impacting youth crime, gender is considered by many scholars to be one of the most important predictors of youth crime.

Chapter Two

The Magnitude and Nature of Youth Crime

INTRODUCTION

If the debates and issues presented in the first chapter are contentious, the same can be said about the nature (or quality) and magnitude (or quantity) of youth crime in Canada. If we are to develop and implement effective youth criminal justice policies, we need to know exactly what we are dealing with. Not only do we need to know how many youths commit crimes, we also need to understand what kinds of crimes they perpetrate and the characteristics of the youths who commit them. In other words, we need an understanding of the qualitative and quantitative dimensions of youth crime. However, there continues to be much disagreement over "who is doing what and how often." The most important controversies are discussed in the following section. In addition to presenting some of the key methodological problems associated with counting crime, this chapter considers what we do and do not know about the levels and types of youth criminality.

THE ADVANTAGES AND DANGERS OF STATISTICS

Imagine you have been asked to comment publicly on the tremendous increase in juvenile crime in your city or town. Before giving your answer, what issues would you have to consider? Assume that the questioner presents you with the "startling" statistical fact that violent juvenile crime has doubled in the past year. What would you have to know before commenting on this apparently dramatic upsurge? Now consider a few additional pieces of information. Let us presume that you know that there were two violent criminal incidents involving youths last year and four this year. In addition, the way police respond to violent incidents has changed due to new laws, and the five largest businesses in your community have laid off thousands of employees in the past 12 months. What remarks would you make now?

People have different assumptions about statistics. Many hold the belief that in addition to being complicated and too difficult to learn, statistics are a modern-day form of voodoo, or a violation of "common sense," while others feel that statistics are equivalent to "scientific truth." As Hagan (1997: 3) points out, when people agree with a particular statistical finding, they often consider such findings to be "obvious," whereas if they disagree, they view the findings as unscientific because "common sense" tells them so.

The example above illustrates the importance of understanding both the strengths and limitations of claims based on empirical data. In answering the question posed in the example, an important piece of information is that there were two incidents last year, but two more this year. Mathematically speaking, this represents a doubling of one type of juvenile violent crime. However, the extent to which this type of crime is a problem—two incidents versus four—is not as grave as the term "doubling" suggests. More important, drawing conclusions solely on the basis of the numbers leaves us with very little information on the causes of the increase. In short, policies designed to deal with the apparent increase in violent crime in our hypothetical community have a high potential for failing if we do not also account for the *context* in which crime is occurring.

Thus, although part of understanding and acting on a social phenomenon such as youth crime requires knowledge of the statistics pertaining to that phenomenon, it also requires some understanding of the strengths and limitations of the ways we gather data and how we interpret them. Before delving into the numbers on youth crime in Canada, we will briefly consider some of the benefits and hazards involved in counting youth crime.

Defining Statistics

Statistics is the science of discovering patterns in data. It involves numerous techniques, many of which are sophisticated and require more than a basic knowledge of mathematics. In this book (and I can hear the sigh of relief already), we will concentrate only on the branch known as descriptive statistics, which provides basic summaries of data or shows relationships between variables such as age and crime.[1]

The chief advantage of using statistics to understand a phenomenon is that they allow us to quickly summarize complex and often large sets of numbers. For instance, it is far more useful to know about the number of crimes committed by youths per 10,000 or 100,000 people in Canada—the crime rate—than it is to know raw numbers of youth offences, because rates allow us to compare trends more accurately over time and place.

In addition to the problems associated with different ways of presenting and interpreting statistical information, the main disadvantage of statistics in criminal justice stems not from the nature of the discipline of statistics itself, but from the *methods* available to researchers and practitioners for gathering raw data. In what follows we will turn our attention to this issue with special reference to the implications for understanding levels and types of youth crime in Canada.

Counting Crime

There are basically only a few ways that we can count crime. *Official statistics* are derived from what authorities such as the police, the courts, or probation workers tell us about crime. Through *victimization surveys*, we can ask people how often and the circumstances in which they have been victimized by crime. Using *self-report surveys*, we can ask people how often and the circumstances associated with crimes they have committed. By using *observational techniques*, we can gain valuable information about crime by observing from a distance or even participating in an environment in which crime occurs. Each of these approaches has advantages and limitations.[2]

Official Data

Most of the data on youth crime used in this book are official statistics—those coming from the police through the Uniform Crime Reporting (UCR) survey, judicial (court), and correctional sources. We focus on these data not because they are necessarily the best sources of statistical information on youth crime, but because they tend to be the only kinds of reasonably comprehensive data on youth crime available in Canada. The UCR is a yearly national survey that counts the number of "criminal code and other statute offences reported to the police across Canada" (Canadian Centre for Justice Statistics, 1998). These data under-represent less serious offences because when a person is charged with more than one offence, only the most serious one is counted. In addition, these official data reflect only those cases that have come to the attention of police and where charges have been laid. This means that factors such as police discretion (e.g., the decision not to lay charges or to divert youth from the system via alternative measures), the willingness of victims to report a crime, and changes in the definition of crime all play a role in restricting our knowledge of the exact number and types of crimes committed by youth.[3]

Judicial sources of data derive from the Youth Court Survey, which provides information on the number of cases heard in youth courts. Each case consists of all charges laid against the individual under federal statute (e.g., the Criminal Code of Canada). Corrections data count the number of young persons who are remanded in custody, in temporary detention, or have been sentenced to a correctional facility. The most important problem with these data, as you might guess, is that they are "post hoc," that is, they only tell us about those youth who have already been caught and processed by the system.

Official data tell us more about the activities of official agencies than they tell us about actual crime levels. Nevertheless, due to the absence of comprehensive and long-term data from other sources, we will need to utilize official data in this book. Where possible, however, we will draw upon statistical and qualitative data from other sources, as discussed below.

Victimization Surveys

Originally intended to reflect a relatively new focus on the concerns of victims of crime, victimization surveys are designed to determine the number and nature of crimes that are often not reported to the police. They do so by asking people to report on the nature of their experiences with crime (DeKeseredy and Schwartz, 1996). In Canada, such surveys are carried out every five years and tap only victimizations of households and individuals. Thus, many crimes against institutions (such as department stores) are excluded. The central problem with this technique, however, is that it tends to underreport crime because survey respondents often forget when, or even if, they have been victimized; they are sometimes unable to determine whether they have actually been victimized by a criminal offence; or they fear reprisal or other negative consequences from reporting their victimization. Particularly important for our purposes is the fact that it is often difficult for victims of crime to determine whether the perpetrator was a youth, especially if the crime was a property crime such as theft or breaking and entering (Doob, Marinos, and Varma, 1998).

Self-Report Studies

Self-report studies attempt to determine the amount of crime that exists by asking people to admit to committing various criminal acts. Nettler (1974: 73-74) lists the methods that could be used in this regard:

- Anonymous questionnaires

- Anonymous questionnaires in which the respondent can actually be identified and their responses checked against police records or later interviews

- Asking people to confess to criminal acts on signed questionnaires that are validated against police records

- Having people complete anonymous questionnaires, identified by number and validated against follow-up interviews and the threat of a lie detector test

- Interviews with respondents

- Interviews with respondents in which responses are validated against official records

The main goal of nonofficial methods of counting crime is to eliminate as much as possible the "interference" associated with official data-gathering techniques. This is because official crime data, such as those available from the Uniform Crime Reports (UCR) or court statistics, only measure the extent to which these authorities process crime. As pointed out earlier, official data really measure police or court activity rather than the number of actual crimes occurring in a community. Thus, self-report studies ask people who may or may not have encountered the criminal justice system whether they have ever committed an offence, in the hopes that they will answer honestly about their behaviour. Of course, the main difficulty with this method is that people may forget what offences they committed and when they committed them, or they may lie because they do not want to admit that they committed a crime. In addition, because it would be expensive and logistically difficult to survey everyone, self-report surveys must rely on accurate sampling procedures so that their results may be generalized to the larger population. Unfortunately, however, studies of crime using this method have often surveyed "atypical" samples, thereby limiting the extent to which they can claim relevance to the entire population (Hagan, 1997). Moreover, with a few exceptions (e.g., Gomme, Morton, and West, 1984; MacLean, 1994), Canadian self-report surveys of youth crime are rare.

Data from Observations

Observing "crime in the making" allows researchers to gain a somewhat different perspective on crime than that allowed by the methods mentioned above. Such "observational" research generally falls into two categories: (1) the researcher can watch and record criminal activity from a distance, not disturbing the social setting (field observation), or (2) researchers can interact with the people they wish to understand either by participating completely in the activities of interest (participant observation) or by observing as a participant to the extent that the participants themselves allow it (observer as participant). Indeed, one of the strengths of gathering data from observation is that it provides information that might be difficult to collect using traditional techniques such as surveys or interviews. For example, you may get some insight into the dynamics of youth gangs by interviewing a few gang members or even administering a questionnaire. However, you are likely to gain new and different insights if you actually watch how the gang members interact with one another, observe how authority relationships are played out, or monitor how particular rituals are conducted. Thus, observational data help us to understand other, more qualitative dimensions of criminal activity. As you might guess, such methods and the data they produce are vulnerable to the subjective interpretations of the researcher. Moreover, it is often difficult or dangerous to gain access to (and the trust of) the people being studied, as many such individuals are suspicious of the motives of researchers. This is especially true of minority or disenfranchised groups such as the very poor, gangs, or certain youth groups (DeKeseredy and Schwartz, 1996).

Other Problems with Data on Youth Crime

Several other "crime counting" issues deserve attention. A significant issue in Canada is that official data sources do not provide comprehensive information on the "race" or ethnic background of those processed by the criminal justice system.[4] One of the main arguments of those critical of contemporary criminal justice strategies in Canada is that the system is biased against particular minority groups. As we shall see, this claim has some validity despite the fact that there are very few studies examining racial discrimination in the Canadian criminal justice system (Henry et. al., 1995). Others, however, contend that the system is not "racist," that it functions according to principles of equality, and that any disproportional representation of particular minorities is related to the qualities of those individuals (see, for example, Herrnstein and Murray, 1994; Wilson and Herrnstein, 1985). We will take up this debate in Chapter Three, but regardless of the perspective one has of the significance of race-ethnicity in the criminal justice system, controversy continues to surround discussions about the value of collecting statistics on crime that include "race" or ethnic background (see Box 2.1).

A principal keystone of the debate is that it is scientifically impossible to classify people according to race. The concept of "race" is dated and in fact is not used by many social scientists any longer. This is because, genetically, human beings cannot be divided into discrete categories based on biological properties (Rex, 1983). However, although we all belong to one "human race," people often act *as if* there are many races, and the consequences of their actions are often harmful. Accordingly, while we can talk meaningfully about "racism" and the fact that aspects of human behaviour are often "racialized," the concept of race is virtually useless. Thus, collecting crime statistics that include race involves balancing knowledge of the degree to which the criminal justice system is racist (in terms of the way police or courts act toward people of colour, for instance) with the potential stereotyping that might also arise when particular groups are singled out as being overrepresented in the system because they are supposedly genetically predisposed to crime.

Gabor (1994), who has commented extensively on the race-crime data debate, draws our attention to some additional points:

- Differences in crime rates vary more *within* racial groups than they do between them. Collecting race data will therefore distract from what should be the real focus of concern.

- Any racial differences in crime rates could be the result of the discriminatory practices of criminal justice personnel such as police, judges, and prosecutors. By collecting data on race and crime, our understanding of the intersection of race and crime will not only be improved, it will bring the issue into the open. Open discussion is preferable to the negative stereotyping that tends to occur when people have few facts.

- Even if we did find links between race and crime, what could we do about it? Unlike poverty, "race" is a characteristic we can do nothing about. On the other hand, the criminal justice system already collects data on other factors over which we have no control, such as age and sex.

Another issue unique to the Canadian context is that official charge rates may be sensitive to the rate at which young people *are not* charged under the Young Offenders Act. Put differently, the existence of alternative measures means that some youths who commit offences may not be formally charged or may be dealt with informally (e.g., when police give a warning or discuss the incident with the youth's parents). However, data on youths not charged from several jurisdictions in Canada show that the rate of youths not charged has been declining since 1991. Thus, any overall decline in youth crime charges is not likely to be the result of more young persons participating in alternative measures programs (Juristat, 1997).

A further gap in our empirical knowledge of youth crime concerns our lack of knowledge of the number and type of certain kinds of crimes being committed by youths. For example, while we know something about the kinds of hate crimes that are perpetrated in Canada, we have very little information on the extent to which youths under 18 are the perpetrators.

There are other issues with counting crime that will not be taken up here, but one significant issue is the matter of female crime and victimization. As we will see in Chapter Three, women's experiences in relation to crime have traditionally been ignored in mainstream criminology, owing to a perception that the level and seriousness of crimes committed by women are trivial or insignificant. Generally, even those accounts that purport to take account of gender are characterized by an "add women and stir" approach that ignores the *gendered* nature of women's and men's lives. In other words, approaches that simply break up aggregate data into categories that tell us "how many" males and females were victims or perpetrators disregard the different consequences and experiences of male and female young offenders. In short, simply pulling out data on males versus females assumes (incorrectly) that male offenders and female offenders are the same except for their sex. For example, although most would agree that youth prostitution is problematic, we do not know precisely how many young boys and girls are engaged in this activity in Canada, nor should we forget that most adult female prostitutes began their careers when they were juveniles. Furthermore, while we understand something about the nature of youth gangs in Canada, we know next to nothing about the role and experiences of females in such groups (Esbensen and Winfree, 1998). Simply discussing "how many" girls and boys participate in gangs or prostitution tells us little of the "lived experiences" of these individuals.

In terms of gang activity, there is a definitional issue at the core of the lack of statistical data on such groups, namely, what is a youth gang? There are big differences between actual gang activity and groups of unsupervised youths "hanging out" and perhaps getting into trouble together. Further, youth gangs vary greatly in terms of their composition and the kinds of activities they carry out (Bala, 1997), and this often complicates our ability to provide detailed statistical profiles and analyses of such groups.

Another problem is that with the exception of a few case studies (e.g., Baron, 1997; Hagan and McCarthy, 1997) we have no Canadian national data on the characteristics and experiences of street youths, such as their family backgrounds, patterns of criminality, school problems, and unemployment history (Baron, 1997). This is a particularly important gap in our knowledge of youth crime because data from these studies have indicated not only that there are increasing numbers of homeless persons in Canada, but that many homeless youths are both the victims and perpetrators of large amounts of criminal activity.

To summarize, we have seen that there are important strengths and limitations associated with the kinds of data we have on crime in general and youth crime in particular. Indeed, these limitations have prompted many to call for a "data triangulation" strategy of gathering crime data that combines several of the techniques discussed above to obtain a more rounded or "more substantive picture of reality" (Berg, 1995). Over all, relying on only one method of gathering data contributes to what criminologists have called the "dark" or "hidden" figure of crime—a term referring to the reality that such methods almost always underrepresent actual levels of crime.

We have also seen that there is much we do not know about youth crime (or adult crime, for that matter) in relation to "race" or ethnicity and gender. Keeping in mind the limitations we have discussed so far, we will now examine data on the nature and levels of youth crime, and the characteristics of youths who commit them.

Box 2.1

In This Robbery, Race Wasn't Relevant

October 17, 1998
Don Sellar, *The Toronto Star*

A few hours after the holdup at the City Savings and Credit Union Ltd. in North York, the police issued a news release that described three suspects.
Here they are:

Suspect #1: Male/black, mid-20s, 6 ft. 1 in., slim build, wearing a light green army style jacket, black mask, dark pants, purple sunglasses. Armed with a long-barrel rifle.

Suspect #2: Male/black, early 20s, 5 ft. 8 in.-5 ft. 10 in., average build but stockier than #1, wearing black 3/4-length jacket, black pants, black mask and dark sunglasses. He was armed with a black handgun.

Suspect #3: Male/black, 25-30 years, black short dreadlock hair, wearing a green army fatigue mask with a black hat. This suspect was driving a stolen red Chrysler Caravan license 863 YWP.

Next day, *The Star* on Page A24 ran a concise 250-word story about the robbery, one in which no shots were fired but staff were advised to hurry up with the cash—or else.

Box 2.1, *continued*

The aftermath of this robbery seemed like something out of *The Gang That Couldn't Shoot Straight*. Suspects #1 and #2 ran away with an undisclosed amount of money, but couldn't find their getaway car and wheelman, Suspect #3.

When the gun-toting duo tried to steal a car in the nearby neighbourhood, they were twice outwitted. First, they were unable to con two children into getting mom out of the house so that she could be robbed of the family car. Next, they tried to force a woman from her van at gunpoint, but she sped away unhurt.

On the third try, they grabbed a 1988 white Pontiac 6000, whose 67-year-old owner acquiesced only after being hit in the face with a gun butt.

"Police are looking for three men," *The Star*'s story ended, laconically.

"Do you not think that this crime is vicious and callous and serious enough to provide a full description of the people involved?" a reader asked the Bureau of Accuracy.

"The radio stations and other papers indicate they are black, but *The Star* in its political correctness describes the suspect as police looking for three men. If this ludicrous policy doesn't change, I'll be cancelling my subscription," the man said.

"When they're black, they're black, and it should be stated so in the paper," a second caller said. "How in the dickens are you going to find these people without the proper descriptions?"

What did other papers do?

A check of *The Globe and Mail* revealed that Canada's national paper was otherwise engaged. No story.

The tabloid *Sun* devoted nearly a page to the crime—Kids, granny foil thugs; Fleeing bank robbers on carjack terror reign—and reported the suspects' race.

In my view, there was little point in doing so. The descriptions were hopelessly vague. They fitted thousands of young black men in Canada's largest city. Two of the suspects wore masks.

By the time the paper came out the next day, unless the holdup men were vying for the "stupid crooks" feature in Ann Landers' column, they could easily have changed clothes and licence plates.

Frankly, the chance of a reader turning in this trio of crooks on such flimsy descriptions seems so slight that it isn't worth the risk of branding thousands of law-abiding black men as potential criminals.

So *The Star*'s sensible policy of not reporting a person's race, colour or religion "unless it is pertinent to the story" must be applied in this case.

It doesn't always. The policy is flexible enough to allow race or colour to be reported, say, when a detailed suspect description is available or grave danger exists. If the crook has a scar across the left cheek or a remarkable tattoo, his race might be the clincher.

Once an arrest is made, there is usually less justification for injecting race into the story. An exception might be when police shoot a criminal suspect and the issue of racial motivation is being hotly debated.

But to those who periodically tell a news ombud that race is an essential ingredient in defining the criminal classes—or, "I want to know who I should be afraid of"—sorry, I can't buy those arguments.

Source: Toronto Star Syndicate. Reprinted with permission.

THE MAGNITUDE AND NATURE OF YOUTH CRIME

In this section, we will examine data pertaining to youth crime. We will focus on changes in the levels of youth crime, the types of crimes youths commit, and the characteristics of the youths who are committing them.

The Crimes

Most studies show that almost every young person in Canada has committed some kind of delinquent act (Doob, Marinos, and Varma, 1998). In a study of 3,000 youth in Montreal, for instance, Leblanc (1983) found that 90 percent of youth had committed a crime. Similarly, West (1984) used self-report data to show that more than 90 percent of Canadian high school boys had committed some "deviant" act such as swearing, shoplifting, drinking, or experimenting with drugs.

If the law were applied uniformly and strictly to these individuals, most young people in Canada would encounter the criminal justice system at one point in their lives. The crux of the matter is that there are big differences between so-called minor "delinquent or antisocial acts," committing a criminal offence, and actually being caught or charged for that offence. In general, the incidence of minor delinquencies among most youth tends to decrease over time, and hence, a very small proportion of young people actually come into contact with the criminal justice system. In fact, in 1997, less than 5 percent of young Canadians were charged with a criminal offence (Canadian Centre for Justice Statistics, 1998); of these, about 5 percent are responsible for the majority of crimes (see Box 2.2). So what crimes do these individuals commit?

Box 2.2

Youth Crime in Canada Has Small Hard Core: Poverty and Abuse Common Factors Among Many Boys and Girls Charged with Offences

Wednesday, December 16, 1998
Timothy Appleby
The Globe and Mail

Almost a quarter of all the criminal charges laid in Canada last year were against youths, but a small pool of hardcore kid criminals accounted for most of the charges.

The bad apples—about 5 percent of all youths aged 12 to 17—share some common traits. A composite profile shows that he (and the odds are still 4-1 it will

---

Box 2.2, *continued*

be he rather than she, although criminality among teenage girls appears to be rising) is likely to be poor, abused and perhaps bored.

"For the vast majority, it's poverty and a lack of family structure," says Staff Sergeant Chuck Ferry, a veteran of some of Toronto's meanest streets and now the supervisor of the Toronto Police Service's youth program. "Numerous of the kids are the products of abuse, and have themselves become abusive."

"Single-parent families—where the father is not in the picture—that seems to be a common element. We all have a sense of wanting to belong to something, and if kids can't belong to a family, they find their own family.

The Statistics Canada figures, culled from 179 mostly urban police forces, found the most typical young offender, among the 121,122 Canadian youths charged with a criminal offence in 1997, was a male aged 16 or 17.

Of those 121,122 accused, 78 percent were boys and 22 percent female—a shift from an 84-16 ratio 10 years earlier.

The current percentage places the male-female ratio approximately in line with the adult criminal world. Adult geographical patterns are reflected similarly, generally rising from east to west.

Where violence is involved—18 percent of the charges, about double the percentage compared with 1987—the bulk (56 percent) is directed at other youths, usually male, though more than 20 percent of the youth-violence incidents reported to police last year occurred on school property.

In the adult world, by contrast, violence chiefly occurs within homes.

The young criminal also has a good chance of getting caught, though not of being incarcerated. More than two-thirds of the charges laid against youths result in a guilty plea, with two-thirds of those convictions resulting in probation. Just 16 percent of those convicted go to jail.

Source: Staff, Copyright © 1998 *The Globe and Mail*. Reprinted with permission of *The Globe and Mail*.

We begin our statistical tour of youth crime by taking an overall look at the charge rates of young offenders over time, and the type of crimes with which they were charged. The data in Table 2.1 show that there has been an overall decrease in crime rates for youths since a peak in 1991. However, the overall decrease in the rate of youths charged with criminal offences reflects a decrease in the number of charges for nonviolent crime, which in turn reflects the "get tough on violent crime" concerns of the public, criminal justice officials and practitioners, and recent legislation. The data in Table 2.1 come from Uniform Crime Reporting and Homicide survey data, and show at first glance that the total level of violent crime charges has doubled between 1987 and 1997. However, when we look at the subcategories making up violent crime, we see that most of the increases occurred in the categories of major and common assaults and robbery involving violence.

Homicide rates have remained relatively stable in this time period, as have charges for sexual assault, but we must be careful in interpreting these data. First, recall that certain kinds of crimes, particularly sexual assault, tend to be underreported, while others, such as homicide, are usually always reported. Thus, we can be relatively certain that the number of youths charged (not necessarily convicted) for homicide, and represented in Table 2.1 accurately reflect the true homicide rate. However, we cannot say the same for sexual assault, because many victims of such acts are reluctant to report them to the police, do not file charges due to embarrassment or fear of repercussions, or may not understand that they have been sexually assaulted. Thus, the sexual assault figures probably underrepresent the actual number of sexual assaults perpetrated by youths in Canada, a conclusion supported by much of the literature on woman abuse (see DeKeseredy and Schwartz, 1998).

Table 2.1
**Youths Charged in Selected Federal Statute Offences, Canada, 1987-1997
(Rate per 10,000 Youth)**

Offence	Year										
	1987	1988	1989	1990	1991	1992	1993	1994	1995	1996	1997
Total Violent	45	50.8	61.4	69.4	82.8	86.5	91.7	91.6	94	93.2	91
Homicide	0.15	0.21	0.21	0.22	0.21	0.23	0.15	0.22	0.26	0.2	0.22
Sexual Assault	5.4	5.5	6.6	7.1	8.3	9	9.1	8	6.6	6.5	6.1
Major Assault	9.5	10.6	12.2	14.1	16.9	17.1	18.8	19	18.4	17.9	17.9
Common Assault	20.9	23.5	28.9	33.6	39.2	41.5	45.1	46.1	48.4	48	46.3
Other Assaults	2.8	3.2	3.8	4	5	4.5	4.4	4.1	4.5	3.8	4.1
Robbery	5.3	6.9	8.7	9.1	12	12.8	12.8	12.7	14.8	15.5	15.4
Total Property	330.7	330.4	339.8	370.5	401.2	361.0	320.3	291.9	285.3	275.9	243.4
Break and Enter	112.0	106.2	98.7	106.5	117.7	106.9	93.7	84.7	78.1	76.7	70.1
Motor vehicle theft	25.9	28.6	32.6	35.2	38.4	35.1	35.1	31.7	28.8	29.0	26.6
Theft	161.0	161.7	173.2	188.1	197.9	171.2	150.8	136.5	141.4	134.3	116.7
Possession of stolen property	21.0	22.3	23.4	26.5	32.0	32.3	30.3	29.2	27.3	26.4	21.9
Total Other Criminal Code Offences	100.7	107.3	115.2	120.0	138.9	136.8	130.0	123.2	126.2	124.9	122.5
Failure to appear	15.1	15.6	19.0	21.6	28.9	31.6	31.6	29.9	33.4	34.5	34.5
Escape custody	6.6	6.5	6.0	6.4	5.8	6.3	5.0	5.4	5.5	5.4	5.1
Mischief	34.6	38.4	37.8	38.3	42.6	39.2	35.1	32.6	32.4	31.8	29.2
Total Other Federal Statutes	17.8	18.6	19.2	20.4	20.1	21.9	26.0	31.6	34.1	37.8	38.4
Drug Offences	14.4	14.5	13.9	13.7	11.5	11.5	14.6	20.3	21.2	22.5	20.8
Total Federal Statute Offences	494.2	507.1	535.6	580.3	643.0	606.2	568.0	538.4	539.6	531.7	495.3

Source: Canadian Centre for Justice Statistics, 1998: 63.

Similarly, we should be careful about jumping to conclusions about violent behaviour based on the increases in major and common assaults reported in this table. In fact, the increases probably reflect an attitude of "zero tolerance" by authority figures toward incidents and behaviours such as bullying or schoolyard fighting that in the past might have been seen as somewhat "normal" and therefore subject to informal resolutions (Bala, 1997; Gartner and Doob, 1994; Schissel, 1997; Tanner, 1996). As one scholar points out, the reality is that "the vast majority of assaults are minor and do not cause bodily harm" (Reitsma-Street, 1993). This does not mean that they do not cause psychological or emotional damage; the point is that *official responses* to such incidents have changed in that there is a greater chance today that such behaviours will be criminalized. Finally, the rate of robbery charges against youths tripled between 1987 and 1997.

With respect to property crimes, we can see that despite a few minor increases between 1987 and 1997, rates in every category have generally decreased. In the "other" category, both mischief and escaping custody have decreased slightly, with only failure to appear in court increasing over the 10-year period. This last point is worthy of further consideration. In addition to suggesting that some youths may not be taking their encounters with the criminal justice system seriously, the trends indicated in this data suggest that a significant number of young people are receiving formal sanctions as a result of not showing up in court, a relatively benign offence that has more to do with hindering the justice process than threatening public safety (Schissel, 1997). In the same light, charges levied against young persons for drug violations have also increased, despite the fact that criminalizing drug use has done little, historically, to curb drug use (Currie, 1993).

We can draw some other important conclusions about youth crime if we reconfigure Table 2.1 another way. Table 2.2 provides a breakdown of each type of offence as a percentage of the total charges laid against youth in 1997.

In this table we can readily see that the vast majority of charges laid against youths involve nonviolent offences. Property crime accounts for about one-half of all charges laid, while about one-fourth of all charges fall into the "other" category. Only about one-fifth of all charges laid involve violence. More important, in light of the media-driven perceptions of extremely violent youth discussed in Chapter 1, homicide made up less than 1 percent of all charges laid in 1997. Further, the Canadian Centre for Justice Statistics reports that in 81 percent of cases of violent crime in 1997, no weapon was used, while a firearm was used in only 3 percent of cases (Juristat, 1997: 23). Again, the point here is not to trivialize those incidents in which severe force or harm to victims was involved, but to illustrate the reality of youth crime as distinct from media accounts and popular images.

Table 2.2

Type of Charges Laid Against Youth as a Percentage of Total Criminal Charges Laid for Selected Offences, 1997

Offence	Percent of all offences
Total Violent	18.4%
Homicide	0.04%
Sexual Assault	1.2%
Major Assault	3.6%
Common Assault	9.3%
Other Assaults	0.8%
Robbery	3.1%
Total Property	49.1%
Break and Enter	14.2%
Motor Vehicle Theft	5.4%
Theft	23.6%
Possession of Stolen Property	4.4%
Total Other Criminal Code Offences	24.7%
Failure to Appear	7.0%
Escape Custody	1.0%
Mischief	5.9%
Total Other Federal Statutes	7.8%
Drug Offences	4.2%

Source: Adapted from Canadian Centre for Justice Statistics, 1998: 63.

If we were to track charge rates *prior* to the implementation of the Young Offenders Act in 1984, we would gain one more important insight. Schissel observes that soon after the Young Offenders Act was enforced, youth crime rates "were driven upward, almost in a linear fashion," and that while some of the initial increases can be attributed to the YOA's inclusion of 17- and 18-year-olds, the shifts cannot be explained by actual increases in crime, particularly in light of the remarkable coincidence between higher charge rates and the implementation of the act (1997: 75). He also points out that the use of informal, diversionary ways of dealing with youthful transgressions—a central principle of the Young Offenders Act as laid out in Section 4—has not grown proportionately with the increase in formal approaches. He has concluded that the spirit of the Young Offenders Act is being violated (Schissel, 1993). In effect, a good deal of what we know about youth crime from official data such as these underlines the view that variations in crime rates are a function of law-making and law enforcement practices (Carrington and Moyer, 1994).

So far, we have looked at aggregate data on youth crime in Canada. In the next section, we consider the characteristics of the perpetrators of youth crime in terms of three important sociological categories: gender, "race"/ethnicity, and class. Keep in mind, however, that in discussing youth crime in terms of these separate categories, we are ignoring the reality that "race," class, and gender *interact* in important ways (Schwartz and Milovanovic, 1996), a theoretical point that we will take up in Chapter Three. Unfortunately, the limitations of official data do not yet permit us to examine how membership in these categories interacts in relation to the causes and consequences of youth crime.

Youth Crime and Gender

We are often told that there are certain factors that allow us to "predict" the likelihood that someone will become a criminal. In the next chapter we will consider this argument and many of the factors that are said to correlate with youth crime. Here, we will focus on what some scholars consider to be the most important predictor of youth crime: gender.[5] Table 2.3 provides a breakdown by gender of charges of violent crime levied against youths in Canada. The first thing you will notice is that violent youth crime is overwhelmingly committed by males—a fact that directly undermines the often heard and increasingly tiresome argument that women (young or old) are as violent as men.[6]

Table 2.3
Male and Female Youth Charged with Violent Offences, 1987-1997 (Rate per 10,000 Youth)

	Males										
	Year										
Offence	1987	1988	1989	1990	1991	1992	1993	1994	1995	1996	1997
Total Violent	71.7	79.6	96.6	107.2	128.7	132.5	136.5	138.4	141.3	139	132.8
Homicide	0.21	0.38	0.37	0.3	0.35	0.41	0.27	0.4	0.41	0.37	0.34
Sexual Assault	10.2	10.4	12.4	13.5	15.8	17	17	15.1	12.6	12.4	11.4
Major Assault	15.4	16.7	19.5	22.9	27.3	27.2	29.2	30.2	28.8	28.3	28
Common Assault	30.8	33.7	41.4	46.5	55.3	56.9	59.8	62.7	66.3	65.1	60.7
Other Assaults	4.4	5	5.7	6	7.6	6.9	6.5	5.9	6.5	5.4	5.7
Robbery	9.4	11.9	15.4	15.7	20.5	21.7	21.5	21.5	24.6	25.4	25.1
	Females										
	Year										
Offence	1987	1988	1989	1990	1991	1992	1993	1994	1995	1996	1997
Total Violent	16.9	20.8	24.5	29.8	34.6	38.1	44.7	42.4	44.3	45.1	47.2
Homicide	0.1	0.04	0.05	0.13	0.07	0.04	0.03	0.03	0.11	0.03	0.1
Sexual Assault	0.3	0.5	0.5	0.4	0.5	0.5	0.8	0.6	0.4	0.4	0.6
Major Assault	3.5	4.3	4.5	4.9	6	6.5	8	7.1	7.4	7.1	7.3
Common Assault	10.6	12.9	15.9	20.1	22.3	25.3	29.7	28.7	29.1	30.1	31.2
Other Assaults	1.1	1.3	1.8	1.9	2.4	2	2.2	2.1	2.4	2.2	2.5
Robbery	1	1.6	1.6	2.1	3.1	3.4	3.7	3.5	4.5	5	5.4

Source: Adapted from Canadian Centre for Justice Statistics, 1998.

The data also indicate that between 1987 and 1997, charge rates for male and female offenders have increased most significantly in the violent crime categories of major and common assault and robbery. As noted above, it is important to remember that the increase in assaults is likely related to lower tolerance of bullying, schoolyard fighting, and the like. However, we should also take note that there seems to be less tolerance of this kind of behaviour among females than males, given that charges in the category of common assault for females tripled, while charges for males doubled over that decade. In other words, if charge rates are a reflection of the effectiveness of policing, then boys and girls are being policed differently, at least when it comes to common assault. As we will see later in this book, there is additional evidence that females and males are treated differently in the criminal justice system.

As we saw earlier, crime rates have been declining for both males and females, but the rate of decline is more pronounced for males. The last rows of Tables 2.4 and 2.5 show the overall crime charge rates for males and females, respectively. Note that male rates dropped from a high of 1,021.8 in 1991, to 751.5 in 1997, (a decrease of 27 percent), while for females, the drop was from 248 in 1992 to 226.8 in 1997 (a decrease of only 7 percent).

The final set of tables we will look at in this section concerns gender differences in nonviolent offences between 1987 and 1997. Compare the data in Tables 2.4 and 2.5. In addition to the overwhelmingly male character of nonviolent charges laid against youth in Canada, we can see that the most common offences differ for males and females. While theft under $5,000 is the most common charge for both males and females, for boys, the charge was imposed in one-fifth of cases and, for girls, one-third. In order, the next most common charges for females are common assault, failure to appear in court, and break and enter; for males, it was break and enter, common assault, and mischief.

The data in these tables obscure the fact that females are more likely than males to be charged with certain kinds of offences. For instance, in 1996, Canadian police reported 165 incidents of prostitution for females, compared to just 20 for males (Juristat, 1996). Once again, these figures greatly underestimate the level of actual prostitution, given the reluctance of prostitutes and their clients to reveal their activities, and the odds that some young prostitutes may be diverted from the criminal justice system toward social services agencies. Moreover, as pointed out earlier, most *adult* prostitutes start their involvement in this activity as teenagers (Lowman, 1986). It should also be noted that the main reason young people get involved in prostitution is for money, and not because they are "promiscuous" or channeling "unbridled sexual energy" (DeKeseredy, 2000).

Table 2.4
Male Youths Charged in Nonviolent Federal Statute Offences, Canada, 1987-1997
(Rate per 10,000 Youth)

| | Males | | | | | | | | | | |
| | Year | | | | | | | | | | |
Offence	1987	1988	1989	1990	1991	1992	1993	1994	1995	1996	1997
Total Property	542.0	540.4	546.7	591.2	635.4	560.6	493.4	451.7	432.9	419.5	369.5
Break and Enter	206.8	196.2	181.3	194.1	214.8	194.1	169.8	152.5	139.6	136.4	123.4
Motor Vehicle Theft	46.7	51.4	58.4	63.4	68.3	61.7	61.5	55.2	49.7	50.2	45.0
Theft	237.3	238.5	251.0	268.3	277.2	233.6	198.6	182.8	186.2	177.0	155.0
Possession of Stolen Property	35.7	38.4	39.6	45.3	55.0	52.9	49.0	48.2	44.8	42.9	35.3
Total Other Criminal Code	166.3	176.3	188.3	198.2	226.5	219.3	207.9	198.6	199.5	194.3	189.3
Failure to Appear	23.4	23.7	28.6	32.1	42.7	45.6	45.9	44.0	48.4	48.9	48.3
Escape Custody	10.9	10.8	10.3	11.3	10.2	11.3	9.0	9.3	9.3	8.9	8.4
Mischief	61.9	69.0	67.1	68.6	75.9	68.6	61.5	57.0	56.6	54.4	50.3
Total Other Federal Statutes	30.1	30.6	31.6	32.5	31.2	34.2	41.7	51.0	55.2	60.3	60.0
Drug Offences	24.8	24.6	23.5	22.9	18.7	18.6	24.6	34.5	36.7	38.6	35.1
Total Federal Statutes	810.1	826.8	863.2	929.2	1021.8	946.6	879.4	839.6	829.0	813.0	751.5

Source: Adapted from Canadian Centre for Justice Statistics, 1998.

Table 2.5
Female Youths Charged in Selected Nonviolent Federal Statute Offences, Canada, 1987-1997
(Rate per 10,000 Youth)

| | Females | | | | | | | | | | |
| | Year | | | | | | | | | | |
Offence	1987	1988	1989	1990	1991	1992	1993	1994	1995	1996	1997
Total Property	109.6	110.8	123.4	138.9	155.2	151.0	138.1	123.8	130.2	125.2	111.4
Break and Enter	12.7	12.2	12.2	14.5	15.8	15.0	13.7	13.4	13.6	13.9	14.2
Motor Vehicle Theft	4.2	4.8	5.7	5.5	7.0	7.1	7.2	6.9	6.8	6.7	7.3
Theft	81.1	81.4	91.8	104.0	114.7	105.6	100.5	87.8	94.4	89.5	76.5
Possession of Stolen Property	5.6	5.4	6.4	6.7	8.0	10.6	9.9	9.2	8.9	9.0	8.0
Total Other Criminal Code	32.1	35.2	38.6	37.9	46.9	50.0	48.0	44.0	49.1	52.0	52.5
Failure to Appear	6.4	7.2	8.9	10.6	14.3	16.9	16.7	15.1	17.7	19.4	19.9
Escape Custody	2.2	2.0	1.5	1.3	1.2	1.2	1.3	1.4	1.5	1.6	1.6
Mischief	6.1	6.4	7.1	6.4	7.6	8.2	7.2	6.9	7.1	8.1	7.2
Total Other Federal Statutes	5.0	6.1	6.2	7.6	8.4	8.9	9.6	11.3	11.9	14.1	15.7
Drug Offences	3.6	3.9	3.8	4.1	4.0	4.0	4.1	5.4	5.0	5.5	5.8
Total Federal Statutes	163.6	172.9	192.7	214.2	245.2	248.0	240.3	221.6	235.5	236.4	226.8

Source: Adapted from Canadian Centre for Justice Statistics, 1998.

Another important way gender matters with respect to the types of crimes with which young females are charged has been highlighted by Chesney-Lind and Sheldon (1992). Using data from the United States showing that young girls who run away from home are more likely to be arrested than young boys who do so, they maintain that young women are more likely to be charged with offences that violate taken-for-granted notions of appropriate female behaviour (Tanner, 1996). In effect, although we could argue that there are some minor differences between the sexes in terms of the types of offences they commit, we should also be aware that differences may also reflect divergent attitudes and responses of police toward young women, particularly in terms of the tendency for male police officers to act in more "chivalrous" and paternalistic ways toward women. In Chapter 4, we will see if data on sentencing and corrections support this contention.

Youth Crime and Race/Ethnicity

As noted earlier, there are reasons why we do not have systematic data on the relationship between race/ethnicity and youth crime in Canada. Mosher (1996: 413) suggests that "Canadian research on racial discrimination in the criminal justice system is generally quite sparse," owing both to the lack of data and the false perception that Canada has not had a problem with the treatment of minority groups within the criminal justice system. Nevertheless, there are a few studies that illuminate our understanding of the link between racism and youth crime. One official source of such information comes from the Report of the Commission on Systemic Racism in the Ontario Criminal Justice System (Ontario, 1995). Keeping in mind that with the exception of aboriginal youth, there are no national data on charge rates for youth by race/ethnicity, data on admissions to prison for young offenders in Ontario (Table 2.6) show at first glance that whites make up the bulk of youths incarcerated in Ontario prisons. However, when we note that groups such as aboriginals and blacks make up far less of the general population than would be indicated by the figures noted in this table, it is difficult to disagree with the general statement that visible minorities are overrepresented in the criminal justice system.[7]

Similarly, studies conducted on the experiences of aboriginal youths consistently point to aboriginal youths' overrepresentation in the criminal justice system at every stage of the process (Bala, 1997; LaPrairie, 1983; LaPrairie and Griffiths, 1984; Morin, 1990).

Table 2.6
Admissions of Youths Aged 16 and 17 to Ontario Prisons, by Sex and Race, 1992/93 *

	Female	Male	Total
White	70.8%	71.9%	71.8%
Black	1.5%	13.3%	12.5%
Aboriginal	22.0%	6.3%	7.5%
Asian	2.4%	3.0%	3.0%
East Indian	0.3%	1.3%	1.3%
Arab	0.9%	0.8%	0.8%
Other/Unknown	2.1%	3.3%	3.2%
Total Percent(*)	100.0%	99.9%	100.1%
Total Number of Admissions	336	4,369	4,705

Source: Ontario Ministry of the Solicitor General and Correctional Services, as quoted in *Report of the Commission on Systemic Racism in the Ontario Criminal Justice System.* © Queen's Printer for Ontario, 1995. Reprinted with permission.

* Percentage estimates may not add up to 100% due to rounding.

In addition to the debates about collecting data on the race/ethnicity of youths encountering the criminal justice system, there is a critical question in terms of the relationship between race/ethnicity and youth crime: Does overrepresentation indicate the racism of criminal justice officials such as police or are there links between racial and ethnic background and other factors related to criminal behaviour, such as poverty and educational achievement? We know from anecdotal and court case information that police discretion plays a critical role in charges laid against visible minority youth (see Box 2.3). There is also some evidence that racism is more likely to occur at earlier stages (e.g., policing) in the criminal justice process than later ones (e.g., the courts) (Mosher, 1996). In addition, it is clear that some groups (such as aboriginal youths) are far more likely to experience high levels of economic deprivation and social isolation than their nonminority counterparts. Accordingly, more definitive conclusions on the intersection of youth crime and race/ethnicity in Canada await the benefit of comprehensive, reliable, and valid data. Until then, we are left with the sad reality that groups of young people from particular racial and ethnic backgrounds are at considerably greater risk of being charged with offences than those belonging to dominant social groups in Canada.

Box 2.3

Excerpted from *Report of the Commission on Systemic Racism in the Ontario Criminal Justice System* (1995), Chapter Six.

On February 19, 1993, P, an 18-year-old black male, was stopped by the police. He and his younger brother were coming from their church's youth basketball game and were standing at Birchmount and Finch [a major intersection in Metropolitan Toronto] when a police car drove by. By way of a dare he raised his left arm, gave the peace sign and shouted "peace out, copper." The car made a U-turn and stopped in front of them. Two officers came out of the car; one white, the other Asian. The white officer approached him asked what he'd said. P explained to the officer, who then said that P had picked the wrong officer to mess with. The officer then asked him for ID [identification]. P asked if he was being arrested, and his brother pointed out that P didn't have to show any ID unless he was being arrested, so P agreed with his brother not to show any ID. The next thing he knew was that he was being thrown up against the police car. There was a struggle, and the officer put handcuffs on him while P was yelling and screaming, "What's going on?" P was taken to the station, where he was charged with resisting arrest, assault, mischief and disturbing the peace. At trial, P was acquitted of all charges. The trial judge concluded that "[t]he evidence of the Crown's case through the officers suffered significantly from inconsistencies, which impacted on credibility . . . the overall evidence of the police left me with a distinct impression that they were overreaching, and filling in the lacunae of their case."

. . . . A study of 248 randomly selected Youth Bureau files, drawn from completed cases at two Metropolitan Toronto police divisions, indicates that black youths are over-represented among young persons whose charges are initiated solely by the police rather than in response to a complaint. The data show that 41% of the sample as a whole, but 52% of the youths whose charges are solely initiated by the police, are black. By contrast 40% of the sample as a whole, but only 29% of youths whose charges are solely initiated by the police, are white.

Source: *Report of the Commission on Systemic Racism in the Canadian Criminal Justice System.* © Queen's Printer for Ontario, 1995. Reprinted with permission.

Youth Crime and Class

There has been a great deal of theorizing about the relationship between class and crime. Some scholars argue that one's class position (e.g., middle or working class) has a direct association with the chances of committing a crime, being caught for one, or the type of punishment one receives. Others, such as Andrews and Bonta (1998) and Tittle and Meier (1990), maintain that no such relationship exists. Much of the disagreement stems from differing theoretical understandings of the concept of class, or differing approaches in the use of data. As these are largely theoretical arguments, they will be dealt with in Chapter Three.[8] What can we say about the empirical data on the relationship between class and youth crime here?

As with race and ethnicity, there is very little that can be said empirically about class because Canadian criminal justice agencies do not collect official data on the economic background of young offenders. However, Tanner (1997) points to a general pattern with respect to the relationship between class and crime—official data from the United States generally point to an inverse relationship between socioeconomic status and crime (the lower the status, the higher the crime rate), while self-report data typically show no such relationship. He contends that the reason for this difference is that self-report surveys typically involve high-school student samples, which exclude hard-core serious offenders who have dropped out of school, and that such surveys rarely ask questions about serious wrongdoing (1997: 57).

In Canada, we have some data on the relationship between poverty, low income, and delinquent behaviours. For example, the National Longitudinal Survey of Children and Youth (Canada, 1996) shows that youths of lower socioeconomic status are more likely to be "aggressive" than those from higher-income earning groups. In Chapter One we saw similar kinds of relationships between economic background and delinquency or delinquency-related behaviours.

What are we to make of these seemingly contradictory conclusions about the role of economic relationships and youth crime? Again, we need data that taps not just the offenders' income levels, but also the nature of their experiences in the labour market, the extent of their underemployment or unemployment, and the nature of the work they do. In addition, we need to further explore the possibility that the linkage between class and youth crime may be one in which economic and social positions are related to other factors (a *mediated* relationship) that are more directly related to crime, such as "race," gender, urbanization, the nature and availability of work, and educational attainment (Crutchfield and Pitchford, 1997; Farnworth et al., 1994; Elliot and Ageton, 1980). In the next chapter we will examine the idea that the concept of social class needs to be reconsidered in criminological literature if we are to finally understand its role in relation to crime.

So far we have merely described differences in crime rates for youths in Canada. In the next section, we will briefly examine youth involvement in several specific crimes; namely, hate crimes, drug-related crimes, and gang-related crimes.

Hate Crime

Hate crimes are crimes characterized by harm motivated by animosity toward an individual and the group to which they belong. National data on hate crime perpetrated by youths are not collected in Canada, although several police forces have started to collect data on incidents of hate-motivated activities. Hate-and bias-motivated crimes are commited on an individual level as part of a group (e.g., some types of Skinheads).[9] Roberts (1995) estimates that about 40 hate organizations, many of whom actively recruit young people in schoolyards or via the Internet, are actively operating in Canada. Research estimates that there are approximately 60,000 hate crimes committed in Canada's three largest urban centres each year, the bulk of which are directed at racial minorities, and include assaults, robbery, threats, and hate literature. Other target groups include religious minorities (particularly Jews) and gays and lesbians.

Roberts (1995) has stated that the majority of hate crime offenders are "youthful" males acting in groups. Gilmore (1994) points out that offenders are mostly in their "teens or twenties." However, we know little else about the role and involvement of young people in these often lethal acts. Our understanding of the level of hate crime is also complicated by the fact that it is one of the most underreported crimes, and because of differing definitions of hate crime used by police forces across the country (Roberts, 1995).

Crime and Drugs

Youth drug use in Canada appears to have fluctuated for some drugs, and declined, or stayed stable for other drugs over the past 20 years (see Table 2.7). For example, the use of cannabis seems to be up from a period of low usage beginning in the early 1980s; cocaine use seems to have gradually declined; and heroin and LSD use is up from low points in the early 1990s. In addition, several "new" drugs, such as Ecstasy and Ice (forms of methamphetamine), have appeared on the scene in this decade.

The exact relationship between drugs and crime is also something of a controversy in criminology. Some argue that drugs "cause" criminal behaviour in that the drug user's addiction to drugs compels him or her to commit crimes to pay for the habit, or lowers inhibition levels so that otherwise docile, law-abiding individuals engage in criminal activities. Others suggest that criminal behaviour leads to drug use because participation in criminal subcultures may also entail the use of drugs. Still others contend that the relationship is bidirectional: drug use sometimes causes crime, while in other instances the reverse relationship occurs (Lyman and Potter, 1996). According to Parker (1996), the reality is that youth crime and drug use is a complex phenomenon, not lending itself readily to simplistic interpretations. He points out that to understand the relationship between drug use and young people's criminal activity, we need to appreciate the social and cultural context in which drug use occurs and the impact of "polydrug" use (the use of many drugs). Above all, he contends there is much to be gained by using qualitative (observational and ethnographic) research techniques to more fully appreciate the multifaceted relationship between drugs and crime.

Regardless, the crime rates for male and female youths reported in Tables 2.4 and 2.5 show that the incidence of drug charges has not increased dramatically, though males are more likely than females to be charged with drug-related offences. Most of these charges would be related to possession or trafficking.

Table 2.7
Drug Use Among Students by Selected Characteristic, Ontario, 1979, 1983, 1985, 1987, 1989, 1991, 1993, and 1995

	Year							
	1979	1983	1985	1987	1989	1991	1993	1995
Drug	Percent using substances during past 12 months							
Cannabis	31.7%	12.7%	21.2%	14.1%	14.1%	11.7%	12.7%	22.7%
Glue	4.3	3.2	2.0	2.4	1.9	1.1	1.6	2.4
Other Solvents	6.2	4.1	2.7	3.7	3.1	1.6	2.3	2.9
Barbiturates (M)	12.8	11.0	9.0	7.8	7.8	4.4	5.6	4.8
Barbiturates (NM)	6.8	6.0	4.4	3.3	2.2	2.2	3.0	2.7
Heroin	2.3	1.6	1.5	1.4	1.2	1.0	1.2	2.0
Methamphetamine	3.6	3.9	3.1	3.1	2.5	1.8	2.0	4.6
Stimulants (M)	5.9	5.2	4.3	4.3	3.3	2.6	4.0	4.1
Stimulants (NM)	10.6	15.4	11.8	7.9	6.5	4.0	5.4	6.3
Tranquilizers (M)	6.9	6.5	4.7	4.9	3.1	2.9	2.2	1.8
Tranquilizers (NM)	5.9	5.0	3.3	3.0	2.4	1.6	1.1	1.6
LSD	8.6	8.6	7.4	5.9	5.9	5.2	6.9	9.2
Other Hallucinogens	5.3	6.0	4.8	4.5	4.3	3.3	3.1	7.6
Cocaine	5.1	4.1	4.5	3.8	2.7	1.6	1.5	2.4
PCP	–	2.0	1.7	1.3	1.1	0.5	0.6	1.7
Crack		1.0	1.0	1.0	1.7			
Ice					–	0.8	1.2	1.1
Ecstasy					–	0.2	0.6	1.8
Steroids					1.1	1.8	1.7	1.5

Source: Adlaf E.M., F.J. Ivis, R.G. Smart, and G.W. Walsh, *The Ontario Student Drug Use Survey: 1977-1995* (Toronto: Addiction Research Foundation, 1995). Reprinted with permission.

Gangs

Youth gangs in Canada are not understood very well, due again to difficulties with gathering data on such groups and problems of definition. The importance of making distinctions between real gangs and groups of youths who are merely "hanging out" together was highlighted earlier. While police in Canada distinguish gangs by their participation in criminal activities and high level of organization, the lack of standardized definitions and systematic strategies of gathering information makes it very difficult to know how much "gang-related" crime actually occurs (Solicitor General, 1994). Moreover, scholarly research on youth gangs in Canada has been hampered by a lack of good historical and contemporary statistical data on their nature and makeup. In addition, there are problems with gaining access to such groups, gaining trust, and the willingness of gang members to voluntarily disclose criminal activities to researchers. Much of what we know of the nature of gang activity, then, comes from largely anecdotal accounts presented in newspapers, magazines, and the like (see Box 2.4). Other than this type of information, we really only know that gangs exist mainly in large urban centres; that they exist in most social, ethnic, and economic categories; and that there are very few *highly organized* youth gangs in Canada (Solicitor General, 1994). In addition, although there are no systematic scholarly studies of youth gangs in Canada, particularly those examining the role of female gang members, some individuals and media maintain that youth gangs are becoming more violent and younger and that they increasingly include girls, involve more weapons, and are creating tremendous fear among students through violence, extortion, and drug dealing in schools (see, for example, Mathews, 1994).

Despite such warnings, and the underlying fear that if Canadians do not act on this issue quickly they will face problems similar to those in the United States, there is, as yet, little good evidence from which to create responsible and scientifically grounded policies addressing youth gangs.

Box 2.4

Special Report
October 24, 1998

Teen Gangs

Fear in Our Schools

More Than 180 Youth Gangs are Carving Out Territories Across Greater Toronto. Their Weapon is Intimidation. Their Shield—Students' Frightened Silence

By Michelle Shephard
Toronto Star Education Reporter

They call themselves Looney Toons, Boys in Blue, Punjab X-Ecution, Nubian Sisters, Trife Kids, Vice Lords, The Tuxedo Boys, Mother Nature's Mistakes and The 18 Buddhas. They are teen gangs. And they are an increasingly violent part of life in our communities and high schools.

More than 180 of them are carving out territories across Greater Toronto.

Not all are dangerous. Some youths just band together, think up a name and try to act tough. But they are learning the art and power of intimidation. And they are using it daily in our schools.

Box 2.4, *continued*

At least 30 gangs are known by police to carry firearms.

"Anybody who thinks the kind of violent incidents that kids face today is the same as 20, 10 or even five years ago is so out of touch, they're not even worth talking to," says Toronto police Detective John Muise, who has watched gang violence grow over the past nine years.

"You rarely see one-on-one fights," Muise adds. "It's gangs, it's weapons and it's definitely more sophisticated in a brutal way."

Students know exactly what they face.

The *Star* surveyed 1,019 students in 29 of 275 public and Catholic high schools across Toronto, Durham, Peel, Halton and York during May, June and July.

The survey focused on teenagers in Grade 10, mainly 15 or 16 years old—a vulnerable age where peer pressure, teenage insecurities or troubles at home can make the gang culture particularly alluring. It revealed a frightening reality:

Gangs and their activities have become an unavoidable part of high school life for many students throughout Greater Toronto.

The majority—767 of the 1,019 students surveyed—said they still feel safe at school. But more than 1 in 5—22 percent—say they have gone to school filled with fear and anxiety about their safety.

More than half of the students surveyed—53 percent—said there were gangs in their schools. One in 10 said they belonged to a gang.

And just 1 in 10—only 10 percent of respondents—said they would report a violent incident in their school to a teacher, vice-principal, principal or any staff member.

The Star survey clearly illustrates one of the biggest problems police and school authorities face every day: Silence.

Most gang-related crimes—extortion, intimidation, assaults—are never reported. Fear breeds silence.

The public rarely sees gang-related violence and usually only finds out about flare-ups that can't be hidden. Consider these incidents in the past year:

Yesterday: Police brace for trouble outside Scarborough's Albert Campbell Collegiate, where they expected a retaliatory attack by the Ghetto Boys for an earlier stabbing of an 18 Buddhas gang member. Nothing happened, but police fear it's just a matter of time.

The Oct. 13 stabbing was itself a payback for a previous mall brawl between the two gangs.

Sept. 21, Scarborough: Two Sir Wilfrid Laurier students are stabbed in the head, neck and chest during a lunch-hour fight. Five Woburn students—police say they are members of the Tuxedo Boys, a Sri Lankan gang—are charged with aggravated assault. Police say the victims required "hundreds of stitches," and are under police protection.

Box 2.4, continued

June 9, East York: A 15-year-old girl is knifed in the chest and stomach at a 7-Eleven store across from Marc Garneau Secondary School at Don Mills and Gateway Blvd. The fight, involving about 40 students from nearby high schools, many armed, has been brewing for months between two female gangs.

Jan. 20, Toronto: The Spadina Girls—five 15-year-olds from Jarvis and Harbord collegiates—are arrested after a "reign of terror" inflicted on other students. Charges include assault, extortion and uttering a death threat. The two ringleaders served eight, and six months, in protective custody.

School boards, administrators and provincial education authorities—and until recently, the police themselves—have downplayed the presence of gangs in the city's classrooms and communities.

But with youth violence escalating, that's starting to change.

"To say (youth gangs) don't exist is a mistake because they do exist," Police Chief David Boothby said in an interview.

"A bigger mistake is to say they don't exist and to not do anything about it."

The new wave of organized youth gangs in Toronto appeared in the late 1980s, against a backdrop of "Gangsta" rap and the growing notoriety of drive-by shootings in south-central Los Angeles.

In 1989, the Untouchables—initially a group of suburban, white, middle-class boys—formed an alliance police consider one of the first organized gangs.

They cruised downtown on weekends, swarming victims for their jackets and shoes, and marking out their turf.

Slowly other gangs—the downtown B-Boys, the suburban Bayview Milliken Posse—began forming alliances to fight back and get in on the game.

Today, the downtown core boasts more than 50 groups—with names ranging from the Silver Boys to Young Guns, Pentagon, Lynch Mob and Gators—that police identify as gangs.

Membership can be fluid. Two years ago, Latino-based La Familia was considered one of the city's largest gangs. Today, according to police, La Familia is smaller and more dispersed.

And today's Untouchables—a downtown multi-racial gang—bear little resemblance to their notorious predecessors. They simply adopted the name.

Defining and following youth gangs is difficult.

Police and the courts use the definition of "criminal organization" as outlined in Bill C-95, which says a gang must include five or more people involved in criminal activity.

Psychologist Fred Mathews, a leading Canadian expert on youth violence, defines gangs as a group of three or more whose members impulsively, or intentionally, plan and commit anti-social, delinquent or illegal acts.

Box 2.4, *continued*

The consensus among high school students interviewed by The Star was four or five people who carry weapons, have some loose sort of organization, are involved in criminal acts and have a name.

If you're in a gang, the definition is less formal.

"They're my boys," says one 15-year-old male member of a west-end gang affiliated with The Untouchables.

A Latin Nation (NLs) gang member defined his group as "insurance" or "back up," and says he sometimes felt he had no other option but to join a gang—or to prove his loyalty by fighting.

"Sometimes you hafta do it (get in a brawl). If you don't do it, you can't show your face. It's like if you've lost your shit, you're gonna get picked on for the rest of your life."

Girls fight too—often more fiercely than their male counterparts. At least five of the 180 city gangs identified by police are strictly female, including the Ghetto Girls, Lady Crew and the Rucus Girls. Many have both male and female members.

One North York student talked about exclusive girl gangs in his Catholic school.

"Oh they're killers. They're worse than us. I wouldn't go near them," he says, waving his hands as he talks.

"Girl gangs are . . . crazy. I don't go near those ones, they'd kill me. They grab rocks and put them (in their) purses and when someone comes they'll crack 'em with it. They also carry those bandanas with locks on the bottom of them. I don't go near them."

Toronto Constable Wendy Gales, of 54 division in former East York, says female violence is often the most severe.

"During the last year, definitely the most violent-type crimes are where the female gang members have been suspects," says Gales, who is investigating the June stabbing outside Marc Garneau school.

Gales' observations are supported by data collected by Statistics Canada. In the past decade, the rate of females aged 12-17 who were charged for violent offences in Canada has increased by 179 percent.

In Toronto, total violent crimes reported by police in that female age group rose 198 percent—from 242 reported crimes in 1987 to 529 last year.

But StatsCan figures also show an overall 7 percent drop in youth crime, continuing a six-year trend.

Police say those figures are misleading. Today's violence is not reported. It's no longer one-on-one. Teenagers are afraid to speak up.

The gangs' strongest weapons are fear and intimidation. And their shield is their victims' frightened silence.

"Statistics only reflect reported incidents," says Toronto 52 Division street Detective Colin McDonald.

"We are on the streets every day begging kids to report crimes that we know have occurred."

Says a 15-year-old North York boy: "Telling someone would just make it worse."

Box 2.4, *continued*

Police do not indicate gang affiliations in their crime statistics, which makes outside tracking of their activities difficult. Similarly, crown attorneys, who deal with hundreds of gang cases every year, do not classify them as gang-related.

In fact, says Toronto senior crown Calvin Barry, evidence of gang activity is rarely mentioned during trials because it is considered prejudicial and could cause a mistrial or draw criticism from the judge.

"The problem is that if you start alleging an accused is a member of a gang, that is a prejudicial assertion . . . because you are making allegations that are very difficult to prove," he says.

The dangerous nature of the city's gangs varies. Police say many have members with some sort of criminal record—offences ranging from shop-lifting to assault to murder.

A criminal record or brief trip through the justice system—most are young offenders—is considered a badge of honour.

But police say many fringe members, sometimes known as "wannabes" or "foot soldiers," eventually will be involved in some of the worst activities—brutal assaults, armed robberies, swarmings—in attempts to earn respect from the leaders.

Some of the more dangerous gangs have adopted an American-gang-style initiation ritual called "jump in" or "beat down." Other gang members, en masse, gather around kicking and punching the newcomer for at least a minute. . . .

Source: *Toronto Star*, October 24, 1998.

VICTIMS OF YOUTH CRIME

No discussion of young offenders would be complete without considering the victims of youth crime. Recent studies of public opinion indicate that many people are dissatisfied with the apparent lack of attention paid to the role and experiences of the victim in criminal offences. Indeed, much of the public's dissatisfaction with the Young Offenders Act has been fueled by perceptions that the legislation demonstrates little concern for victims who are not receiving "justice" in the form of "harsher punishments" for perpetrators or whose experiences as victims were not being uniformly taken into account at sentencing.[10] In this section, we will briefly consider some data on the types of people who are victimized by youth crime, their relationship to the offender, and where the criminal acts tend to take place.

The majority of victims of violent youth crime are youths themselves (see Box 2.5) and in most cases the victims know the perpetrator as "acquaintances" (57 percent), "family members" (13 percent), or "close friends" (4 percent). The remaining cases (26 percent) of victimization involved strangers.

Box 2.5

Victims of Youth Violence

The most likely victims of youth violence are other youths and male youths in particular. In 1997, more than half (56%) of all victims of youth violence were other youths, while an additional 10% were children (A Profile of youth justice in Canada pp. 31). Twelve- to 17-year-olds were identified as victims in common assault cases involving young accused as often as adults (55% in both cases), while youths were slightly more often the victims of robbery (16% versus 13%). Children less than 12 years old were most often the victims of youths in common assault (43%) or sexual assaults (34%).

Six in ten victims of youth violence were male. Males were more often victims of robbery (17% versus 8%) and serious assault (21% versus 13%) compared to females. Three in four victims of youth violence knew the accused. . . .

Source: Juristat 1999: 6.

Table 2.8 provides a breakdown of violent offence victimizations by sex. We can see that, like adult crime, youth crime is gendered in that males are more likely to be the victims of major assaults and robbery, while females are more likely to be sexually assaulted.

Unfortunately, there are no data on the victims of nonviolent crimes committed by young persons. However, we can be reasonably confident that the victims of a good portion of property crimes are store owners (in the case of theft under $5,000) and those whose homes are broken into (break and enter offences).

Table 2.8
Victims of Youth Violence by Sex and Offence, 1997

		Sex of victim	
Offence	Total	Female	Male
Common assault	53	57	51
Major assault	18	13	21
Robbery	14	8	17
Sexual assault	8	16	3
Homicide	0.1	0.1	0.1
Other	7	6	8
Total victims of youth	100	100	100

Source: Canadian Centre for Justice Statistics: 32

Summary

In this chapter we have examined some important aspects of what we know about the quality and quantity of youth crime. One of the key points was that there are severe limitations associated with official sources of data for certain types of crimes, thus reducing our confidence in understanding the nature and level of youth crime in Canada. We also examined some of the advantages and disadvantages of particular methods of collecting data on crime, as well as the importance of understanding how to interpret statistics. One conclusion we can draw from this discussion is that good data on youth crime will require a synthesis (data triangulation) of various quantitative methods (e.g., the Uniform Crime Reports, victimization surveys, and self-report surveys) and qualitative methods (e.g., ethnographies, interviews, and participant observation).

In terms of the data presented in this chapter, we have seen that, contrary to most media accounts, youth are *not* getting more violent—and that a significant contributor to the perception of increased youth violence lies in the category of common assault, which is sensitive to changes in official responses to youths' behaviour.

We also examined the relevance of categories such as "race," class, and gender, and explored what we know about the ways these factors intersect and interact with one another. The data on male and female experiences with crime, either as victims or as perpetrators, also point to the reality that boys and girls, like men and women, experience the world differently—a fact that should be taken into account in theorizing and policymaking in relation to youth crime.

We briefly looked at what we know about the nature and frequency of hate crimes, drug-related crimes, and gang-related crimes and concluded that our knowledge about these behaviours in Canada is meager at best.

You will recall that one of the themes of the first chapter was that doing something meaningful about youth crime requires an understanding of the context in which it occurs, how much crime there really is, and who is doing it. In addition, we need to understand the strengths and weaknesses of different explanations of *why* youths commit crime. Accordingly, the next chapter considers (mostly) sociological theories of why youths commit crimes.

NOTES

[1] The other branch, *inferential* statistics, is concerned with drawing conclusions and inferences *from* a particular set of numbers in a research study *to* a larger population. There is another important distinction between *parametric* and *nonparametric* statistics. The former refer to representative samples, whereas the latter refer to nonrepresentative samples. For more on these distinctions, consult any statistics text.

[2] Note that the advantages and disadvantages discussed here are by no means exhaustive. See Hagan (1997) and DeKeseredy and Schwartz (1996) for a more comprehensive treatment.

[3] The revised Uniform Crime Reporting Survey (or UCR-II) was developed in 1984 and is nonrepresentative data collected from mostly urban police departments in various provinces. It collects information on incidents reported to the police but includes information on age, sex, relationship of the accused and victim, location of the incident, presence of weapon, and degree of injury to the victim.

[4] It should be noted that several agencies responsible for collecting crime data, such as the Canadian Centre for Criminal Justice Statistics, have proposed to collect data on race, but have consistently abandoned these plans.

[5] You should remember that there is an important sociological distinction between the concepts of "sex" and "gender." Sex refers to biological factors, whereas gender refers to the idea that "masculinities" and "femininities" are socially constructed.

[6] For a detailed empirical critique of the "women do it, too" position see DeKeseredy et. al., 1997.

[7] For example, aboriginal people make up approximately 2 percent of the total Canadian population (Fisher and Janetti, 1996)

[8] For instance, theoretical problems associated with the determination of class position include whether class should be thought of in the Marxian sense as a relationship to the means of production, in terms of socioeconomic status or income levels, or in terms of status.

[9] For more information on Skinheads in Canada, see Young and Craig (1997) and Baron 1997).

[10] As Bala (1997) reminds us, the Young Offenders Act was amended in 1995 to uniformly permit courts to receive victim impact statements.

Discussion Questions and Problem-Solving Scenarios

1. If statistical data is open to interpretation, can we really "know" *anything* about youth crime?

2. Hold a class discussion focusing on the argument that young women's experiences with crime both as perpetrators and as victims differs from that of males, and speculate as to why this is the case.

3. Write an essay speculating on the *ways* in which "race," class, and gender interact in relation to youth crime.

Suggested Readings

Hagan, F. (1997). *Research Methods in Criminal Justice and Criminology.* 4th ed. Boston: Allyn & Bacon.

Schwartz, M.D., and Milovanovic, D. (1996). *Race, Gender, and Class in Criminology: The Intersection.* New York: Garland.

Juristat (1999). *Youth Court Statistics 1997-98 Highlights.* Vol. 2, No. 19, 85-002 XIE. N.

Statues of Karl Marx and Friedrich Engels loom symbolically behind a group of children. Among the many theories exploring the causes of youth crime are the Marxist theories of left idealism and left realism, which locate the causes of youth crime within the context of capitalist social relations.

Chapter Three

Why Do Youths Commit Crimes?

INTRODUCTION

As with statistics, many students wonder about the utility of theory. Preferring to "get their hands dirty" in the so-called real world, many see theory as bordering on the esoteric, a practice conducted only by absent-minded professors asleep in an "ivory tower" that is totally divorced from the reality of what goes on outside academia. While some scholars do conduct their research in a political and social vacuum, for other social scientists, theory and evidence are inextricably linked. The importance of this connection cannot be underestimated, particularly in light of the fact that so many criminal justice practices aimed at young offenders appear to be divorced from valid empirical and theoretical insights about crime. Indeed, applying appropriate theories about youth crime to the real world is critical, given the "common sense" perception by many people that crime is a consequence of factors like poor parenting, drug use, or low moral standards (see Table 3.1).

Each of the perceptions reported in Table 3.1 are in fact "theories" about criminality. When people make judgments about the causes of crime, they are "theorizing." It matters a great deal whether perceptions of the causes of crime are correct, because, as we have seen, public pressure often drives legislators to make laws (such as the Young Offenders Act) that purport to address youth crime. But how do we know these perceptions are right? The only way to determine the validity of "hunches" about crime is to assess the degree to which these factors fit with the evidence we have about crime. In turn, the only way to determine the "goodness of fit" is to *test* the theories in question (Williams and McShane, 1994).

Table 3.1
Percentage of Canadians Reporting Factors Very Important in Causing Crime, 1998

Perceived causes of crime	Percentage reporting "very important factor"
Poor parenting	64
Increase in illegal drugs	63
"Soft" justice system	53
Poverty	52
Low moral standards	51
Unemployment	50
Violence on television	49
Lack of discipline in schools	48

Source: As reported by Canadian Centre for Justice Statistics, 1998: 55.

In this chapter, we will focus on some of the most widely read and cited theories of crime as they apply to young offenders, and will consider the relevance of these theories to policy issues.[1] Before doing so, however, we will briefly consider what a theory is and the problem of classifying theories into a meaningful framework.

What is a Theory?

Technically, a theory is a set of interrelated propositions, constructed and fitting together logically, which claim to explain one or more aspects of the world around us. Theories can be abstract, in the sense that they speculate on the nature of things that are not directly observable (for example, the "big bang" theory of the origin of the universe), or they can be concrete, focusing on observable and measurable aspects of reality to help explain that reality. Theories represent different ways of looking at the world, but in most cases they must lend themselves to something called *empirical verification*, that is, they must be testable. In addition, to be accepted in scientific communities, the results of tests of theories should consistently be replicated. Think of it this way: If one were to assert that the reason youths commit crime is because "it's God's will," it would not be a testable theory because we cannot (at least not scientifically) "measure" the extent to which God plays a role in human life, let alone determine whether God exists in the first place. These notions are a matter of *belief and faith* rather than scientific fact and are not testable. Therefore, they would not constitute a good theory.

Williams and McShane (1994: 4-6) list several other important aspects of a good theory:

1. It should be logically sound—it should not propose illogical relationships and should be internally consistent.

2. It should be able to make sense of *conflicting positions*—that is, it should be able to reconcile different facts or evidence about particular phenomena.

3. It should have *sensitizing ability*—meaning it should focus our attention on aspects of social reality that may have been ignored or forgotten.

4. It should be seen in light of the problem of *popularity*—that is, some theories are seen to be "good" because they are popular. However, popularity is not a good indicator of the validity of a theory.

The criteria making up a good theory are relatively simple to understand. Unfortunately, the same cannot be said for the way criminological theories can be classified. This is why students often have difficulty understanding where a particular theory "fits" in relation to others. For instance, theories of crime have been categorized in a myriad of ways, including but not limited to: (1) sociological or nonsociological, (2) positivist or classical, (3) macro or micro, (4) radical or conservative, (5) individualistic or environmental, (6) consensus or conflict, and (7) modern or postmodern.

This book will classify criminological theories according to whether they are individualistic or environmental. Nevertheless, the proliferation of frameworks for classifying criminological theories can sometimes be confusing. Illustrating that there are many ways of categorizing theories of crime, and that some theories overlap two or more categories, Table 3.2 provides one way of organizing theories—a typology—into a framework compatible with the way they are presented in this book.[2] This book examines theories of youth crime utilizing the labels of "individualistic" versus "environmental" causes, a distinction that will be covered fully in the following sections. In addition, however, consider the other elements of the table, reading from left to right. The first thing you will notice is that some theories of crime are "individualistic," "positivist," *and* "determinist," while others are "macro," "sociological," *and* "critical." However complicated these terms may seem, each is important because, as we shall see, applying such labels tells us something about the theory's basic assumptions.

Table 3.2
A Typology for Understanding Criminological Theories

Category	Focus	Type	Actions	A few key ideas, concepts, and theories	A few theorists
Individualistic	Micro level	Classical Philosophical Traditional	Free will	• People choose their actions • Rational self-interest • Hedonism • Rights	Bentham James Q. Wilson
		Psychological Positivist Traditional	Determined	• Inadequate self-control • Attention Deficit Disorder • Egocentric personality • Antisocial personality	Andrews & Bonta
		Biological Positivist Traditional	Determined	• Genetic deficiency • Body type • Low blood sugar • Schizophrenia • Personality disorder	Lombroso Sheldon
Environmental	Macro level	Sociological Positivist Traditional	Free will within determined circumstances	• Social structure is criminogenic • Anomie, strain • Status frustration • Illegitimate (or no) opportunities • Inadequate social bonds • Labeling • Differential association • Social disorganization • Subculture	Durkheim, Merton Cohen, Cloward & Ohlin Hirschi Lemert, Becker Sutherland Shaw & McKay Cohen
		Sociological Philosophical Positivist Critical	Free will within determined circumstances	• Social structure is criminogenic • Class, ethnicity, and gender • Poverty, inequality • Racism • Patriarchy, feminism, masculinities • Crimes of the powerful • Left realism • Peacemaking • Constitutive postmodernism	Quinney, MacLean W.J. Wilson Messerschmidt, Chesney-Lind Simon, Friedrichs Young, DeKeseredy, MacLean, Currie Pepinsky Henry & Milovanovic
Integrated	Macro/micro level	Sociological Biological Psychological Positivist Critical	Free will within determined circumstances	• Crime is a complex psychosocial and/or a biosocial phenomenon	Barak

A second point you might notice is that "positivism" appears to be connected to almost every type of criminological theory. This is because positivism is more a "method of inquiry" or philosophical position than a criminological theory per se (Williams and McShane, 1994). It emphasizes the centrality of scientific method in understanding human behaviour, and posits that behaviour is determined by forces (psychological, biological, or social) over which human beings have limited control. Positivism has had and continues to have a major influence on criminal justice policy for both youths and adults, and so we must be aware of its relationship to criminological theories.

In the fourth column of the table, the term "actions" refers to the assumptions made by theoretical perspectives regarding basic ideas about the role of human action in theories of crime. This is important because policies are often based on assumptions about people's motivations—assumptions that may or may not be true. Is it true, for example, that people are "rational self-maximizers," "pleasure-seeking" beings who rationally weigh the costs and benefits of their actions? Or is it the case that people are "puppets on a string," that is, their behaviour is "determined" by forces beyond their control? What are the implications of these two very different positions for crime control and prevention? If young people choose to commit crimes, should they not get what they deserve? That is, should the punishment not fit the crime? However, does this change if we assume that young people have very little control over the circumstances that condition and shape their behaviour, such as school, parenting, or income?

Finally, note the table's distinction between "traditional" and "critical" criminology. There are many varieties of theory within these two schools of criminological thought, just as there are many variations *within* subcategories such as "feminist" criminology.

Crime theory is obviously far more complex than any table or diagram can describe. This chapter will examine theories and perspectives that have been influential, controversial, and enduring in criminology, particularly in relation to youth crime. There are many other theories of crime that are not discussed here. As you encounter these in other books and in your lectures, I invite you to use the table to help you conceptualize their basic arguments and relationship to other theories.

YOUTH CRIME IS A PROPERTY OF INDIVIDUALS

Individualistic approaches to crime assume that people commit wrongdoings because they are simply doing what comes naturally to them (Barak, 1998). Whether these natural behaviours are caused by psychological or biological deficiencies, or constitute "rational" choices, the main idea is that the causes of—and therefore the solutions to—crime can be found "inside" the individual.

At the same time, those adhering to individualistic models contend that social structural conditions have little relevance to predicting and controlling crime. They variously argue that criminal youth are simply "out of control," "lack morality," "have anti-social personalities," or show "little respect" for authority, people, or their property. Accordingly, solutions to youth crime call for a range of policy responses, including "sending women back to the home to provide care and nurturing for their children," "returning to traditional family structures and values," and "making young people more accountable for their actions." Other researchers in this category maintain that crime is an outcome of "bad genes," "lower intelligence," "psychological maladjustment," "neurological dysfunction," or "chemical imbalances." They stress the importance of medical treatment and intervention, counseling, nutrition, or therapy as the most effective response to youth crime (see Box 3.1). Each of these theoretical approaches and their implications for youth justice is considered in more detail below.

Box 3.1

Predisposition to Violence Found

The Toronto Star
Wednesday, December 14, 1994
By Lisa Priest: Health Policy Reporter

Boys who were rejected by their mothers early in life and suffered birth complications are predisposed to committing violent crimes as adults, a new study shows. The 35-year study—the first of its kind—found those baby boys were more prone to commit murders, rapes and armed robberies as adults, according to the American Medical Association's Archives of General Psychiatry. "While only 4.5 percent of the subjects had both risk factors, this small group accounted for 18 percent of all violent crimes," said psychology professor Adrian Raine of the University of Southern California, who was involved in the study published yesterday. "If we can provide pre-natal and post-natal services, we could reduce violence by 18 percent," he said, adding that the violent crimes include attempted murder, assault, illegal possession of a weapon and threats of violence. Birth complications included breech deliveries, forceps deliveries, being delivered with the umbilical cord around the neck and suffering a lack of oxygen, according to the study of 4,269 boys born in Copenhagen between September 1959 and December 1961. The boys were picked because Denmark's National Crime Register holds the "most systematic and accurate crime records in the world," Raine said in a telephone interview. Researchers followed the boys into young adulthood and checked their criminal status from age 17 to 19 with the register, where all police contacts and court decisions involving Danish citizens are recorded. Early child-

Box 3.1, *continued*

hood rejection was defined as whether the pregnancy was unwanted, the mother tried to abort the fetus or the infant was placed in a full-time institution such as a hospital or social service care for more than four months during the first year of life. However, the mere presence of either birth complications or maternal rejection did not predispose a child to violence, Raine said. But "when you place the two together, it's like an explosion." That's because children with birth complications sometimes suffer brain dysfunction that can lead to a lower intelligence, school failure and then work failure, he said. And children who have not bonded with their mothers in the first year of life sometimes become "affection-less" and unable to have "meaningful, intimate relationships." "If you don't care about bonding with someone, shoving a knife in someone's back or blowing a hole in their head may not bother you," he said.

Source: Toronto Star Syndicate. Reprinted with permission.

Classical and Neoclassical Criminology[3]

Classical theories start with the idea that all people have equal rights in a society that is held together by consensus on the belief that crime is morally wrong. Moreover, classical and neoclassical criminology assume that:

1. People are pleasure-seeking, or "hedonistic," beings. They want to minimize pain and maximize pleasure.

2. People make rational decisions about their actions.

3. They weigh the costs and benefits of their actions before acting.

Theories of youth crime informed by classical thinking suppose that young people will naturally gravitate toward behaviours that are pleasurable (e.g., exciting or risk-taking behaviours), or that they will engage in such behaviours to achieve some pleasure in the future (e.g., they will steal to gain the pleasure from a stolen good). In doing so, the young person will "calculate" the costs and benefits associated with his or her actions, weighing the pleasure that might be gained from the activity or the end result against the potential pain of being caught and punished.

According to this type of theory, in order to successfully prevent crime, our society must create an environment in which the costs of committing a crime "outweigh" the benefits. For classical and neoclassical theory, there are two ways in which this can be accomplished. One is through *general deterrence*, which involves creating a criminal justice system that visibly punishes individuals for their wrongdoings, and thus deters others from potentially committing crimes because they fear similar consequences. The second one is *specific deterrence*, which is the principle that those who are punished for a crime will not commit another crime because their punishment has "taught them a lesson." The aim is to remove the offender, and the threat to public order and safety they represent, from the rest of society.

According to classical thinking, if punishment is to work, it must be certain, proportional to the crime, and timely (Schneider, 1990; Williams and Hawkins, 1986). Young people should *know* that if they get caught they will be punished. Moreover, their punishments should fit the crimes, and should occur shortly after the individual is found guilty so that the association between the crime and the punishment is fresh in their minds. Presumably, this will ensure that they will not do it again. To what extent is this approach validated by empirical research? Baron and Kennedy (1998: 27) point to research showing that "empirical tests of this proposition generally suggest that the perceived certainty of legal punishment does provide a moderate deterrent effect. . . . while the perceived severity of punishment does not." However, Tunnell's (1992b) study of the decision-making processes of repeat offenders showed that while the benefits of committing the crime were deliberated, the risks of being caught were considered rarely or minimally.

In a way, classical approaches are not really theories of the *causes* of crime because they assume that individuals are automatically and naturally inclined to commit crimes. As such, classical criminology is more of a philosophical standpoint than a scientific theory. According to this point of view, developing mechanisms in society to curb or control the real and potential levels of crime inherent in all of us is the most important aspect of crime policy. In other words, in the world of classical criminology, young people commit crimes because they are inadequately controlled, and the solution to the problem is to increase the likelihood that they will be caught and punished (DeKeseredy and Schwartz, 1996).

While the general principles of classical criminology are more than 200 years old, its basic philosophy is still pertinent today. One of the principle features of the Young Offenders Act discussed in Chapter One is that young people should be held responsible for their actions. Remember also that proposed amendments to the act call for swifter, more "meaningful" consequences for youth crime, an idea with special relevance in light of public perceptions that young people are "getting away with murder."

As you can see, the ideas embedded in classical criminology tend to dominate contemporary Canadian policies toward youth in conflict with the law. In concrete terms, this means we should expect to see a continued or increased emphasis on policing and incarcerating youth. In Chapter Four, we shall see if this has indeed been the case in Canada.

Does this approach make sense to you? Do you think that people rationally determine the pros and cons of committing a criminal offence before doing so? Some commentators, such as Currie (1985), argue that such a process is unlikely, especially when we consider that violent crimes such as homicide are often committed in the "heat of passion." Moreover, research conducted by Schneider (1990) shows that youths' perceptions of greater certainty and severity of punishment can actually *increase* criminal behaviour, particularly because some youths achieve greater status in the eyes of their peers if they have "done some time" (Katz, 1988). Finally, what if choosing to commit a crime *is* the most rational decision a young person can make? For instance, as we pointed out in the last chapter, prostitution is sometimes the only way young people can make a living, while many homeless youths steal or rob simply to obtain the basic necessities of life (Hagan and McCarthy, 1997). If you were in such circumstances, would the threat of punishment deter you from doing what you had to do in order to survive?

Perhaps the most incriminating evidence against the classical perspective emerges when we think about the relationship between incarceration and crime. The United States has the highest incarceration rates in the world, yet they also have the highest violent crime rates of all industrialized nations. While classical theory suggests that high rates of imprisonment will *reduce* crime, in the United States, this is clearly not the case. Moreover, because we are unsure of exactly how much youth crime there is, it is difficult to accurately assess the impact of a strategy based on deterrence.

Classical and neoclassical theories have been very influential in shaping contemporary justice strategies for Canadian youths. In subsequent chapters we will discuss possible reasons for the popularity of these perspectives and will examine the value of some current tactics based on classical thinking. For now, you should be alert to the linkages between the assumptions of classical thinking, the notion of deterrence, and what you already know about the workings of the youth criminal justice system.

Biological and Psychological Theories of Crime

Whereas classical theory assumes and accepts the existence of the motivation to offend, psychological and biological theories assume that people offend because of biological or psychological abnormalities. More succinctly, they assume that some young people are *predisposed* to crime. While it is impossible to review and assess the variety of psychological and biological theories here, a few major points about these perspectives should be made.

First, a bit of history. Biological and psychological theories of crime have been around for hundreds of years. In earlier years, this author exposed students to such theories with the express purpose of ridiculing them. This was easy to do. For instance, it was easy to point out the flaws in the work of Lombroso, who argued that criminals were identifiable by the physical characteristics of their skulls and concluded that they were "throwbacks" to earlier stages of human development—a notion called *atavism*. Although Lombroso employed scientific methods to reach his conclusions, and can therefore be considered one of the earliest criminological positivists, his scientific methodology was seriously flawed. Moreover, he had no idea how to deal with the fact that female criminals did not seem to have the same kind of "abnormalities" he observed in males—so he simply concluded that *all* women were atavistic (DeKeseredy and Schwartz, 1996).

Or consider the work of Sigmund Freud, who maintained that crime was the result of the battle between id, ego, and superego, where one's conscience (the superego) is underdeveloped to such an extent that the innate desire to commit antisocial acts (the id) dominates behaviour. Let us not forget, of course, that for Freud, women were inferior to men. Freudian theory may well have prompted criminologists to consider the importance of early childhood experiences. However, in addition to being clearly misogynist, the fact is that concepts like the id, ego, and superego cannot be tested.

Relaying information about these early theories to students almost always elicited amusement. However, there was also a collective sense of relief because the students assumed that modern criminology had clearly "moved beyond" such conclusions. Have we, though? And to what extent have new insights into the biological and psychological bases of human behaviour contributed to our understanding of crime?

Regardless of the obvious failures of early attempts to find predispositions to crime, part of sociological criminologists' dissatisfaction with psychological and biological theories stemmed from the need for early sociology to establish itself as a science in its own right. Today, many sociologists are recognizing that crime is a *psychosocial* and/or *biosocial* phenomenon, not because sociologists have "mellowed" with time, but because new evidence compels us, with a critical eye, to entertain new possibilities.

For example, relatively new evidence from biology shows that lowered levels of serotonin (a neurotransmitter) have been observed in the brains of violent criminals (LeMarquand, Pihl, and Benkelfat, 1994). According to Short (1997: 148), "statistical studies of the relationship between violence, other deviant behavior, and possible sources of brain damage and neurological dysfunction find some support for their causal importance." While the evidence in this regard is compelling, it is important that it seems only to be valid for a very *small* proportion of offenders. Moreover, one must consider the relationship between social experiences and conditions and these chemical or hormonal imbalances. Could it be that some young children who engage in criminal conduct suffer chemical dysfunction because they do not eat properly, cannot afford adequate health care, or because they are physically abused? While there can be little doubt that there are connections between biology and crime, one point is clear—biology and criminal behaviour are *mediated* by social factors and environments (Short, 1997).

Psychological theories of crime have traditionally been concerned with the links between Intelligence Quotient (IQ) and crime, with the main idea being that those with "lesser intelligence" are more likely to become criminals. However persuasive this idea may be, the evidence supporting such a claim is not good. First, IQ tests are sensitive to cultural and social bias and really only measure one dimension of overall "intelligence." Second, studies on the relationship between IQ and crime show that there are virtually no differences between those who are criminal and those who are not. Finally, low-level intelligence among criminals is probably related to their ineptitude at evading detection and does not seem to be a factor for white-collar criminals. In short, criminals are not less intelligent than noncriminals (Bohm, 1997).

More recently, consider the claim, advanced by Andrews and Bonta (1998: 143), that antisocial cognitions, antisocial associates, a history of antisocial behaviour, and a number of indicators of antisocial personality are the "most well-established" risk factors associated with crime. Empirical evidence indicates that these are, indeed, reasonably good *correlates* of criminal behaviour, but there are several problems with viewing them as important to the exclusion of the *social context* in which they occur. For instance, how well would the following characteristics— used by Andrews and Bonta to define "antisocial" personality—describe the feelings and attitudes of the average teenager?

- Restless energy

- Adventuresomeness

- Impulsiveness

- Poor problem-solving skills

- Hostility

- Callous disregard for other people and responsibilities

With the possible exception of the last criterion, each of these factors describe aspects of most teenagers. Moreover, none of these factors are eternal constants. Defining someone as having "restless energy" or being "adventuresome" depends upon who is doing the defining and the cultural and social context in which we judge others. In short, as with characteristics such as IQ, these factors are socially constructed.

Like biological theories, psychological approaches demonstrate that *some* (particularly very violent) offenders demonstrate antisocial and even psychotic tendencies. Again, as shown in Chapter Two, such individuals make up a very small proportion of all young offenders. When it comes to other offences committed by young people, psychology and biology have little to say. What biological or psychological risk factors, for example, would explain the offence of escaping custody? If you were locked up in jail, wouldn't you want to run away?

To be fair, some biosocial and psychosocial theories do attempt to account for the influence of antisocial peers and other associates, which have traditionally been the focus of certain sociological theories of crime. Again, though, we are left with the problem of defining the term "antisocial." To illustrate, consider that many young people growing up in the 1960s who smoked pot, wore their hair long, and railed against authority were considered, in that era, to be antisocial. A lot of them grew up to be "perfectly respectable" accountants, lawyers, dentists, and the like. In effect, criminal or "deviant" behaviour *varies* during the course of one's life. It is ludicrous to suppose that *all* people possessing these "traits" are predisposed or at risk for criminal conduct, while all those who do not are "normal" (Curran and Renzetti, 1994).

In addition, if psychological, biological, or genetic dysfunction is related to all criminal behaviour, then why do these factors do such a poor job of explaining corporate or white-collar crime, which causes far more harm to individuals and property than adult *and* youth street crime combined (Frank and Lynch, 1992; Simon, 1996). Similarly, these theories are unable to account for variation in crime rates across time and geography. In other words, if the causes of crime are mostly biological and psychological, then why is there such significant variation in crime between nations like Japan, Canada, and the United States? Do people in these countries have different genetic, psychological, or biological makeups?

One final issue is that of causality. These theories predict that factors like genetic predisposition, antisocial personality, or low levels of educational achievement are predictive of crime. However, they have neglected to consider that these factors may be caused *themselves* by social factors such as inequality, diminished life chances, and the feminization of poverty. As Rothenberg and Heinz (1998: 58) cynically remark, it is a "no-brainer" that biological and psychological research will someday "discover" that:

> . . . . the poorest of the poor have increased rates of alcohol and drug abuse, dysfunctional families, and poor social networks, low IQ, and a high rate of 'maternal neglect'. . . . Given the current establishment of a genetic discourse on crime and "deviance," these findings will be interpreted as the result and not the cause of the misery.

In sum, there is no question that understanding and responding to crime require serious consideration of what goes on in the minds or bodies of individuals, but, just as with some sociological theories, which may make too much of factors such as socioeconomic status or geographical location, the case for particular biological or psychological factors is often overstated. Biological and psychological theories of crime help us to understand some aspects of crime and some types of crime, but fail to explain others. Most variants tend to ignore the relationship between social factors and biological and psychological functioning.

The policy implications of these perspectives include treatment and rehabilitation. While many sociologists generally support such programs, they also argue that our response to crime should attempt to change the social environment in which biological and psychological factors interact. Kelly (1996: 467) puts the matter more strongly, arguing that treatment programs focusing exclusively on the individual are usually unsuccessful because policymakers and practitioners have failed to recognize that those being "treated" exist in a social world to which they must return after treatment. That social world has made demands on them, has played a central role in making that person who he or she is, and will continue to do so after the individual has been "rehabilitated." To ignore this is to misunderstand the realities of that individual's life. Not surprisingly, when individual treatment fails, the fault is often seen as residing with the individual, not in social terms—ironically perpetuating a hopeless cycle of failure. Ignoring the individual's immediate social environment (such as peers, parents, and school) may be one thing, but individualized treatment cannot deal with the larger social environment within which peers, parents, schools, and the offender exist. Put another way, psychological and biological "solutions" to youth crime ignore larger social, political, and economic factors. Such factors include the way market societies operate to create schools that set students up for "success" and "failure," that marginalize those who do not meet "standards," or that create conditions under which families live in poverty from which there is little likelihood of escape.

In the next chapter we will examine other consequences of utilizing biological and psychological perspectives for the administration of youth justice, particularly in light of the reality that, ironically, such approaches, in conjunction with classical thinking, are quite influential today.

YOUTH CRIME IS A PROPERTY OF THE ENVIRONMENT

Those who argue that youth crime is a function of environmental influences usually point to the *criminogenic* role played by socialization agents such as peers, families, and schools, and social structural variables, such as poverty, inequality, and sexism. Before examining these theories, we need to briefly review the essential arguments of four broad sociological theoretical perspectives.[4]

Functionalism, whose earliest proponent was Emile Durkheim, maintains that: (1) people are essentially egoistic; (2) societies survive because of value consensus, that is, most people share a belief in certain basic values; (3) every social phenomenon and institution has a function in society (if they did not play a role (or function) in society, they would not exist); and (4) society can be viewed as a biological organism in which the parts are interdependent and (in properly functioning societies) in equilibrium. This sociological school of thought focuses on macro-level problems.

Symbolic interactionism, pioneered by George Herbert Mead, assumes that while macro-level issues are interesting, what is of real importance is the study of the ways in which people interact with one another using symbols to communicate. In other words, symbolic interactionists contend that social problems such as crime can be understood only in terms of the *meanings* that such actions have for the individuals involved. Accordingly, symbolic interactionists focus on micro-level issues.

Like functionalism, *conflict theory* is concerned with macro-level issues. In direct contrast to functionalism, however, conflict theory, which is associated with the work of Marx and Weber, maintains that people *do not* share equal beliefs in certain basic values; it is conflict, not consensus, that characterizes modern societies. Maintaining order in society therefore requires the exercise of power, usually by a powerful minority. The unequal distribution of power tends, therefore, to create conflict and repression at the expense of the minority.

Feminist approaches to understanding society, while diverse, essentially all start from the idea that women's experiences of the world are different than men's. Daly and Chesney-Lind (1988: 502) refer to feminism as "a set of theories about women's oppression *and* a set of strategies for change." [emphasis in original] Moreover, feminist perspectives emphasize that social roles, while socially constructed, are dominated by male interests, and that gender and sex are distinct. Gender inequality is viewed as the major cause of the continued oppression and marginalization of women. Because they focus on macro-level issues like gender, class, and patriarchy, as well as women's lived experiences, feminist theories can be both micro- and macro-level.

As you consider the following theories of youth crime, you may wish to think about them in relation to these four major perspectives. Doing this will give you a sense of their intellectual tradition and sociological "roots," and will give you an idea of their underpinning assumptions about societies and individuals.

Strain-Subcultural Theories

As the name suggests, *strain theories* of youth crime emphasize the tension between people and social structure. This tension can take various forms, and different theorists within the strain theory tradition have focused on different dimensions of the tension. In general, however, all varieties of strain theory start with the proposition that social structures exert pressure on individuals to conform to basic kinds of behaviour, which could be conformist or deviant. As pointed out in Chapter One, for instance, our society encourages young people to perform particular roles: that is, to be obedient, ambitious, individualistic, and so on. We also raise the goal of accumulating wealth to an extraordinarily high level, while socializing youth to consume and behave "like adults." The resulting "strain" between the goals transmitted by our culture and the legitimate opportunities to achieve these goals underpins criminal behaviour. Thus, supporters of strain theory contend that we must consider ways in which society can better support people who are "falling through the cracks" by creating more useful social supports, such as universal child care, or by changing the structure of the economy so that fewer people are victimized by job loss, diminished work opportunities, or welfare (Currie, 1993; Wilson, 1996)

Thus, the essential argument of strain theory is that when young people are unable to achieve these "culturally prescribed" goals legitimately, they experience strain because they are not able to "fit in" to society (Barak, 1998). So, they find other ways to fit in, which may involve engaging in *illegitimate* (i.e., criminal) activities to achieve particular goals (i.e., money or status). Of course, not all youths who are unable to achieve these goals turn to illegitimate activities. In fact, Robert K. Merton (1938), the "father" of strain theory, maintained that several outcomes of strain were possible (see Table 3.3). In contrast to those who accept society's goals and have the legitimate means of achieving them (conformists), or those who do not really subscribe to these goals but go through the conventional motions anyway (ritualists), some people face blocked opportunities to achieve these same culturally given goals and so resort to other, sometimes criminal, means of achieving them (innovators). Still others may reject culturally determined goals and replace them with their own goals while also finding nonconventional ways of achieving them (rebels). Finally, there are those who, having failed to achieve goals legitimately, simply drop out of the game altogether (retreatists).

Table 3.3
Merton's Typology: Modes of Adaptation to Strain

Modes of Adaptation	Cultural Goals	Institutionalized Means
Conformity	Accept	Accept
Innovation*	Accept	Reject
Ritualism	Reject	Accept
Retreatism*	Reject	Reject
Rebellion*	Reject but replace with new goals	Reject but replace with new means

* denotes that criminal activity could be associated with this mode

It is important to remember that Merton was more concerned with all potential forms of deviant behaviour (of which crime is only one possibility) as an outcome of strain. In addition, he pointed out that cultural goals could be *anything* emphasizing achievement in the extreme—it did not necessarily have to be acquiring wealth (Williams and McShane, 1994).

Albert Cohen (1955) provided an important twist to Merton's theory that is particularly useful for our topic. Cohen felt that Merton's version of strain theory was unable to explain juvenile delinquency because his research found that young delinquents did not really "buy in" to the culturally transmitted goal of financial success that seemed to motivate adult offenders. In his examination of youth gangs, he observed that much youth crime seemed to be aimless, malicious, and negative. Instead of financial gain, he argued that these young people wanted status and respect, something they were unable to get in their schools and community because these were largely middle-class institutions that used "middle class measuring rods" to judge them. While middle-class children were able to meet the "standards" set by schools and teachers, working-class kids often could not, resulting in *status frustration*. As in Merton's typology, the outcome of this kind of strain could vary. According to Cohen, some youths might work harder to meet middle-class standards, while others could "reject" the standards and accept a working-class stature. Others might find like-minded individuals in the same situation and form a *delinquent subculture* that would provide the missing status because the standards in such groups *can* be achieved. Finally, achieving status in the subculture might involve *inverting* middle-class values, or doing exactly the opposite of what is expected of "good" middle-class youth.

Although there are obvious similarities between Cohen's and Merton's theories, it was left to Cloward and Ohlin (1960) to provide another insight—that crime as an outcome of strain could be driven by a quest for financial gain and at the same time could be a strategy for gaining status. Cloward and Ohlin's theory of *differential opportunity* maintained that it was not just about youth (or adults) gaining access to legitimate opportunities to pursue the Canadian or American dream, but also that some individuals had access to *illegitimate* opportunities. By this they meant that some people live in stable, but criminal environments (*criminal subcultures*) in which they can both learn and internalize criminal norms, techniques, and values. There could be other outcomes as well. *Conflict or violent subcultures* could arise in situations in which there were neither legitimate or illegitimate opportunities, and where youths both achieved a "reputation" and released their frustrations via gang violence. Finally, *retreatist subcultures* occurred when youths were unable to join or form either violent or criminal subcultures and so retreated into the haze of alcohol and drug addiction.

A more recent variation of strain theory advanced by Agnew (1985) argues that in addition to being aware of blocked opportunities, we should pay attention to the strain that arises in attempting but failing to *avoid* stressful situations such as family violence, bullying peers, or sexual harassment. For Agnew (1985: 163), then, "adolescents located in aversive environments from which they cannot escape are more likely to be delinquent."

As mentioned earlier, the essence of strain theory perspectives on youth crime is that youths are motivated to commit crimes because they are unable to achieve goals that are prescribed for them, or because they cannot escape from difficult personal circumstances. One important contribution of strain theory was that it shifted attention away from the properties of individuals, toward the ways in which societal variables affect crime. However, there are some shortcomings to this approach. While we cannot examine all the problems with strain theory, we will look into several key ones.

One criticism that was leveled against strain theory is that it assumes that all individuals aspire to middle-class values and successes (Miller, 1958). While this critique was debated for a time, research generally indicates that most working-class youth *do* in fact desire the same things as their middle-class counterparts (Kornhauser, 1978).

Another criticism leveled at strain theory is that it fails to ask where the strain is coming from in the first place. Put differently, if some youths experience an inability to achieve certain goals legitimately, then why is this so? Where do these goals come from? Who propagates them? And why are some people blocked access to legitimate opportunities for achieving them? In effect, strain theory does not go far enough in locating its key ideas in the broader political and economic structure of society. In the same vein, strain theories neither question why some actions are defined as criminal in the first place, nor who has the power to define them as such.

Another issue stems from the expectation that the problems faced by today's youths in accessing legitimate opportunities (see Chapter One) would result in higher levels of crime than what we currently know of. Put simply, if strain is such a problem today, then why do we not see more youth crime? A related and more damning criticism is that strain theories, as developed by Merton and Cloward and Ohlin, ignore the gendered nature of crime (Hackler, 1994). Given women's fewer opportunities to participate in paid work and their concentration in low-paying job ghettos, we would, once again, expect that females would have higher crime rates than males, which (as Chapter Two illustrated) they do not.[5]

The policy implications of strain theory center on its two key pillars—legitimate opportunities and culturally prescribed goals. In other words, if strain causes youth crime, then the solution is either to provide young people with better access to legitimate opportunities for success, or to help them to redefine success in a different way. The last strategy seems somewhat unlikely, given the emphasis in modern North American society on achieving the highest financial and personal goals imaginable. However, a great deal has been invested (principally in the United States) in the notion of increasing the number of, and access to, legitimate opportunities. The greatest difficulty with this strategy for reducing crime, however, is that ultimately the logic of free-market societies implicitly and explicitly discourages and blocks certain people from realizing their aspirations. It is very difficult to provide people with truly equal opportunities for success in societies built on a foundation of inequality, and in which certain groups of people have a vested interest in reproducing inequality. Despite this difficulty (and perhaps because of it), programs designed to reduce crime by increasing opportunities have had limited success. Programs in the United States and Canada, such as "workfare," "retraining," Headstart, the Job Corps, and—more broadly—the "war on poverty," have clearly failed to create a level playing field for all citizens. Indeed, such programs may well have reproduced inequality and strain by pathologizing their clients, by acting as a conduit into dead-end jobs, and by controlling a potentially troublesome class of individuals while merely appearing to "do something" about the problem (Davis, 1975). As we saw in Chapter One, Canada continues to maintain a child poverty rate of one in five, and high youth unemployment rates while proudly crowing about its ranking by the United Nations as the best nation in the world to live (unless you are a woman or a child).

Although strain theory has been very influential in sociological criminology, few have actually attempted to empirically verify its hypotheses with data on groups (Williams and McShane, 1994). Nevertheless, strain theories have been very important in diverting attention away from individual causes of crime and toward the role of the social environment. Readers should practice applying this theoretical approach, as well as others we have discussed so far, with the exercise in Box 3.2.

Box 3.2

Exercise: Which is More Relevant in Explaining This Incident: Psychological, Biological or Strain Theories?

A Look at the 'Trenchcoat Mafia'

Source: AP Online Date: 21-Apr-1999 23:08 Document ID: ED19990421090000050 Subject(s): National
Author(s): DAVID FOSTER, Associated Press Writer
Story Filed: Thursday, April 21, 1999 11:08 PM EDT

LITTLETON, Colo. (AP)—Dylan Klebold and Eric Harris hurled insults at Jews, blacks and Hispanics at Columbine High School. But they REALLY hated the athletes, who had power and popularity—everything they didn't.

"All jocks stand up!" one of the attackers yelled during their murderous spree Tuesday. "We're going to kill every one of you."

They killed 13 people in the deadliest school massacre in recent years. Then Klebold and Harris turned their guns on themselves.

As horrible as their assault on classmates was, it did not come out of the blue: Klebold, Harris and others in a band of outcasts who called themselves the Trenchcoat Mafia had a long-running feud with Columbine athletes, including a recent confrontation in which the "mafiosi" showed up carrying swords and brass knuckles.

The Trenchcoat Mafia was no secret society. Members posed for a yearbook photo last year. They had their own special spot in the cafeteria, near the stairs. They wore black trench coats—no matter the season—and berets with German crosses. They openly admired Hitler. They spoke constantly of war and guns, and Harris had made a video at school in which he bragged about his new guns.

After Paducah and Edinboro, Jonesboro and Springfield, how could such provocative behavior not raise alarm?

Rather easily, it turns out.

If fellow students at Columbine were concerned—and some now say they were—they said little to adults, figuring they could handle these troublesome misfits themselves.

If teachers and police noticed, they passed it off as teen-age rebellion, unpopular kids looking for a sense of belonging.

And if parents like Steve Cohn worried about their children's safety, they rested easy knowing that Columbine High was the nicest of schools in the nicest of areas.

"We moved here 11 years ago because of the schools," Cohn said. "It's been a great neighborhood. Until now."

Cohn's son, Aaron, 15, narrowly escaped execution Tuesday. Lying on his stomach in the library, Aaron cowered as one of the masked gunmen leveled a shotgun at his head. A few moments earlier, a girl had jumped on Cohn's back, covering the baseball slogan on his shirt. The gunman moved on and chose another victim.

A few weeks ago, the big news at Columbine High was pranksters putting Superglue in all the outside door locks.

Most cliques here would be familiar on any U.S. high school campus: band kids, nerds, stoners, skateboarders and, at the top of the pecking order, athletes.

Box 3.2, *continued*

Harder to label were the dozen members of the Trenchcoat Mafia. Some fellow students described them as resembling "Gothics," sharing a penchant for black clothes and ghoulish makeup. Their long black dusters fit the Gothic style, but also that of Old West villains. Members of the group simply said the coats kept them warm.

Their interest in Hitler and World War II was well-known around school. They played war games and bragged about their guns. Harris and Klebold sometimes spoke German in the hallways and made references to "4-20," Hitler's birthday, said Aaron Cohn, who lives five doors down from the tidy, two-story home on a quiet cul-de-sac where Harris' family moved in a couple years ago. The massacre took place on Hitler's birthday.

Cohn said Harris, 18, was nonetheless a quiet kid who hadn't caused him any problems in the past. Other neighbors echoed that.

"He was a nice guy," said Matt Good, 16, who lives two doors away. "Shy person, didn't say much. I'd see him walk from the car to the house, and that's about it."

Harris' parents were nowhere in sight this week as reporters streamed past their home. Neighbors said they didn't know much about the family, except that the father was a retired military man.

Harris and Klebold were arrested last year for breaking into a car and completed their probation in January.

Klebold, 17, and other Trenchcoats had reputations for being smart and skilled at computers. Choir teacher Lee Andres remembers the 6-foot-4, blond Klebold as a smart kid. He ran the sound for one of last year's school musicals.

"They were extremely bright, but not good students," Andres told the Denver Rocky Mountain News. "They disliked authority. They did not like to be told what to do."

By all accounts, they held a special hatred for athletes—a contempt returned in good measure. John Duven said his teen-age son, a jock, almost got into a fight with them last year, but Duven talked him out of it.

The hostilities resurfaced this year.

"A couple of months ago, the jocks were supposed to fight them," said Good, a football player. They made a date to rumble: a Friday night at a baseball field. The jocks showed up, but the Trenchcoats were two hours late, and they went to the wrong spot, Good said. They also showed up carrying swords and brass knuckles—not the jocks' idea of a clean fight. The rumble was never rescheduled.

"The jocks said forget it," Good said.

School officials said they'd had no discipline problems with Klebold or Harris, and they passed under the radar of the Jefferson County Sheriff's Department, said spokesman Steve Davis.

After the shooting, investigators questioned other members, but Davis said there was no indication other members took part in the actual shooting.

Steve Cohn finds it hard to believe that school authorities or police didn't notice the group.

"Wasn't it obvious, to someone?" he asked. "All the kids knew about it. You'd think a teacher would notice. You'd think the sheriff's department would know."

Differential Association Theory

As a novice parent, I once asked friends with older children how they had managed to raise such good kids. They told me that the key had been to provide the children with lots of love, to keep them busy with legitimate things to do, and to keep an eye on with whom they were "hanging around." For these parents, this was a common-sense approach to dealing with the potential of all children to engage in deviant, and possibly criminal, behaviour. It was based on the premise that young people *learn* how to be bad from others.

The idea that crime is something that is learned is one of the most attractive theories of youth crime. Most people share the belief that young people are especially susceptible to learning new and sometimes deviant lifestyles. Hence, the role of parents, peers, and others from whom young people learn skills, norms, and values cannot be underestimated.

This basic idea forms the core of Edwin Sutherland's (1947) *differential association* theory of crime. Sutherland, whose ideas belong within the tradition of symbolic interactionism, maintained that deviant behaviour is learned in interaction with others in a process of communication. Further, he argued that most of this process occurs in intimate groups, and includes learning the techniques, attitudes, motives, and ways of rationalizing deviant behaviour.

In the process of learning, people gravitate toward deviant behaviour based on their favourable or unfavourable assessment of the meaning of legal codes. If this assessment is more heavily weighted in favour of violating the law, they will engage in delinquent behaviour. Sutherland also provided a series of concepts for understanding how differential associations vary in their quality—in terms of: (1) *frequency*, the number of times one is exposed to ideas; (2) *duration*, the length of time one is exposed to ideas; (3) *priority*, the extent to which people are exposed to learning at early stages of their development; and (4) *intensity*, the importance to the potential delinquent of the individual from whom he or she is learning.

Finally, Sutherland suggests that learning deviant behaviour is like learning any other kind of behaviour, and that one cannot explain crime by reference only to criminals' general needs and values because these generally tend to be the same as the needs and values of other, law-abiding individuals. (For example, while some people steal for money, law-abiding people simply work for money. Therefore the need for money is not the cause of crime.[6]) Moreover, association with prosocial, anticriminal associates can provide people with opportunities to learn conforming, noncriminal behaviour.

Sutherland's theory has been very influential. It pointed out the role of learning and relationships with others in criminal behaviour, and provides us with a way to understand, theoretically, why some people commit crimes while others do not, even though they exist in similar situations. In addition, Sutherland was aware that learning can be enhanced and inhibited by virtue of the context in which it takes place. Thus, he maintained that communities had a role to play in an individual's learning process because they could, depending on their level of organization, either promote or discourage criminal associations (Vold, Bernard, and Snipes, 1998). Sutherland not only suggested that who a person associates with and learns from can determine whether they become criminal, but he also alerted us to the *quality* of those interactions. Thus, the theory of differential association alerts us to both the *content* of what is learned and the learning *process* in relation to criminal behaviour.

Several criticisms of differential association have been advanced. The most important of these may be that the theory is likely untestable because it is difficult, if not impossible, to measure "definitions favourable or unfavourable to violation of the law" (however, see Matsueda, 1988, for the argument that differential association theory can be tested). Another critique is related to the problem of causality. It may be the case that crime is caused by youth associating with other criminal individuals, but the opposite may be true instead. That is, youth may *seek out* other like-minded individuals as a form of social support (Vold, Bernard, and Snipes, 1998), and they may learn crime in the process of interacting with people they have chosen or need to be with. The question remains, then, what causes youth to be drawn to these others in the first place?

Since the advent of Sutherland's theory, a great deal of attention has been focused on learning as the mechanism for criminal behaviour. One of the most important "subsets" of learning approaches—cultural and subcultural theories—have some interesting applications to youth crime, so we will consider them briefly.

Differential association emphasized the content and process of learning and the environment in which such learning takes place. Similarly, cultural and subcultural theories focus on content but pay a little more attention to the role of ideas (and what they contain) in creating crime. For instance, some scholars, such as Miller (1958), argued that the lower class had distinctly different values (e.g., whether to stay out of or get into trouble, toughness, excitement, and so on) than middle-class people who supposedly valued achievement. Working-class culture, then, could easily result in the creation of an environment that could generate gang delinquency (Vold, Bernard, and Snipes, 1998).

Other learning approaches focus on the learning process, arguing that behaviour is not only learned in intimate or primary relationships, but also in other environments. Akers's (1998) *social learning theory*, for example, states that young people could learn criminal behaviour by observing the consequences of such behaviour for other people, through imitation or through identification with other groups that could be quite distant from the learner.

While theories of crime that emphasize learning have been very influential in criminology generally, modern discoveries about the learning process have enhanced what we know about learning crime behaviours. However, focusing solely on ideas and how they are learned denies the influence of social structure. This is problematic because most sociologists assume that ideas (or the ways one thinks) do not exist in a vacuum. Hence, it is clear that for continued relevance, learning approaches need to account for and integrate the influence of the social environment on the content and process of learning criminal behaviour.

The criminal justice policy implications of learning theory are quite straightforward: if crime is a normal learned behaviour, it can be *un*learned. Equally important, and as we saw in the critique of biological and psychological approaches, if the source of learned behaviour is in the social environment, policy should focus on altering the environment as well. As the brief story at the beginning of this section illustrates, policies and programs that take the perspective of learning theory attempt to encourage young people to choose to participate in *legitimate* activities. More specifically, such strategies would attempt to encourage better socialization of children. Some examples of strategies and policies that would reflect an emphasis on learning include family therapy, parenting courses, and behavior modification, or creating better opportunities for young people to participate in school-based or extracurricular activities.

Labeling Theory

Labeling theorists such as Lemert (1951) and Becker (1973) maintain that societal reaction to deviant behaviour is a key factor in explaining how young people (and adults) move from minor delinquencies to more serious types of crime.[7] As such, *labeling theory* is not really a theory of the "first causes" of crime, but instead focuses on the consequences of being labeled an "offender." This approach, which has its roots in symbolic interactionism, is concerned with the process by which people come to see and define themselves as deviant or criminal, and thus behave like criminals. The basic idea is that in the process of interacting with formal authorities of social control, such as police, courts, or even teachers, young people are defined as "incorrigible," "delinquent," "criminal," or as "offenders." Even though they may only have committed a few delinquent acts, the redefinition of their identity by formal authority figures leads to individuals defining themselves in the same terms as the labelers. It is the negative social reaction of those who have the power to define others that is important here. Hence, the focus of labeling theories is not on those who are controlled, but on how those who control have an impact on the individual.

There are different variations within labeling theories with respect to who gets labeled, how, and why. As Erich Goode (1994: 141-142) notes, some labeling theorists argue that it does not matter what you do, labels tend to be applied randomly and are dependent on the levels of power and status of the labelers. Others, argue that it *does* matter what you do, and that one's actions, in conjunction with factors such as race/ethnicity, class, and gender, play a part in the societal reaction to that behaviour. Goode argues that this latter "version" of labeling seems to fit the empirical facts better than an approach that discounts the importance of specific actions taken by an individual. In effect, he and most other labeling theorists maintain that those who are likely to be labeled and suffer the consequences of labeling are more likely to be people who have violated some societal norm. With respect to the consequences of labeling, he makes a distinction between saying that "going through the process of labeling" *always* results in the individual's stronger commitment to deviant behaviour, and contending that living through such a process usually, but may not, result in the individual seeing himself or herself as a deviant/criminal. For instance, a young offender who is caught shoplifting may or may not see himself or herself as a "shoplifter/thief/criminal" after being processed through the formal criminal justice system (which is, incidentally, an unlikely event, given today's emphasis on diversion for first-time offenders in this offence category). The youth may or may not steal again.

Above all, labeling theorists suggest that the labeling process is but one in a host of factors that may increase criminal behaviour. They are suggesting that one's social position, status, and personal characteristics play an important role in determining the societal reaction to deviant behaviour, but that these factors are not the only ones to take into consideration when examining these reactions.

There are many detailed discussions on the process by which labeling occurs, and these cannot be covered here. However, one widely cited and discussed model comes from the work of Lemert (1951) who alerts us to the distinction between primary and secondary types of deviance. Primary deviance or criminal activity refers to violations of societal norms that are "symptomatic and situational." Lemert (1951: 75) argues that for those who are engaged in primary deviance, "normal and pathological behaviours remain strange and somewhat tensional bedfellows in the same person." As you might guess, pretty much all of us have engaged in primary deviance at one time or another, but what is important according to this perspective is the *reaction* of the "audience" that is observing and monitoring the behaviour. According to Lemert, when people begin to see themselves as deviants or criminals, via the process outlined in Figure 3.2, they can be said to experience *secondary deviance*—they are identifying themselves as "criminals" per se, and the label becomes a self-fulfilling prophecy. In addition, the remainder of society may have difficulty seeing the individual in terms other than "criminal," even after such an individual has paid his or her dues. It may be difficult to find and keep a job, for instance, or the person might be

shunned by the community or their peers, thus perpetuating and inten-
sifying the tendency to engage in the same behaviours that "got them in
trouble" in the first place.

Figure 3.1
Lemert's Sequence of Interaction Leading to Secondary Deviance

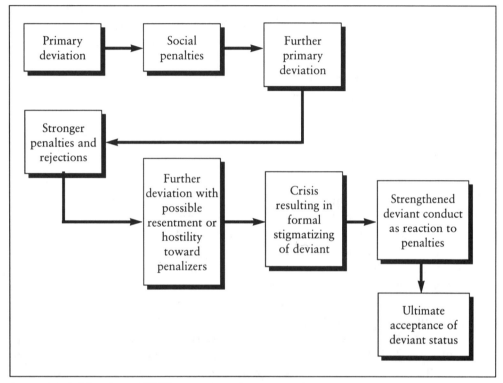

Source: Adapted from Lemert (1951).

One criticism of labeling theory is that while it might be very good
at explaining the process by which young people become "secondary"
deviants, it is not good at explaining why they engaged in "primary"
deviance in the first place. However, labeling theorists have generally
argued that they have never really been concerned with the causes of primary deviance (see Becker, 1973). In addition, however, one problem
with the approach is that it tends to be linear (one thing leads to another, which leads to the next, and so on), which may not necessarily be the
way the labeling process works. Further, the theory tends to place too
much stock in the power of official agencies, such as the police and
courts, to influence the "passive offender," who seems to be overcome
with the power of such agencies to label him or her, and then succumbs
to the labeling process. Another related issue is that labeling theory
seems to posit that labeling is almost universally bad. In reality, some
individuals may be deterred from committing further crimes by virtue of

their interaction with the criminal justice system (Bynum and Thompson, 1996). In addition, labeling cannot account empirically for the tendency for most young people to stop committing crimes as they get older, or for the fact that some individuals actively seek out criminal labels as a means of gaining status in the eyes of their peers or community (Bordua, 1967). Finally, the extent to which labeling actually creates more crime than it prevents is unknown (Bohm, 1997), a fact that may have something to do with the reluctance of many labeling theorists to empirically test the theory on the premise that deviance is "largely the product of attempts to measure or record it" (Robins, 1975: 21).

The theories we have covered so far have all been influential within criminology and some have had an impact on criminal justice policy toward youth. Labeling theory is no exception to this, and in fact, has had a major impact on young offenders law because its assumptions have been used to support the idea that young offenders should be *diverted* from the criminal justice system. As we saw in Chapter One, a central component of the Young Offenders Act is Section 4, which provides guidelines for diverting some young offenders from the formal criminal justice system. The basis of this philosophy is that interacting with the criminal justice system will contribute to the stigmatization of the offender, and could result in the intensification of criminal behaviour, rather than its reduction. In general, this idea underpins the policy strategy often referred to as "radical non-intervention" (Schur, 1973). Put another way, the general policy idea is that young persons should be redirected away from the criminal justice system, while acknowledging (under the Young Offenders Act) that they are responsible for their actions. This latter issue has led to another criticism of the policy, namely, that for some young offenders admitting guilt in the context of a less "formal" process might have the same effect as if they had gone through the formal system, an argument that has been referred to as "net-widening," which will be discussed further in Chapter Five.

Social Control Theories

In contrast to theories that speculate about why young people *do* commit crime, social control theories ask why they *do not*. What kinds of basic assumptions are being made here? If you decided that social control theories assume that everyone might commit crimes if they could, you would be right. In fact, *control theories* assume that people would commit crimes if they could but that they do not because they are prevented from doing so (or "controlled") by their socialization (Box, 1971). Underlying this argument is the assumption that people are born morally open-minded, that we are inclined toward self-gratification, and that choosing deviant or criminal acts may often be the most efficient way of satisfying our needs.

One of the most significant proponents of control theory is Travis Hirschi. Hirschi (1969) argues that "proper" socialization will prevent juveniles from engaging in deviant or criminal behaviour because it will create a strong *bond* between that individual and society. This bond consists of four elements, as follows:

1. *Attachment*—the degree of emotional regard and respect one has for other individuals.

2. *Commitment*—the degree to which an individual entertains and pursues ideas about conventional objectives such as a "respectable career."

3. *Involvement*—the time and energy one invests participating in conventional activities.

4. *Belief*—the degree of respect held by individuals for the framework of moral order and law of conventional society.

Basically, Hirschi's argument is that lower levels of these four dimensions of the social bond are more likely to lead to delinquent behaviour, whereas higher levels will lead to conforming behaviour. More recently, Gottfredson and Hirschi (1990) have argued that unsuccessful child-rearing practices (such as poor parental supervision or ineffective punishment), in conjunction with situations that are conducive to delinquency, are primarily responsible for youth crime because they contribute to low self-control. In a more problematic vein, they also argue that the influx of women into the paid labour force creates conditions under which youth crime might flourish because mothers are not able to supervise their children properly, children are left on their own, and homes are left unguarded. While research on this hypothesis does show a relationship between women's employment outside the home and delinquency, there is much that we do not understand about the possible mediating effects of other factors, such as type of employment, stress due to women's "double day," work-family conflict, the role of abusive fathers, and family breakdown. Keeping this in mind, empirical tests of Gottfredson and Hirschi's general contention that parental behaviour is a primary influence on children's self control have shown some support for their views (Gibbs, Giever, and Martin, 1998). The question is, what *other* factors inhibit parental ability to provide child supervision?

As with some of the other theoretical categories we have examined, there are many variants of control theory. For instance, *containment theory*, as proposed by Reckless (1961), holds that individuals refrain from commiting crimes because they are socialized to resist temptations and to strongly believe in conventional social norms. He refers to this "self-control" as inner containment. Control does not just reside in the individual, though, it is also demanded by society. Thus, Reckless maintains that there is another set of controls, *outer containment*, that functions to restrain people, and that these controls consist of legal demands and prohibitions. Within this framework, young people are subject to personal factors that "push" them toward delinquent behaviour (such as anxiety or frustration) and factors within the social environment (such as membership in a gang, or criminal subculture) that "pull" them to engage in criminal behaviours.

Another important variation of control theory comes from the work of Sykes and Matza (1957), whose "techniques of neutralization" approach suggests that young people lose their self control because they are able to rationalize and justify their actions. Sykes and Matza assume that the majority of young people fully understand the moral implications of committing a crime, that most believe in conventional moral standards and laws, and that most feel shame and remorse over their illegal actions. Moreover, in a later development of the theory, Matza (1964) argued that young people "drift" between conformity and delinquency. But why do they drift? Because, they are able to "neutralize" the impact of nonconforming actions by verbalizing about them in five major ways:

1. *Denial of responsibility*—the youth contends that his or her behaviour is not his or her personal responsibility, but that of another person or situation.

2. *Denial of injury*—the youth contends that no one was actually hurt by his or her actions.

3. *Denial of the victim*—the youth argues that the victim "had it coming to them" or "deserved it."

4. *Condemnation of the condemners*—the young person attempts to "turn the tables" on his or her accusers, with statements like "well, you do it, too," or "you're just as bad."

5. *Appeal to higher loyalties*—the youth contends that his or her commitment and allegiance to groups more important than society or conventional others (such as gangs or friends) forced him or her to do what he or she did.

The idea that young people drift between delinquency and conformity is persuasive because it makes sense to say that most youth are neither "all bad" or "all good." Rather, over the course of their development, youth tend to gravitate between moments of delinquent behaviour, and moments of conformity.

Although it could be categorized as a gender-based, or "neo-Marxist" theory, *power-control theory* (Hagan, Simpson and Gillis, 1987; Hagan, 1989; Hagan and Kay, 1990) is categorized here as another variant of control approaches. As the name suggests, this theory explains crime by reference to the exercise of power deriving from ownership and control over the means of production (a macro-level issue) and, ultimately, control over the youth within the family (a micro-level issue)

(Hagan et al., 1987). The basic idea is that power relationships in general society (particularly those experienced in the workplace) are mirrored in the family. Given that female youth have a far lower rate of crime than males, there must be something going on in the way youths are controlled in the family that varies by gender and family type. Hagan and his colleagues argue that *egalitarian families* are those in which mothers and fathers both work outside the home in positions of authority. The equality of authority experienced by parents in the workplace translates into control over children that includes socializing girls to take as many risks as boys. Conversely, *patriarchal families*, in which mothers are at home and fathers work in paid labour, provide stronger controls over daughters compared to sons (who are encouraged to take risks). Thus, the delinquency rates of girls in patriarchal families should be lower than egalitarian families.

Although Hagan and his associates (1987) have tested this theory with some success, further attempts to replicate their findings have been unsuccessful (Jensen and Thompson, 1990; Morash and Chesney-Lind, 1991). In addition, the theory should predict increasing rates of female youth crime given that women have entered the work force in increasing numbers since the 1970s. However, as we saw in Chapter Two, youth crime continues to be the prerogative of *male* youths, and there have been no sharp increases in female youth crime corresponding with women's entry into the paid work force. As feminist critics such as Morash and Chesney-Lind (1991) have argued, the theory is to be commended for taking gender seriously, but ultimately amounts to a variation of the discredited notion that "women's liberation causes youth crime" (discussed further below). At the same time, the theory does not do justice to the realities of women's participation in paid and unpaid (domestic) labour because it does not adequately deal with the fact that while women have entered the workforce in large numbers, they are still primarily responsible for housework and child care, and are often physically, emotionally, and economically dominated by their husbands. Thus, the extent of their "authority" in the family is not likely to be a simple reflection of the authority they have in the workplace (DeKeseredy and Schwartz, 1996).

Although control theories continue to be popular and are some of the most tested theories in criminology, a number of criticisms have been leveled at them. The most basic of these is directed at its core assumption—that people have an innate inclination to choose to commit crimes to satisfy needs. As we noted earlier, some control theorists, such as Matza (1964), argue that crime is not a matter of people being *naturally* motivated toward "doing bad things." Rather, he claims that it is the level of temptation young people encounter in everyday life that may or may not motivate them to commit delinquent behaviour. Nevertheless, it is important to ask why, when tempted, it is assumed that youths or adults will generally choose deviance over conformity unless their urges are curbed?

Another criticism of control theory is that it underestimates the influence of delinquent peers, a weakness Hirschi himself has acknowledged. More fundamentally, control theory makes the assumption that youths and adults violate norms upon which the rest of society uniformly agrees. That is, it is presumed that consensus, not conflict, characterizes social values. Finally, there is the issue of causal direction: does delinquency result from poor bonds to society or is it the other way around (Bohm, 1997)?

As with learning theories, the policy implications of control theory are straightforward: if inadequate socialization produces weakened social bonds resulting in crime, then the "cure" is to make the socialization process more effective. Hirschi argues that the most important areas of focus for improving socialization are families, schools, and the law. For instance, parents could be taught how to provide better control over their children through the use of meaningful, nonphysical punishments; rewards for good behaviour; and positive interaction in the family (Larzelere and Patterson, 1990). One such program, called "Catch 'Em Being Good," developed parenting skills in the areas of: monitoring and supervising children's behaviour, using appropriate punishments and rewards, being consistent with discipline, communicating effectively, and involving children in family activities (Hawkins, Von Cleve, and Catalano, 1991). As with learning theory, policies based on control theory would also emphasize creating opportunities for youths to participate in conventional activities (thereby strengthening their bonds to conventional order). In addition, some have suggested that helping youths develop skills to live in society without violating its rules, as well as making social expectations clear and consistent, are fruitful strategies for reducing youth crime (Weis and Hawkins, 1981).

Ecological Theories

Ecology is the study of environments. In the case of theories of crime, the term generally refers to the study of the impact of social environments on communities, individuals, and criminality. The most famous line of thinking in the ecological tradition was developed at the University of Chicago in the 1920s. The theoretical orientation that developed there, which came to be known as the "Chicago School," focused on the ways in which human societies resembled the organization of and interrelationship between plants and animals in nature. Shaw and McKay (1931, 1942), who specifically studied youth crime, argued that crime was a consequence of the shape and character of neighbourhoods and their role in creating conditions under which criminal behaviour could take place. As such, they emphasized the links between crime and *social disorganization* within neighbourhoods. Sampson and Groves (1989), two more recent social disorganization theorists, have defined these as:

1. low socioeconomic status

2. a mix of different ethnic groups

3. high levels of social mobility (transience)

4. family disruption and broken homes

The basic argument here is that communities that exhibit these characteristics are more likely to be criminogenic (that is, they generate crime) than those that do not because the social controls that should operate to prevent people from committing crime are low or absent in the "disorganized" communities. Moreover, if communities are integrated and cohesive (that is, if they are places in which neighbours "look out for each other" and share common goals), they are less likely to be criminogenic.

Shaw and McKay maintained that the values held by young people who commit crime in such neighbourhoods have been culturally transmitted by the higher number of people in these communities who hold criminal values. As you may have surmised, then, their theory shares much in common with the social control theories discussed earlier.

Several criticisms have been leveled at social disorganization approaches. The first is that there may be factors other than social disorganization that contribute to youth crime in a community. For instance, it may be that poverty, family disruption, and underemployment *all* play a role in creating social disorganization, which in turn is related to crime (see Sampson and Lauritsen, 1994). A related criticism is that the roots of social disorganization itself—inequality, changing economic conditions, and so on—tend to be ignored, and in that sense, the approach does not go far enough. More recently, however, others such as Wilson (1996) have attempted to address this issue by putting social disorganization in the context of larger economic and social processes.

As with many theories we have encountered, there is also a problem of generalizability inherent in this approach, in that not *all* youths in disorganized or disadvantaged neighbourhoods commit criminal offences. Moreover, there is a danger that this theory can pathologize neighbourhoods because it assumes that disorganization is perceived by community residents in the same way that social scientists might view it. In other words, what may be "social disorganization" to the scientific observer, may in fact be "acceptable everyday life," "richness," "diversity," or "dynamism" to community inhabitants.

The policy implications of this theoretical approach is that rather than concentrating on treating the individual, crime can be prevented by treating the community. Thus, as Shaw pointed out, programs should be developed in socially disorganized communities to help improve the quality of neighbourhood life. This could be accomplished by marshaling community resources to help deal with problems, providing community members with ways of improving their life chances, and creating opportunities for residents to achieve higher levels of community cohesion and social support.

More recent variations of the ecological model have departed from the more critical and political nature of versions, which as we have seen, implied that reducing crime means changing communities for the better. For instance, Cohen and Felson (1979) contend that we need not try to understand why people commit crimes, we can just assume that there are always going to be people who are likely to offend. Their approach—*routine activities theory*—supposes that crime varies according to: (1) whether likely offenders are present, (2) whether there are capable guardians present, and (3) if there are suitable targets available to be victimized.

What this theory suggests is that there are certain places that, because of their characteristics, are more conducive to criminal activity. Further, it implies that the behaviour and characteristics of potential crime *victims* are very much a part of the causes of crime. Put another way, routine activities theory places the onus of responsibility for crime reduction on the potential victim's shoulders. While it does not, as stated earlier, purport to provide any answers to the question of why offenders are motivated in the first place, the theory is particularly interesting for its implications for youths. Consider, for a moment, the fact that the youths most likely to be physically assaulted on the street or arrested for disorderly conduct are white males, and that these individuals are also the most likely to frequent public places where the situation can get out of control very easily (e.g., bars, clubs, or sporting events). Thus, routine activities theory concurs with what our mothers probably told us—to avoid being victimized, it is wise not to drink too much and stay out too late. While this "target hardening" strategy may be good advice, this theoretical approach still individualizes crime and, like control theories, assumes that all individuals will commit crimes unless they are prevented from doing so. That is, it sees crime as a problem of good individuals learning how to avoid (innately) bad ones. Another policy focus of this approach is on the "built environment," which consists of creating better or higher surveillance in areas perceived as "crime zones" or establishing barriers (such as lower hedges or more lighting) that will supposedly reduce the likelihood of criminal victimization. Again, increasing the level of public safety is good common sense, but does little to combat the root causes of crime. In the end, as some critics have charged, cleaning up and making an environment safer for potential victims will merely *displace* crime to other locales less able to implement such strategies.

Critical Theories

What does it mean to take a "critical" perspective within criminology? Beginning with the idea that society is characterized by conflict between interest groups over values and resources, critical criminologists argue that it is impossible to separate one's principles from the criminological enterprise (Schwartz and Friedrichs, 1994). It is argued that all perspectives on crime have inherent biases toward particular views of the world. Hence, critical criminologists choose to examine crime on behalf of the underprivileged or weak. Further, because they locate the causes of crime in the nature of the social structure, critical criminological perspectives generally seek to solve the crime problem by radically transforming the social structure.

In this section, we will examine only a few of the many critical theories for understanding youth crime.[8] We begin with the basic arguments of early Marxist theories. Although not as influential as they have been in the past, their relevance continues to be debated, and they have greatly influenced the thinking of later critical criminologists.

All critical theories, including those that could be called "Marxist" in orientation, start with the idea that people make decisions and choices about their actions and lives, but within circumstances that they have *not* chosen themselves. Put another way, young people may well choose to commit violent crimes, but critical theorists would be interested in the ways in which social structural factors (such as poverty, dropping out of school, or some other disadvantage) contributed to a youth's decision to commit his or her crime.

Marxist Theories: Left Idealism and Left Realism

Beginning with the idea that human beings are conditioned by their social circumstances, Marxist-oriented theories maintain that factors such as exploitation, alienation, power, and social class are central to understanding crime, and that crime is a "rational response" to the demands of capitalist society (Gordon, 1973; Greenberg, 1981). Moreover, Marxist approaches share some commonalities with the learning, control, and strain theories discussed earlier, because they maintain that people learn to commit crime in circumstances in which their attachment to the conventional social world has broken down and when they lack legitimate opportunities to participate in conventional social life. Unlike more mainstream theories, however, Marxist approaches locate all factors, such as juvenile offenders, their peers, schools, families, and the strain they experience, within the context of capitalist social relations. It is capitalism as a social system, and the relationships that characterize this system, that in the final analysis are responsible for crime.

For instance, *left idealists* would contend that many youths who commit crime are simply reacting to their position in the class structure. They have little connection with the working world, little or no hope for the future, and diminished life chances. Thus, their crime is a reaction to these circumstances. These youths are, in effect, modern-day "Robin

Hoods," whose actions symbolize the plight of the working and under-privileged classes and their resistance to the political and economic system (capitalism) that represses them (DeKeseredy and Schwartz, 1996).

There are many criticisms of this position. One of the most important is the fact that the vast majority of crimes committed by working-class people victimize other working-class individuals, not the middle or capitalist classes who repress them. Another problem with left idealism is its tendency to assume that being poor or working-class automatically predisposes one to commit crime. We know empirically that not all poor young people commit crimes and that many harmful crimes are committed by the wealthy and powerful in our society.

Because they dismiss working-class crime as inconsequential and as "proto-revolutionary" activity, idealists focus most of their attention on crimes of the powerful, thereby ignoring some crucial realities. Moreover, because street crime is ignored in this way, and because the causes of crime are said to be so fundamentally rooted in the nature of capitalism, idealists tend to have very few concrete proposals for reducing crime. Instead, they argue that nothing short of a fundamental "revolution" in the way we produce—that is, a transformation to socialism—will solve the problem of crime once and for all.

More recent, neo-Marxist theories of youth crime have made some advances over left idealism. Colvin and Pauly (1983) maintain that adults' experiences of authority and control at the workplace create particular perceptions and responses to authority in general. These bonds are translated into family relationships between parents and between parents and children, and are reinforced by educational and peer experiences. In short, delinquency is a consequence of the authority bonds that exist in workers' lives. While conditional empirical support for this theory has been found, it remains relatively untested and ignores a range of other factors that contribute to juvenile crime, particularly gender (Simpson and Elis, 1994).

More recently, Colvin (1996) argued that crime is linked to the process of social reproduction, defined as involving the institutions of socialization that prepare people for productive roles in society (1996: 60). When such institutions fail to prepare youths for participation in the economy, society loses the productive potential of these individuals and experiences higher costs of welfare and prisons as well as higher rates of crime and other social pathologies. Colvin takes the explicitly Marxist position that crime is a consequence of social structural inequality stemming from the class structure of capitalist society, which in turn determines the priorities and resources allocated to major institutions of socialization such as families and schools. That is, youths who do not do well in school or go to disadvantaged schools, hang out with peers in the same social situation, and/or come from disadvantaged families are more likely to commit crime.

According to this view, then, the keys to reducing crime include better supports for poor people; comprehensive job training; nationwide parent-effectiveness programs; preschool programs; expanded and enhanced public education; service programs that encourage youths to participate in adult and community life; enhanced workplace environments that emphasize democratic control and collective bargaining and that encourage the development of self-directed, creative employees; economic investment in industries meeting human needs and services; and a more progressive income tax system (Colvin, 1996).

Left realists take some of the arguments made by idealists seriously, but build a much more "practical" or "realistic" theory of crime and what is to be done about it. In addition to arguing that crime is a serious problem for the working class, John Lea and Jock Young (1984: 81), two of realism's most important defenders, argue that the cause of crime can be placed in the context of the equation:

Relative Deprivation = Discontent

Discontent + Political Marginalization = Crime

Discontent is a product of relative deprivation because it occurs when comparisons between groups are made, which suggests that unnecessary injustices are occurring. *Relative deprivation* is the notion that people perceive their position in society in different ways and relative to other people. For instance, poor people might not view themselves as worse off than others if everyone around them is poor, but in the midst of a society that is blatantly unequal, their perspective might be different. It is "poverty experienced as unfair (relative deprivation when compared to someone else) that creates discontent" (1984: 88). For Lea and Young, *political marginalization* consists of two components: "isolation from the effective channels of pressure-group politics, and isolation from processes whereby political interests can be clearly and instrumentally formulated" (1984: 214).

In addition, left realists use the metaphor of the *"square of crime"* to illustrate the relationships between key people and institutions in the study of crime. The square consists of: (1) the state, which is responsible for law-making, policing, and sentencing; (2) the general public, which reacts to crime; (3) the offender; and (4) the victim. Young (1992: 27) argues that:

> It is the relationship between the police and the public which determines the efficacy of policing, the relationship between the victim and the offender which determines the impact of crime, the relationship between the state and the offender which is a major factor in recidivism.

The implications of this theory are particularly interesting for understanding youth crime because, as we have already shown, most young people are socialized to believe that the future holds promise, that it can be realized with a little hard work, and that failure to achieve these goals is a failure of the individual, not the system. When their expectations are not fulfilled, they replace legitimate and conventional interests with a "diffuse set of resentments and grievances"—they become discontented. This discontent, when combined with the inability to change things through legitimate avenues (such as voting, or through access to powerful interest groups), and in conjunction with relative deprivation, greatly increases the chances of criminal activity among youth.

In summary, then, left realists argue that crime is not just a "moral panic" manufactured by the ruling elite. To be sure, they argue, we should take crimes of the powerful seriously, but we should also focus on the fact that working-class people are victimized by the powerful and other members of the working class in capitalist society. Moreover, crime is a relational phenomenon that demonstrates the antisocial nature of our society.

Left realism has been subject to a number of criticisms, including the fact that it may have departed too far in philosophical orientation from its more left-wing counterpart in left idealism. As a consequence, some may claim that left realism is nothing more than liberal theory in a new guise (or that there is nothing "left" about left realism). A related concern is that in claiming to offer a realistic strategy for reducing crime and the harm it causes, realists must automatically engage with, and potentially embrace current strategies that are conservative and oppressive (Schwartz, 1991). Moreover, some theorists, such as Einstadter and Henry (1995), have argued that realists focus too much on working-class crime and not enough on crimes of the powerful. Others have claimed that the left realist perspective on the role of the community in responding to crime assumes that our communities are homogenous rather than diverse, and that the possibility therefore exists that community members with particular interests will create strategies (such ass vigilantism) as oppressive as the current system (Michalowski, 1991).

Because realists focus on access to legitimate opportunities for self-fulfillment as well as political expression, the practical implications, particularly for youth justice, are similar to other theories emphasizing inequality.

The solution to crime, according to Lea and Young, consists of:

1. The *demarginalization* of offenders by providing alternatives to prison that serve to *integrate* the offender into the community again.

2. *Pre-emptive deterrence*, which involves deterring crime *before* it is committed

3. The *minimal use of incarceration*, given that prisons simply serve to create hardened, bitter criminals and diminished chances of "going straight."

The Young Offenders Act contains the promise of demarginalizing and diverting young offenders through Section 4 (Alternative Measures). Thus, there is a possibility that the existing legislative framework, if implemented properly, could be effective in reducing crime. By removing young offenders from the court process and at the same time allowing them to confront their behaviour in the presence of a victim, we may be able to return some control of the situation to the actors involved while reducing the costs of processing through the criminal justice system (Alvi, 1986).

The question remains, however, as to whether there is any real political will to create environments that reduce relative deprivation and discontent (see Box 3.3). As will be shown in the next chapter, the notion of minimizing the use of incarceration for youth has clearly not been taken seriously in Canada.

Box 3.3

Tories Demand Apology After Liberal Leader's Comments on Crime

Ontario Debates Issue: 'Poverty Breeds Despair and Despair Breeds Crime'

John Ibbitson
National Post

"I'm depraved on accounta I'm deprived," chirped the juvenile delinquent in West Side Story. The Ontario government disagrees.

Bob Runciman, the Solicitor-General, says that Dalton McGuinty, the Liberal opposition leader, has insulted the poor by saying poverty breeds crime.

Mr. McGuinty has "slighted countless parents who, despite fiscal difficulties are working hard to instill proper values in their children," Mr. Runciman said in a speech yesterday.

"He should be apologizing for . . . coming out and equating income levels with propensity to commit a crime," he told reporters afterward. The solicitor-general cited numerous studies that show there is little or no link between income level and criminal activity.

The question is fast becoming a political issue in Ontario, as the Conservatives and Liberals stake out opposing ground over how to attack youth crime in the run-up to an expected spring election.

Mike Harris, the Conservative premier, brought the issue forward in a speech earlier this month, when he decried what he considers the general decline in civility by the younger generation.

"Are you appalled when you hear young people swearing at their bus driver, or their teacher, or at their mother?" Mr. Harris asked, rhetorically. "Are you shocked when you read of youth vandalizing a cemetery, or swarming a subway passenger, or causing someone great personal injury or even death? I am."

The government promptly launched a "consultation" into whether the province needed a uniform code of conduct and dress for students and whether Ontario should mimic Manitoba by enacting legislation that holds parents accountable for crimes committed by their children.

Box 3.3, *continued*

Mr. McGuinty responded by saying the Conservatives didn't understand the true causes of youth crime and had actually contributed to it by cutting welfare and other financial supports for the poor.

"If you want to be tough on crime, you have to be tough on the causes of crime," he told reporters. "Poverty breeds despair and despair breeds crime."

For the Tories, it was the opening they were looking for.

"Mr. McGuinty is a former defence lawyer for young offenders," said Mr. Runciman, who has "insulted numerous young people who confront economic challenge without resorting to crime."

Numerous studies, he said, have proved there is no connection between income level and crime.

"Mr. McGuinty misunderstands the true nature of the problem as much as he claims society misunderstands the young offenders who used to be his clients."

In fact, Paul Whitehead, a criminologist at the University of Western Ontario, said yesterday, neither Mr. McGuinty nor Mr. Runciman appear to understand the causes of youth crime. "They're both right and they're both wrong," Prof. Whitehead said. While income level alone is not a major determinant of criminal behaviour, factors that predispose young people toward crime are more common among the poor, he said.

Those factors include lack of education, lack of parental support, and lack of a sense of community.

Neither stricter discipline nor additional money for the poor, taken in isolation, will make any serious dent in youth crime, he said.

Rosemary Gartner, director of the Centre of Criminology at University of Toronto, said the government is blowing the issue of youth crime out of proportion. Crime rates are on the decline, including major acts of violence by youths, she observed. Minor acts of violence by youths are on the increase, but that may well be the result of new zero-tolerance policies toward violence that have been adopted by schools.

"A lot of this rhetoric is around an epidemic increase in violence by youths that simply is not the case," she said.

Mr. McGuinty said yesterday the Tories were attacking his comments on youth crime to distract the public from the government's more controversial policies on health care and education.

The opposition is after the government over reports that cuts to the Ministry of the Environment have forced inspectors to ignore environmental abuses.

"You want to crack down on crime? Crack down on corporate crime. Crack down on polluters," he said.

Source: *National Post.*

Feminist Theories[9]

Have you noticed something about the theories we have discussed so far? Except in stereotypical or negative ways, not one of them mention women. If you noticed this, at some level you understand the importance of women's different experiences in relation to crime. If you did not notice, this is not surprising. The treatment of women in the criticisms of the theories you have read about so far has been downplayed purposely because this reflects the fact that, until very recently, criminology has dismissed or ignored the concerns of one-half of the world's population. Therefore, we can add one more criticism to each of the theories we have examined up until this point: the fact that, with minor exceptions, women have historically been disregarded or misrepresented in theories of crime (Beirne and Messerschmidt, 1995). Why did this happen?

There are many reasons for the absence of women from criminological discourse; criminological theorizing has historically been dominated by men, resulting in much of the "malestream" criminology we see today. In addition, in the past, women did not (or were not allowed to) participate in academic life, thus precluding them from contributing their insights to theoretical and empirical debates. In addition, many people, heavily influenced by the media, some religious groups, and conservative politicians, equate feminism with demonizing or hating men, being gay or lesbian, or being pro-choice. This anti-feminist backlash has resulted in an "automatic" rejection of any analysis that uses what some have termed "the other 'f' word." It has thus been very difficult for feminist approaches to gain ground, though this is changing.

Generally, feminists are united by a commitment to put gender at the forefront of the analysis of society and by their efforts to eliminate gender inequality. Further, the goal of most feminist scholars is "not to push men out so as to pull women in," but rather to gender the study of social problems (Renzetti, 1993: 232).

Contrary to popular images, "feminism" is not a single thing, but a diverse body of thought. For example, Tong (1989) identifies eight distinct types of feminism, and there are major debates within each type (Schwartz, 1991). For the purpose of this book, however, we will utilize Daly and Chesney-Lind's (1988: 502) definition (mentioned earlier), which refers to feminism as "a set of theories about women's oppression *and* a set of strategies for change." Feminist perspectives can be distinguished from nonfeminist or "malestream" perspectives on the basis of the following shared attributes:[10]

- Gender and power are key elements of social problems.

- Sex and gender are distinct. Sex is determined by bio-physiology, and the concepts "men" and "women" are used in referring to sex differences. Gender, however, is socially constructed, and the concepts "male" and "female" are used in referring to gender differences.

- Gender inequality is viewed as the major cause of the continued oppression and marginalization of women.

- Scholarship and research should be used to support women.

- Gender and gender relations order social life and social institutions in fundamental ways.

- Women should be at the center of the study of social problems, not peripheral, invisible, or appendages to men.

- Male social constructions of gender and gender relations, which are inauthentic but useful props for gender inequality, should be replaced with authentic social constructions supporting gender equality.

Although there are many types of feminist thought, we will focus here on four widely read and cited perspectives: (1) liberal feminism, (2) Marxist feminism, (3) radical feminism, and (4) socialist feminism.

Liberal feminism argues that women are discriminated against on the basis of their sex, and that they are denied access to the same political, financial, career, and personal opportunities as men (Messerschmidt, 1993). Discrimination can be eliminated, they argue, by removing all obstacles to women's access to education, paid employment, political activity, and other public institutions; having women participate equally with men in the public sphere; and changing laws (Daly and Chesney-Lind, 1988: 537).

Marxist feminism argues that class and gender divisions of labour determine male and female positions in any society. The gender division of labour is viewed as the product of the class division of labour. Because women are seen as being primarily dominated by capital, and secondarily by men, the main strategy for change promoted by Marxist feminists is the transformation from a capitalist society to a democratic socialist society (Daly and Chesney-Lind, 1988; Messerschmidt, 1986). Thus, crime is theorized as a consequence of the ruling-class power to define as criminal any actions that threaten the existing capitalist social order.

Radical feminism sees male power and privilege as the "root cause" of all social relations, inequality, and other social problems. According to radical feminists, "the most important relations in any society are found in *patriarchy* (institutionalised male dominance which includes masculine control over the labour power and sexuality of women); all other relations (such as class) are secondary and derived from male-female relations" (Beirne and Messerschmidt, 1991: 519). Some strategies for change advanced by radical feminists include: overthrowing patriarchal relations, developing biological reproduction technologies that enable women to have sexual autonomy, and creating women-centered social institutions and women-only organizations (Daly and Chesney-Lind, 1988: 538).

Socialist feminism is informed by some elements of Marxist and radical feminism. For example, class and patriarchy are considered key variables in socialist feminist analyses of social problems. However, neither class nor patriarchy is presumed to be dominant. Rather, class and gender relations are seen as equally important. These relations interact in determining the social order at any given time in history (Jaggar, 1983; Messerschmidt, 1986). Socialist feminists argue that "to understand class...we must recognize how it is structured by gender, conversely, to understand gender requires an examination of how it is structured by class" (Beirne and Messerschmidt, 1991: 520). In sum, socialist feminists contend that we are influenced by both class and gender relations, and that strategies for change should simultaneously focus on transforming patriarchal and class relations (Daly and Chesney-Lind, 1988). Having laid out the foundation of four key feminist perspectives, what can be said about their applicability to youth crime?

There are three general problems in criminology and criminal justice that are of interest to feminist theorists (Bohm, 1997; Daly and Chesney-Lind, 1988; Vold, Bernard, and Snipes, 1998).

1. Women's victimization

2. Gender differences in crime, which include two problems:

   a. The generalizability problem—Can theories about male crime be generalized (or applied) to women?

   b. The gender ratio problem—Why do women commit fewer crimes than men?

3. The differential treatment of women and men in the criminal justice system

As suggested earlier, early attempts to theorize about female youth crime tended to apply concepts appropriate for *male* offenders to the experiences of females or utilized stereotypical constructs of "appropriate" male and female behaviour. Thus, while women's voices, concerns, and experiences were excluded in the study of crime, female crime was still theorized from the perspective of men. We saw, for instance, that Freud had made some extremely objectionable statements about women. Similarly, biological theorists argued that there was something in women's physical makeup that predisposed them to crime, or that women used their physiology to hide their crime (Pollock, 1950). Likewise, Cohen (1955) argued that girls are "naturally" inhibited from committing crime. Another example of this phenomenon is found in the work of Thrasher (1927), who, in attempting to explain why there were so few female gangs, contended that girls who did join gangs had merely taken on male roles.

Some 20 years later, Adler (1975) maintained that women did not commit crime because they lacked the opportunities that men have. Adler's argument, often referred to as the *emancipation thesis* or *liberation hypothesis*, is that as women have become more "like men" in other spheres of life such as work or politics, they have also gained new opportunities for and sensibilities about crime that are similar to men's. Thus, for Adler, as female youths have gradually departed from their "traditional" roles, and as they have taken on new ones, rates of crime for young women have increased. (See Simon, 1981, for a related but slightly different viewpoint.)

One immediate difficulty with this argument is that it is difficult, if not impossible, to determine whether rates of female crime *have* in fact increased based only on official police statistics.[11] Regardless of this major limitation, and as Chapter Two showed, even official data show that rates of female youth crime in Canada have generally remained stable and that male youths commit a greater number of (and more serious kinds of) crimes. In addition, empirical tests of the emancipation thesis have generally failed to support the theory, with some studies actually showing that delinquent girls are *more* traditional and supportive of patriarchal values than nondelinquent girls (e.g., see Cernkovich and Giordano, 1979).

What about contemporary feminist theorizing in criminology? To begin, we need to be careful not to completely dismiss the utility of existing theories that ignored or stereotyped women's relationship to crime (Chesney-Lind and Sheldon, 1992). In fact, some of the theories you have read so far have potentially useful applications in explaining female youth crime. There is no reason why differential association, strain, control, or other theories cannot be modified to account for gender variations in criminality or women's experiences with the criminal justice system (Smith and Paternoster, 1987). For example Hagan et al.'s power-control theory, while categorized in this chapter as a control theory, explicitly attempts to account for gender variation in crime. Heidensohn (1985) has argued that rather than study women's criminality, we should be studying the strikingly high number of women who conform. Similarly, labeling theory has been applied to the study of female criminality, as in the case of Rosenblum's (1980) study of prostitution, and modified differential association theory has been used to explain aspects of female delinquency (see Mears, Ploeger, and Warr, 1998).

Notwithstanding the potential in modifying existing theories to understand female juvenile crime, more current feminist approaches have focused on a variety of problems, including differences in rates of rape in "socialist" versus capitalist societies (Schwendinger and Schwendinger, 1983), understanding and exposing the violent victimization of women at the hands of men (Kelly, 1988), and applications of theories of masculinities to crime[12] (Messerschmidt, 1993). Meda Chesney-Lind (1995), a key figure in theorizing female crime from a feminist perspective, argues that understanding female crime requires recognizing that girls are often the victims of sexual abuse and violence, to which they respond differently than boys. In addition, those who victimize them typically wield the power to keep them vulnerable and at home through their ability to influence the actions of police, courts, and the like. Finally, when girls run away from abusive homes, they are often forced into engaging in survival crimes like theft or prostitution. Thus, Chesney-Lind's argument attempts to account for what is different in the lives of girls and boys, the ways that such differences contribute to female offending, and the importance of locating crime in the context of a male-dominated society.

While feminist theories show great promise in enriching our understanding of criminality, to be sure, they have been subject to criticisms. One of these is an objection to the tendency of some feminist theories to see gender as the "first cause," thereby ignoring its relationship with race/ethnicity and class. While there are some implications of this for the problem of causality, seeing gender in homogeneous terms also masks variations in women's experiences (for example, women of colour, poor women, or lesbian women). In addition, as Messerschmidt (1993) points out, feminist theories that are "essentialist" are problematic because they assume that *all* men and *all* women have essentially the same nature, a contention that denies the role of socialization into sex roles, and precludes the possibility of change (see also Goodey, 1997).

In sum, feminist approaches to criminology have provided us with new and important insights and corrected many falsehoods within criminology (Vold, Bernard, and Snipes, 1998). Nevertheless, there remains much work to be done, particularly with respect to the generalizability issue, the construction of theories that take women's ways of knowing seriously, and the application of feminist methods to criminological research.

SUMMARY

This chapter has focused on some of the most widely cited theoretical perspectives on youth crime. We began with an emphasis on the linkage between theory and policy and then discussed the idea that although criminal justice policies for youths reflect theories of crime causation, they do not always reflect the most coherent or relevant theories.

Even if they are outdated, flawed, or clearly wrong, each of the theories discussed here have made some contribution. Scientific knowledge (and, therefore, practical solutions to problems) depend greatly on the extent to which theories can be supported or refuted. If we know that particular factors are related to youth crime, we ought to be able to design and implement policies that should be effective in curbing youth crime. At the same time, our society gains something when (and if) we reject or modify policies because they are erroneous or based on unsound assumptions. Accordingly, understanding the assumptions of theories, their logic, the extent to which they are supported by evidence and their implications for policy is a crucial exercise if we are to do something effective about law and order.

We also briefly discussed the essence of good theory, and the problems of classification that permeate the field of criminology. Having identified some of these issues, and recognizing that there are always theories that do not fit as neatly as we would like, we nevertheless offered one way of classifying theories: a distinction between theories that emphasize properties of individuals and those that focus on the role of social environments. Theories in these two broad groups were then discussed and evaluated, with the bulk of attention given to sociological theories of crime.

One important conclusion many come to in the course of learning about criminological theories is that no *one* theory can explain youth crime. Youth crime is a consequence of both individual and social factors and the key is to understand the relative importance or "weight" of these factors. For example, although youth crime is most definitely not a result *only* of "bad parenting" or "neurological dysfunction" or "bad friends" or "poverty," it is almost certainly the result of a complex interactive web of these things. Indeed, this idea is central in the motivation of those attempting to create new "integrated" theories of crime. For example, Barak (1998: 5) defines his integrative criminology as an attempt to "bring together the diverse bodies of knowledge that represent the full array of disciplines that study crime" (see also, Elliot, Ageton, and Canter, 1979; Sullivan and Wilson, 1995; Thornberry, 1987).

In this author's view, if criminology is to advance better theories of youth and adult crime, it must come to terms with the multifaceted nature of crime. This means nothing less than rigorously studying the great variation in psychological, familial, sociological, and community factors that interact to produce criminal behaviour, within a society that is defined and shaped by power relationships of many kinds. We must not only take what is useful from existing theories of crime, but challenge and discard all that is not. There is much at stake here—for to continue to hang on to criminal justice policies based on theories and assumptions that are outmoded or inadequate is to deny justice to young people and the society in which they live. In the next chapter, we will examine the realities of current criminal justice practices for youths in Canada in order to determine the extent to which we have done this.

NOTES

[1] As the majority of influential theories on youth crime and crime in general are American or European, we will focus on these.

[2] A typology is a hypothetical construction of elements useful for making comparisons. The idea here is not to "pigeonhole" theories into strict categories but to provide a useful framework for thinking about the properties theories have and do not have in common.

[3] The term "neoclassical" refers to a return to older "classical" ideas. Because the approaches are essentially the same, we will use the terms interchangeably.

[4] We cannot delve into the nuances and details of these theoretical perspectives here, but we do need to have a sense of their basic foundations before proceeding. Those (particularly nonsociologists) interested in deepening their understanding of sociological approaches should consult any of a number of excellent theory texts, including: Collins,

Randall (1994), *Four Sociological Traditions* (New York: Oxford University Press); Levine, Donald N. (1995), *Visions of the Sociological Tradition* (Chicago: University of Chicago Press); Fraser, Nancy (1989), *Unruly Practices: Power, Discourse, and Gender in Contemporary Social Theory* (Minneapolis: University of Minnesota Press); as well as the ones suggested at the end of this chapter.

[5] On the other hand, strain theories may help to explain the *kinds* of crime women commit (see DeKeseredy and Schwartz, 1996: 214).

[6] Sutherland presented these ideas as nine separate but related propositions, which have been simplified here.

[7] Becker (1973) himself, however, is not happy with the term "labeling," and prefers to talk about the interactionist approach rather than "labeling theory."

[8] This chapter will not cover other "critical" but less widely cited theories such as peacemaking and newsmaking criminologies or postmodernism. For an introduction to these, consult Bohm, 1997, or Vold, Bernard, and Snipes, 1998.

[9] Parts of this section draw upon Alvi, DeKeseredy, and Ellis, 2000

[10] See Bograd (1988), DeKeseredy and MacLeod (1997), and Yllö (1993) for more detailed descriptions of the principles included in this list.

[11] Indeed, Adler based her conclusions on official data.

[12] Messerschmidt (1993) argues that there are many kinds of masculinity.

DISCUSSION QUESTIONS AND PROBLEM-SOLVING SCENARIOS

1. Taking any case of criminal activity by youths as discussed in the media, prepare an essay comparing and contrasting how two of the theories discussed in this chapter would explain this crime (see Box 3.2)

2. Hold a debate on the following statements: If women's liberation has contributed to women's equality, then we should expect to see more crime from women. The solution to female crime is therefore to reduce women's equality.

3. Speculate as to which of either psychological or sociological perspectives provide the most useful understanding of youth crime.

SUGGESTED READINGS

Vold, G., B,T. Bernard J, and J. Snipes B. (1998). *Theoretical Criminology*, 4th ed. New York: Oxford University Press.

Curran, D.J., and Renzetti, C.M. (1994). *Theories of Crime*. Boston: Allyn & Bacon.

Barak, G. 1998. *Integrating Criminologies*. Boston: Allyn & Bacon.

A teenage offender faces the criminal justice system. Canada's youth justice system continues to emphasize the control and punishment of young offenders and to discriminate on the bases of gender and ethnicity.

Chapter Four

Youths in the Criminal Justice System

INTRODUCTION

Technocratic approaches to youth justice focus on the "nuts and bolts" of the system but neglect its consequences for young people, the ideas that underpin it, and whether it works. For administrative criminologists concerned with the technical or managerial aspects of criminal justice, it is sufficient to contemplate flow charts of the system and ruminate over how it can be made more "efficient." In this world of "actuarial" justice, then, what counts depends on what can be counted, whether books can be balanced, how well risk can be managed, and the extent to which costs can be controlled (Rigakos, 1999).

As a whole, this book is intended to help you develop a critical sociological understanding of the workings and consequences of the criminal justice system for youths in Canada. In this chapter, we will not discuss the many nuances and subtleties of court processing or police arrest procedures, as these are better left to more technically oriented manuals. Moreover, focusing only on the "guts" of the system tends to distract us from what this author considers to be the most vital aspects of criminal justice practice—the impact of the system on the offender and society, the rationale behind policies and procedures, and the capacity of policies to achieve justice for society and young offenders.

Having said this, it is important to have at least some grasp of the steps and institutions making up the youth criminal justice system. We will briefly consider its structure. We will then consider the consequences of the justice system for youths by weaving fact with fiction. We will follow the fictional stories of three youths as they progress through the criminal justice system. This will provide you with a sense of the variations in experiences that occur for youths in trouble with the law, and the ways in which personal characteristics and biographies make a difference to those experiences. The data we will examine provide some context and justification for the conclusions drawn from the stories we track.

We will then place these stories in the context of different models of justice. There are many such models, each with different assumptions (resting on some of the theoretical ideas we discussed in Chapter Three) and with differing consequences for offenders.

A Brief Overview of the System

Canada's youth criminal justice system is similar to the adult system in its broad outlines. Generally, when a crime is allegedly committed, it is reported to the police, who investigate the incident and then may or may not lay charges against that individual or issue a document for them to appear in court. Depending on the circumstances, charges are followed by court appearances, a decision or plea of guilt or innocence, then sentencing, punishment, and release.

There are some aspects unique to the youth system. Referring to Figure 4.1, you will notice that youths are tried in a court specifically designed to deal with young offenders, a consequence of Section 2 of the Young Offenders Act, which compels provinces and territories to create a "youth court" in each jurisdiction (Bala, 1997).

At each stage of the process, an individual encounters various actors in the system, beginning with the police. The police are among the most critical of all the players in the justice system, as they have the ability to exercise *discretion* in deciding whether to charge individuals with a criminal offence. That is, they can choose, on the basis of several legal and nonlegal factors whether they will lay charges, and in some provinces, decide whether a youth is a candidate for alternative measures. Legal factors considered by police in deciding whether to lay charges include the nature and seriousness of the offence and whether the youth has been in trouble with the law before. Nonlegal factors are less "objective" in the sense that they involve police perceptions of the young person's demeanor and attitude, and include the ways in which officers interpret and act with regard to the "race," class, and gender of the alleged offender (Bala, 1997).

Figure 4.1
The Youth Justice Process in Canada

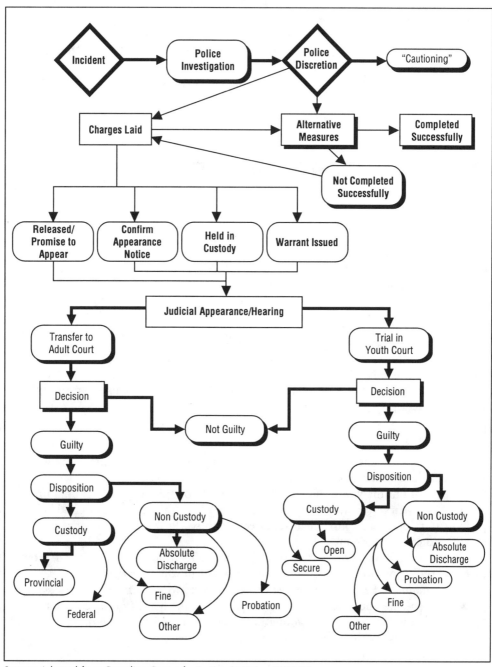

Source: Adapted from Canadian Centre for Justice Statistics, 1998:12.

In most cases, when juveniles are formally charged, they will enter the formal system, which (depending on the circumstances) entails being held in custody pending a trial or being released into the community after promising to appear in court at a later date. At the next stage, the youth appears in court, and a decision is made as to whether the case should proceed to adult court (for those committing more serious crimes) or through the youth court system. In both cases, a trial is held, a decision of guilty or not guilty is made, and the youth is committed to one or more *dispositions* or sentences, such as custody, community service, probation, or a fine (see Box 4.1).

Box 4.1

Sentences For Canadian Youths

There are two categories of sentences (or dispositions) in youth court: custody-based and community-based.

Custody Sentences

Custody sentences require the young person to spend time in a designated correctional facility. There are two types:

Secure (Closed) Custody: The young person is committed to a facility specially designated for the secure detention of young persons.

Open Custody: a young person is committed to a community residential center, group home, child care institution, forest or wilderness camp, or any other similar facility.

Community Dispositions

Community dispositions can be served in the young person's community. They include a variety of sentences:

Probation: the youth must abide by a set of conditions for a maximum period of two years. At a minimum, the youth must keep the peace, be of good behaviour and appear in court when required to do so. Probation is often combined with other types of sentences.

Fine: the youth is ordered to pay up to $1,000 within a set time period. However, credits for work performed in lieu of payment can be earned.

Community Service: the young person is ordered to perform community service work (a specified number of hours without pay for the benefit of the community.)

Absolute Discharge: The young person is found guilty of the offence and is discharged absolutely (does not have to serve a sentence for his/her offence). However, a record is kept of the decision.

Other: various dispositions including conditional discharge, compensation, compensation in kind, pay purchaser (money for the innocent purchaser of stolen goods), restitution, prohibition/seizure/forfeiture, essays, apologies and counselling programs may be ordered.

Source: Canadian Centre for Justice Statistics, 1998: 38.

CONFRONTING JUSTICE: STAGES AND OUTCOMES

In this section, we will learn about the youth criminal justice system by following the stories of three fictional youths in conflict with the law. It has already been suggested that an adolescent's personal and social characteristics play a role in determining outcomes and experiences with the criminal justice system. Thus, before embarking on our exploration of the system, we need some background on our three fictional youths.

- Julie is an aboriginal girl of 14 who occasionally lives with her mother in public housing in Winnipeg, Manitoba. Julie's parents' marriage ended years ago, when her father left the family just before Julie was born. For the past two years, she has been under the care of a child-welfare agency, from which she has run away numerous times. She was born with fetal alcohol syndrome as a consequence of her mother's alcoholism. She has a learning disability and has great difficulty in school, which she rarely attends. Julie has no brothers or sisters, and she and her mother live on welfare. Julie has been in trouble with the law before, having been arrested for disorderly conduct and shoplifting. She has been neglected but has managed to survive, spending a fair amount of time on the streets or staying with acquaintances.

- John is a white, 16-year-old boy who lives in Oakville, Ontario. His parents are both working professionals and together they earn a comfortable income. John is a good athlete and scholar and has earned top marks in school. He hopes to become a computer programmer after going to university, which he will enter next year. Although he likes to drink beer and smokes an occasional marijuana joint, he has never been arrested.

- David is a white, 17-year-old boy living in Vancouver, British Columbia. He has one younger brother. His parents both work in low-skilled, low-paying jobs but they manage to make ends meet. David has grown up in a violent household. He has been the victim of physical and verbal abuse by his father ever since he can remember, and his mother has been sexually and physically abused by his father as well. David's teachers say he is bright, but he has little interest in school, which he skips regularly. He has been in trouble with the law many times, beginning at the age of 12 when he was arrested for shoplifting. Through his early teens he has been charged and convicted of theft under $5,000, common assault, and assault with a weapon. As a result of his criminal record, he has "done time" in closed and open custody facilities.

The Police and Arrest

It is Friday night in the middle of June in Winnipeg. Julie is hanging around the streets, smoking marijuana and drinking with a few friends. She does not have the money to buy any of the drugs or liquor she consumes, but is able to do so because her older friends have access to money. Bored, the teens decide to walk further down the road to see if there is anything going on. In the process, they walk by a few cars, and a few of the group take keys and knives to the doors, scraping the paint. As they come to the corner, a police car pulls up. Several of the group run away, but Julie is apprehended. She is charged with mischief, released into the custody of her mother, and ordered to appear in court in one month.

In Ontario, John and some of his friends go to the mall, where they purchase clothing and some computer games. As they exit a store, a security guard approaches them and asks if he can see inside their bags. The guard discovers a computer game in John's bag and asks to see the receipt, which John is unable to produce because he has stolen the game. The guard escorts him to the main office, calls John's parents and calls the police, who charge John with theft. John is then sent home with his parents with an order to appear in court in a few weeks.

On a rainy night in Vancouver's Gas Town area, David and his friends are drinking in a local pub after having consumed some amphetamines (speed). As the night wears on, David becomes increasingly aggressive and challenges another man to a fight outside the bar. In the ensuing scuffle, David punches and kicks the man until he is unconscious. The police arrive, and David scuffles with them. He is arrested and charged with assault and resisting arrest. The police call his parents and decide to keep him in jail overnight.

Although our fictional characters are not representative of the entire juvenile population in Canada, their experiences are germane to understanding some important aspects of the police-youth interaction.

First, there is considerable variation by jurisdiction in the ways in which youths and police interact (Conly, 1978). Thus, what happens when a young person comes in contact with police depends very much on *where* the interaction takes place. For instance, if John would have committed his offence in Manitoba, he would stand a greater chance of being warned or diverted immediately to an alternative measures program. However, he lives in Ontario, where youths are automatically charged. Accordingly, although he may end up participating in an alternative measures program, he must first attend court to find out if this will be his fate, a strategy that flies in the face of the basic logic of alternative measures (and which we will discuss later).

Second, the police exercise considerable *discretion* in their dealings with youths. Depending on the nature of the offence (e.g., not much discretion can be exercised in a murder charge) and the laws in the juris-diction, police possess extraordinary power to determine the fate of alleged young offenders. As we noted earlier, police discretion is influenced by legal factors (such as laws and type of offence) and nonlegal factors (including race, class, and gender). Thus, in addition to the fact that he is charged with assaulting someone with a weapon, David's attitude, the fact that he fought with police during his arrest, his record of prior offences, and his inebriated condition all probably contributed to his arrest and the decision to hold him in jail until his court appearance.

Third, although all three of our fictional characters are charged, not all youths are charged by police. In fact, approximately one-third of all youths who are apprehended by police are *not* charged (Doob, Marinos, and Varma, 1998), and a host of factors contribute to the police officer's decision to lay charges against a youth. Relationships between some of these factors and the decision to charge are evident in Table 4.1.[1]

According to most studies, the most important of these factors is the seriousness of the offence and whether the young person has had prior charges (Doob and Chan, 1982). In addition to these objective factors, police reactions to the suspect's demeanor or attitude, gender, and colour also play a significant role (Leiber, Nalla, and Farnworth, 1998; Neugebauer-Visano, 1996; Sealock and Simpson, 1998). The data in Table 4.1 also highlight the different experiences of aboriginals and the greater proportion of older youths who are charged, probably because they generally have longer records of offending. Also striking is the fact that of the youths who are apprehended for offences involving property, about one-half are charged, even though one-third of these charged cases involve property worth less than $100.

We should also take note that the police tend to have a fairly standard view of justice and the causes of crime. A recent study of police attitudes toward the effectiveness of sentences (see Table 4.2) showed that many police officers feel satisfied with the dispositions young offenders are receiving for a first offence, but are less satisfied with the outcomes of the justice process when it comes to repeat offenders (Solicitor General Canada, 1997). To a large extent, then, police sentiments are in line with those who argue that repeated juvenile crime should be met with more severe consequences. In turn, this idea rests on the simplistic notion (critiqued in Chapter Three) that because crime is a rational choice, when people break the law they deserve what they get, and that those who *continue* to break the law deserve ever harsher responses from society because this strategy will presumably "make them see the light." Moreover, it is argued that the most incorrigible offenders are essentially not worth saving because no preventive measures will stop them from committing crimes over and over again, a perspective that completely denies the role of social environments in creating criminogenic societies. (See Box 4.2 for an example of this type of "reactive" thinking.)

Table 4.1

Percent of Accused Youth Charged, or Processed by Other Means,* by Selected Characteristics of the Accused and of Circumstances of the Incident

Characteristics/circumstances	Charged %	Processed by Other Means %	Total N	Total %
Gender of the accused				
Female	60.3	39.7	14,431	15.3
Male	58.8	41.2	79,790	84.7
Aboriginal status of the accused				
Not an Aboriginal	57.6	42.4	89,045	94.5
Aboriginal	83.5	16.5	5176	5.5
Age of the accused				
12	33.7	66.3	4,731	5.0
13	44.5	55.5	8,713	9.2
14	53.4	46.6	15,325	16.3
15	59.2	40.8	19,514	20.7
16	64.1	35.9	22,578	24.0
17	68.1	31.9	23,360	24.8
Evidence that the accused consumed alcohol or drugs				
No	58.9	41.1	93,809	99.6
Yes	87.9	12.1	412	0.4
Coaccused adult in the incident				
No	57.9	42.1	82,242	87.3
Yes	66.8	33.2	11,979	12.7
Number of young persons implicated				
Only the accused	63.6	36.4	50,035	53.1
1 or 2 coaccused youth	55.9	44.1	36,069	38.3
3 or more coaccused youth	44.6	55.4	8,117	8.6
Type of incident				
Against the person	59.5	40.5	13,159	14.0
Against property	54.3	45.7	67,296	71.4
Other	81.7	18.3	13,766	14.6
Closest victim-accused relationship				
N/A	58.8	41.2	82,304	87.4
Stranger	70.4	29.6	3,374	3.6
Unknown	67.3	32.7	892	0.9
Family	62.0	38.0	1,164	1.2
Other	54.4	45.6	6,487	6.9
Type of weapon present				
N/A	58.7	41.3	82,034	87.1
Unknown or none	56.9	43.1	9,139	9.7
Other weapon	73.2	26.8	2,564	2.7
Firearm	80.0	20.0	484	0.5
Modus operandi was shoplifting				
No	63.4	36.6	82,041	87.1
Yes	59.7	40.3	12,180	12.9
Level of injury suffered by any victim				
N/A	58.9	41.1	81,009	86.0
Unknown or none	57.9	42.1	6,886	7.3
Minor injury or death	58.4	41.6	5,571	.9
Major injury or death	84.1	15.9	755	0.8
Value of property involved				
N/A	70.9	29.1	28,085	29.8
0 - $25	52.2	47.8	16,837	17.9
$26 - 99	55.6	44.4	10,321	11.0
$100 - 499	52.6	47.4	17,987	19.1
$500 - 999	47.2	52.8	7,567	8.0
$1,000 +	60.4	39.6	13,424	14.2

Source: Adapted from Carrington, 1998: 5-7.

*Processed by other means includes alternative measures, warnings, or situations beyond the control of police, such as the death of the accused, or their involvement in other incidents for which charges have been laid.

Table 4.2
Police Perceptions of Whether Current Disposition is Meaningful by Type of Crime

Is the Current Disposition Meaningful?	Yes	No	Don't Know
Minor Property 1st Offence	82.7%	16.0%	1.3%
Minor Property Repeat Offence	41.3%	56.0%	2.6%
Minor Violence 1st Offence	75.3%	22.7%	2.0%
Minor Violence Repeat Offence	34.7%	61.3%	4.0%
Serious Property 1st Offence	54.7%	42.7%	2.7%
Serious Property Repeat Offence	34.0%	63.3%	2.7%
Serious Violence 1st Offence	58.0%	38.0%	4.0%
Serious Violence Repeat Offence	38.0%	56.7%	5.3%

Source: Solicitor General Canada, 1997: 10.

Box 4.2

Crime and No Punishment

Friday 5 September 1997
Ottawa Citizen

The Department of the Solicitor General recently released a survey of police attitudes concerning the effectiveness of the justice system in dealing with young offenders. The study, "Police Perceptions of Current Responses to Youth Crime," conducted by Carleton professors Tullio Caputo and Katherine Kelly, offers some common-sense recommendations about where the post-Young Offenders Act legal system can be improved.

Youths who break the law can be divided into three categories. The first and largest is made up of the 75 to 80 percent of young offenders whose crime is a relatively minor, one-time occurrence. According to the police survey, this group of fundamentally "straight" kids who made a one-time error in judgment and committed minor property or violent crimes (such as roughnecking in a schoolyard), can be dealt with effectively through informal measures, such as warning the young person and talking to his or her parents. This is enough to ensure that most never come in contact with the legal system again.

Things are different for the other two groups. At the extreme are the 3 to 5 percent of young offenders who repeatedly commit more serious infractions and

Box 4.2, *continued*

go on to become habitual criminals. This small group, which "can account for as much as 50 percent of all youth crime in a community," is almost impossible to reach with preventative measures.

Between these apparent incorrigibles and the benign majority are 15 to 20 percent of "high risk" repeat offenders who can be prevented from becoming career criminals so long as they are dealt with effectively at a relatively early stage.

At the moment, however, that often isn't happening. Over and over again, the survey quotes frustrated police officers who are reluctant to bring repeat young offenders into contact with the criminal justice system. The reason is that the mild sentences and punishments they so often receive send the perverse message that there are no consequences to re-offending. "So now when a kid gets sentenced it's probation, probation, probation," said one survey participant. "Next time I break the law it's probation." The punishment for breaking the law while on probation? More probation, of course.

There's no need for new legislation in this area. If punishments already on the books were more strenuously enforced, the survey points out, the situation would be vastly different. It cites an instance in which a dusk-to-dawn curfew imposed as a bail condition was rigorously enforced. The result: Punishment stopped being seen as a "joke" and became a "meaningful consequence." But such arrangements remain the exception.

The report closes with a list of "considerations for possible action." Two are worth mentioning here. First, the line between first violations and repeat offences should be starker, even for minor crimes. It is a false kind of mercy to allow someone to continue to offend without serious sanction until finally bringing down the hammer at the very end.

Second, the Young Offenders Act should apply to children between the ages of 10 and 15. Police currently have no tools at all to deal with the small but non-negligible number of instances where children under 12 years of age are involved. And 16- and 17-year-olds can and do commit crimes serious enough to warrant punishment that goes beyond the YOA's strict sentencing limits, which at the moment often seem to be the only limits the current system is capable of enforcing.

In our view, these are sensible recommendations.

Source: *Ottawa Citizen* (September 5, 1997).

Alternative Measures

Because *alternative measures* are meant to divert young offenders from the formal justice system, it is appropriate to discuss them before examining the court experience and sentencing process.

As noted elsewhere in this book, there is a range of alternative measures, including mediation, victim-offender reconciliation, making an apology, writing an essay, providing some form of compensation in the form of work or money, and working in the community (community service orders). Although he must come to court at least once, John is considered an "ideal" candidate for alternative measures, so he ends up working a few hours a week for the store owner from whom he stole, and making a written apology. This outcome is discussed and agreed upon by John, the victim, and the agency that will provide and supervise the alternative measures.[2]

It is very difficult to determine how many youths are actually processed through alternative measures because those who do not go through the formal system will not "show up" in official court statistics. Nor is it possible to distinguish between those who are referred to alternative measures by police and those who are given warnings by police. Nevertheless, it is estimated that only 20 percent of all cases are dealt with via alternative measures programs (Canadian Centre for Justice Statistics, 1994).

There is also some difficulty with determining whether alternative measures actually work. However, Bell (1999) states that while they appear to be highly successful (with "success" being defined presumably in terms of recidivism rates), it is difficult to know definitively whether lowered recidivism is caused by participation in the program or other factors.[3] Hence, although alternative measures programs are promising, we need to conduct more rigorous and systematic evaluation studies to determine how useful they actually are.

Another important issue is that alternative measures programs are not applied uniformly across Canada, and often do not adhere to the basic principles and guidelines set out in the YOA. Put differently, although the basic principles of alternative measures are intriguing and potentially useful, the actual implementation of these measures leaves much to be desired. There is, as always, a difference between the law in books and the law in action.

As Chapter One outlined, there are other criticisms of alternative measures. The Church Council on Justice and Corrections (1996) has summarized some of these as follows. Alternative measures:

- Widen the justice net by involving mainly young people who would not be brought into the justice system, but would merely receive a warning if the program did not exist.

- Often reward service groups and agencies that don't question the existing system, with contracts to manage alternative measures programs.

- Reduce, rather than expand, the range of community-based programs helping to reintegrate young people, by cutting funds to community programs not selected for alternative measures programs.

- Restrict programs to a narrow range of options, such as essay or apology writing, which do not speak to the unique needs and realities of many young people and do little to address the harm done or to reintegrate the young person into the community.

- Exclude aboriginal and minority youths because these youths are not seen to have the skills or family support to benefit from such programs.

The Courts

Although this is not representative of every case, all three of our young offenders must appear in court. Despite his embarrassment, for John, this is a relatively painless process. He and his parents come to the court, where the Crown states that John is being considered for an alternative measures program and John leaves the court knowing he will likely not have to make another appearance before the judge. He is, however, intimidated by the formality of the proceedings, and his parents' disappointment in him makes everything worse. Nevertheless, for the most part, his interaction with the formal components of the youth justice system is over. The other two youths, however, are just beginning their interface with the formal criminal justice system.

Julie makes her appearance in court and her case is recommended for trial. Although her mother has been invited to attend the first appearance, she does not show up. The judge also recommends that Julie be remanded in custody. He feels reasonably sure that she may not show up in court for her trial, because she lives mainly on the streets and because her mother has not given any indication that she will provide lodging for Julie while she awaits trial.

David faces far graver consequences. This is not his first offence, and he has committed other violent crimes. Accordingly, the Crown recommends that his case be transferred to adult court. David is refused bail and the judge orders that he be detained, pending a transfer to adult court hearing. The judge also orders a psychological health assessment. In the hearing, there are some important circumstances and factors that must be weighed before making the decision to transfer David's case to adult court. For instance, the court must take into account that David has had a very difficult life and that he was intoxicated at the time of the incident. At the same time, these facts must be balanced with the rights of society to protection from violent persons, and the reality that the youth justice system that has been part of David's life for many years is clearly not providing him with the rehabilitation and care he requires. Moreover, from the judge's point of view, David may be "unreachable" through the juvenile system. Weighing all the available information, however, the court decides that David's case should not be heard in adult court.

Although each of the court experiences described above vary, they illustrate some basic underlying principles at work in the court-youth process. As we might expect, given the emphasis of the Young Offenders Act on due process and rights, young offenders are given the opportunity to consult with lawyers and their parents, and there are rules governing whether youths should be detained, released into custody, or transferred to adult court. Despite these rules, there is still considerable discretion at work at this stage, this time from the court (Crown prosecutors and judges), which bases its decisions on a host of factors similar to those governing police behaviour and decisionmaking.

In addition, the fact that all three of our characters end up in formal proceedings of varying degrees indicates that in many cases, formal processing has superceded the ideal of diversion from the system, regardless of the offence. Not surprisingly, this also means greater costs to taxpayers, backlogged court systems, and bureaucratic inefficiencies. For instance, according to Kenewell, Bala, and Colfer (1991), in 1989-90 the daily costs of detention alone for youths in Ontario was approximately $80,000 per day.

Another issue has to do with the increased use of diagnosis and assessment tools to attempt to determine the extent to which youths are "at risk" of committing further crimes, and supposedly to understand what "treatment" approaches are likely to be most effective. While such tools can be effective for certain types of offenders, it seems unlikely that they will work for everyone. In these cases, David faces a battery of psychological tests; Julie may have to take some, though she has taken them before; and John will face none. All are different kinds of offenders with varying backgrounds and circumstances. Using such tests to determine what should be done about youth crime presupposes that criminal behaviour occurs in a social and political vacuum, that it is the individual who is responsible, and that the answer to what should be done (which in itself assumes that people can and should be "corrected") resides "inside" the individual. (For one youth worker's opinion of such tests, consider Box 4.3.)

Box 4.3

A Youth Worker's Perspective on Testing to Predict Youth Crime

For several years now, professionals have been developing and implementing an assessment instrument designed to identify and "predict" young offenders at risk of re-offending. Such an instrument claims to be able to capture the wide range of anti-social behaviour committed by adolescents. However, as a front-line worker with adolescents, I have grave concerns with this clinical assessment approach. This approach requires that a youth be declared "at risk" if they meet specific criteria outlined in the assessment. If the youth falls within a high category, functional responses may be provided to youth and their family, however if the youth's score is off by a number or two, resources are almost always not available.

Box 4.3, *continued*

As a youth worker, I have the opportunity to work with many youth, however these experiences can be hindered by political barriers. For example, a youth I had been working with had difficulties dealing with anger, often resulting in aggressive outbursts. His criminal charge was the result of an aggressive outburst. This youth functioned at a twelve-year-old level although he was almost fifteen years old. He had not become actively involved in criminal behaviour, nor did he associate with anti-social peers. I made continual attempts to allocate support for him and his family, however all services were either full or he did not meet the criteria. (He only scored at the moderate level on an assessment.) I knew at the time that if services were not allocated soon, an incident would occur. Soon after, this youth seriously assaulted someone in a aggressive outburst and began engaging in other criminal behaviour. This youth clearly needed help and without support he would continue to deteriorate and fall deeper into the youth justice system. It was not until he had incurred several more charges, that he "qualified" for services.

Although this screening protocol is mechanistic and consistent, its functional abilities are very limited. It is a very individualistic and reactionary approach that clearly does not look at the larger picture. Dealing effectively with youth who have engaged in criminal behaviour cannot be achieved by applying numerical scales. To make effective gains in our youth justice system we must focus on social-investment strategies, not individual and reactive ones.

Source: Contributed by a former student of the author.

This section has considered some aspects of the court process, but in the next section we will take up the most widely studied—and potentially most controversial—component of the process: sentencing.

Sentencing

Our three young persons are now at the stage at which they will be sentenced. We have already discussed John's experiences. It is likely that he will successfully complete his alternative measures program, and he may or may not steal again. For now, though, his encounter with the system has been brief and is unlikely to have future repercussions.

David is sentenced to a secure custody institution for the maximum term permitted under law. For the next two years, his life will be disciplined and structured, and he will be subject to a number of intervention programs. When he gets out, he will be 19 years old, with a long history of involvement with crime, no prospects, and little hope for the future. He will, however, have the opportunity to participate in some post-release programs with several goals, including increasing his job market prospects, skill training, his ability to manage anger, and so on.

In Julie's case, the judge determines that she needs care beyond what her mother is willing to provide. She is a repeat offender but has not committed any violent crime, and she has failed to comply with previous sentences she has received. This latter phenomenon is actually a fairly common occurrence among young offenders, but more so for females. By 1991, one in four charges laid against Canadian girls in youth courts were against the administration of justice, and more than one-fifth of females in custody facilities were charged with violations of administrative laws (Reitsma-Street, 1993).

The judge decides to sentence Julie to an open-custody facility. As Table 4.3 shows, the most common sentence for youths is probation, and young females are more likely than males to receive this disposition. Males, on the other hand, are more likely to be incarcerated either in secure or open-custody facilities. Though these data are not broken down by the age of the offender, overall, the harshest sentences tend to be given to older males and younger females (Bell, 1999; Duffy, 1996).

Could it be that these different sentencing patterns are related to the type of offence, not gender or "race"? We must consider whether there are other factors that could account for the differences apparent in Table 4.3. For example, repeat offenders tend to be sentenced to custody (as David's situation illustrates), and most repeat offenders are male.

Table 4.3
Youth Sentences, 1996-97 by Sex

	Percent	
Sentence	Males	Females
Probation	49	57
Community Service	6	8
Open Custody	19	15
Secure Custody	17	10
Total Custody	36	25
Fines	5	4
Absolute discharge	2	3

Source: Adapted from Canadian Centre for Justice Statistics, 1998: 40.

When sentences are broken down by type of offence, as in Table 4.4, we can see that certain differences among boys' and girls' experiences remain. Girls, for instance, are more likely to receive probation in nearly every category of offence, while boys are more likely to receive a custodial sentence. However, as Bell (1999) reminds us, in the past four years the number of young women incarcerated has *increased* by 26 percent, compared to only a 4 percent increase for boys. Thus, while type of offence and offender history play a role in sentencing, it is clear that there are gender differences as well, most of which can probably be explained by reference to the patriarchal nature of the justice system. Thus, girls are receiving harsher sentencing not because they are committing more serious crimes (they are not) but because of criminal justice officials' desire to enforce patriarchal expectations regarding young girl's "proper" behavior (Chesney-Lind, 1986). We need to keep in mind that while the Young Offenders Act supposedly eliminated status offences for which female youths were punished under the Juvenile Delinquency Act, some scholars (e.g., Boritch, 1997) argue that, under the YOA status offences have merely been reclassified into administrative offences and violations of court-ordered dispositions (also see DeKeseredy, 2000).

Table 4.4
Most Serious Sentence for Youths by Sex, 1996-1997

	Males				Females			
OFFENCE	Sentence (percent)							
	Custody				Custody			
	Secure	Open	Probation	Other	Secure	Open	Probation	Other
Violent	17	17	58	8	8	12	70	10
Property	14	18	55	13	6	10	65	19
Other Criminal Code	24	22	35	19	15	21	47	18
Other Federal Statute	18	20	35	26	15	22	39	23
Total Federal Statute	17	19	49	15	10	15	57	17

Source: Adapted from Canadian Centre for Justice Statistics, 1998: 65.

What about the fact that Julie is aboriginal? Is her experience consistent with the great disparities between native and non-native people that exist in the juvenile (and adult) criminal justice systems at every stage of the process (LaPrairie, 1996; Schissel, 1993)? Schissel (1993: 99) argues that:

> . . . Natives appear to experience consistently more severe dispositions than Whites or Others despite legal and court-specific influences. As well, native juveniles receive more severe dispositions when unaccompanied by a parent, as compared to Whites and Others. Simply put, Native juveniles benefit the most from the presence of a family member or guardian.

Thus, because Julie's mother did not appear with her in court, it is likely that she was at a distinct disadvantage compared to other aboriginal and non-native youth whose parents attended court sessions. Furthermore, because Julie is poor, native, and disenfranchised, it is likely that her experiences with the justice system will differ from non-natives because the system has been constructed to address the needs of non-native youth (Bell, 1999), a reality that consistently mirrors the experiences of ethnic minorities in general (Miller, 1996).

To what extent does the system reflect a middle- or upper-class bias? To be sure, the current youth justice system, like the adult one, is supposed to be blind to socioeconomic differences. But can we say unequivocally that John would have been recommended for alternative measures had he been poor and black? Unfortunately, there are very few good studies of the relationship between class and youth crime in Canada. However, studies in the United States continue to point to the strong relationship between poverty and both criminal behaviour and victimization (see Kasarda, 1992; Wilson, 1987, 1996).

The maximum "time" a young offender can do in a closed- or open-custody facility is two years for most offences.[4] On average, probation terms last approximately one year, although the maximum term is two years (see Table 4.5). In addition, although custody terms have become shorter in recent years, probation terms have lengthened. Finally, about 5 percent of young offenders are fined for their transgressions. With the exception of impaired driving cases, fines tend to be low because most youths would find it difficult to pay high fines (Canadian Center for Justice Statistics, 1998).

Table 4.5
Median Sentence Length in Days, First and Repeat Offenders, 1996-97

	First-time Offenders			Repeat Offenders		
Offence Offence	Secure Custody	Open Custody	Probation	Secure Custody	Open Custody	Probation
Violent	56	60	360	75	45	360
Property	30	53	360	60	60	360
Other Criminal Code	14	30	360	20	30	360

Source: Adapted from Canadian Centre for Justice Statistics, 1998: 54.

Several points should be made here. First, a young offender's sentence for the same crime can vary across jurisdictions depending on the judge. For example, an experiment in simulated sentencing in which 43 judges were given fictional cases to preside over, concluded, among other things, that wide variation in sentencing apparent in the fictional judgments represented different philosophies utilized by judges to determine the fate of young offenders (as described in Doob, Marinos, and Varma, 1998).

Second, the data in Table 4.5 show that although probation is the most common sentence, custody is clearly a common choice among the range of dispositions a judge could hand out. Moreover, in 1994-95, approximately 43 percent of all sentences to custody for young offenders were for property offences. Of those, 39 percent were cases of break and enter (Juristat, 1996). What does this mean in relation to the approaches taken by other nations? Well, the proportion of youths who are sentenced to either open or closed custody in Canada is astounding. Canada incarcerates approximately one-third of all young offenders, and according to Schissel, (1997: 8) ". . . despite claims that Canada is a more desirable country to live in than any other, we incarcerate more children per capita than any other industrialized nation, including the United States."

Third, custody for young offenders in Canada is expensive. Approximately one-quarter of a billion dollars per year is spent incarcerating nonviolent offenders (Doob, Marinos, and Varma, 1998) and, while costs vary by type of institution, Canadians pay about $80,000 per year to keep a youth incarcerated (Bell, 1999).

Fourth, most of those receiving longer custodial sentences are repeat offenders, but it is unlikely that incarcerating such individuals for longer periods and more frequently will "turn them around." In short, except with regard to a handful of truly dangerous individuals who threaten public safety, prisons do not work. Prisons fail because they cannot deal with the broader structural and social forces that motivate crime, they are often brutal and dehumanizing, and they are often in fact excellent places to learn how to become a "better" criminal (Currie, 1998; Faith, 1993). It is not surprising, then, that "most custody programs experience a recidivism rate at or above 50 percent. . . ." (Bala, 1997: 244).

Finally, we should briefly consider the recent arrival (in Ontario and Alberta) of boot camps, seen by many as an "innovation" in corrections. Although they vary in structure, these are essentially strictly supervised camps in which military discipline and strict behaviour codes are used to both punish and deter future delinquencies (see Box 4.4).

Although there is little Canadian data on the effectiveness of boot camps, recent evidence from the United States generally indicates that they are no better than other, traditional dispositions in reducing recidivism; that they have failed to reduce prison overcrowding; and that they do not necessarily reduce costs (Lab, 1997; MacKenzie and Shaw, 1993; Simon, 1995). Nevertheless, a punishment-minded public, an overall perception that they are cheaper than traditional incarceration facilities, and a generally simplistic attitude toward the causes of youth crime in Canada (i.e., "they just lack discipline") all seem to be driving the continued implementation of boot camps.

Box 4.4

Boot Camps: The Jury's Still Out: Angry Youths Grew Up with Abuse, Counsellor Says

Jacquie Miller
Ottawa Citizen
Sunday 14 September 1997

Jim Kragtwyk has spent 12 years trying to figure out what makes teenagers break the law and how to turn them around. A lanky, easygoing man, he chats in his shabby basement office in Chaudiére House, his dog sprawled at his feet. Upstairs are nine guys who have stolen cars, beaten people up, and broken into houses.

The brick house in Ottawa's Chinatown neighbourhood is an "open custody" facility where 16- and 17-year olds serve their time. Mr. Kragtwyk has worked there since it opened in 1985.

He agrees wholeheartedly with the "lofty ideals" behind the provincial government's latest experiment for young offenders. Ontario says it wants to teach teen criminals respect for authority, discipline, self-respect, and work ethics.

But Mr. Kragtwyk doubts whether most of the teens he knows could be transformed by sending them to boot camp.

Ontario opened a military-style camp for young offenders near Barrie, north of Toronto, last month. Solicitor General Bob Runciman says he plans to expand the "strict discipline" regime to the rest of the province's youth jails as well.

Mr. Kragtwyk wonders: Would that help the guys upstairs?

Many teenagers in custody are already angry, he says. Crewcuts, pushups and dawn-to-dusk discipline probably won't force them to change. "They probably had way too much of that when they were growing up. They probably had someone who was overly strict or abusive. They don't respond to that. That is where a lot of their behaviour and anger comes from. They don't need someone else throwing things at them or being really strict with them."

Military-style camps are popular with the public. They appeal to people who are fed up with crime and favour a get-tough approach.

At the camp near Barrie, teenagers are up at 6 a.m. They face 16-hour days of study, marching, work, calisthenics and life-skills programs. There is no TV, no swearing, no slacking off.

When he announced the boot camp, Mr. Runciman warned that the days of "coddling criminals" were over. He has suggested that youths don't take jail seriously because they can watch TV and play pool. The military-style camp is supposed to change attitudes and make jail less attractive.

Experts dismiss the idea. They say boot camps may be good politics, but they won't make the streets safer.

"The research is very clear," says Paul Gendreau, of the Centre for Criminal Justice Studies at the University of New Brunswick. "It shows these programs have virtually no effect whatsoever on the criminal behaviour of participants."

Box 4.4, *continued*

He sounds exasperated. Military camps teach "discipline, being neat and tidy, being obedient, being fit," he explains. "And those aren't predictors of criminal behaviour at all. If being fit and obedient and keeping a nice, neat, tidy bed were major predictors of criminal behaviour, then 92 percent of (average people) would be hard-core criminals."

The United States began introducing boot camps for young offenders more than a decade ago. But they are falling out of favour, says Mr. Gendreau. Some have closed because they didn't work.

Teen criminals need programs that teach them skills and new attitudes, not military drills, says Harry Gow, a criminology professor at the University of Ottawa.

The things that work? "Teaching people how to think, how to count to 10, how to deal in a disarming way with potentially aggressive people, how to handle such things as budgeting, and dating, in a peaceful way," says Mr. Gow. "That requires more classroom time, and less time running around yelling like a bunch of idiotic Marine recruits in the typical boot camp."

But Mr. Runciman says the current system failed. About 80 percent of adults now in jail were young offenders. "The public is pretty well fed up with what they see as lax, kid-glove treatment of young offenders," Mr. Runciman says.

Armchair critics should give the camp a chance, he says.

MPP Gary Carr, who co-chaired a provincial task force on how to implement strict discipline, says the public believes that youths in custody are treated as help-less victims and allowed to run the detention centres.

"We go in and give them a group hug and say, 'Don't worry, it wasn't your fault, it was your mother's fault.' "

Ontario's boot camp was ridiculed last month when the day before the grand opening, two inmates hot-wired a van in the compound, crashed through the gates and escaped. Since then, two youths have been moved to regular juvenile jails for trying to assault a guard, and another two were removed for refusing to co-oper-ate. The jail, built to house 32, had a dozen young offenders this week.

Ontario is not copying the extreme, "shout-in-your-face" U.S. boot camps, where drill sergeants humiliate teenage inmates, says Mr. Carr.

But a military routine will provide young offenders with the structure that is often missing in their lives, he argues. Drills and physical challenges like running obstacle courses build self-confidence and teach youths to rely on each other, he says.

"Most of these kids who are in trouble have never had structure. They have parents that don't care. If they want to get up at 10 a.m. and go to school, fine. And if they don't, who cares?"

Ontario's camp is modelled after a military-style jail for high-risk male young offenders in New York's Catskill Mountains, the Sgt. Henry Johnson Youth Lead-ership Academy.

Mr. Carr said the task force was impressed with what the academy did for its inmates, some of the "meanest, toughest" hoods from Harlem. The youths he met at the academy wore uniforms, didn't swear, and called him sir. One lad was "so polite, you'd want your daughter to marry him."

Box 4.4, *continued*

Mr. Carr came away convinced the academy inspired the boys to renounce crime. The academy also runs an after-care program that gives support and help to the teens when they return home to the ghettos.

In Toronto, in contrast, when the task force visited the Metro West Youth Detention Centre, Mr. Carr said a kid passing by in the hallway blew a raspberry right in his face. The youth wasn't punished, he said.

Ontario's boot camp isn't all drills and running laps. It also offers school and programs, such as anger management and civics lessons. Most experts say the programs are the key to reaching young offenders.

In Ottawa, Mr. Kragtwyk says he tries to figure out what drove the youth to crime and offers programs to attack those problems. His house, operated by the Salvation Army, runs 13 programs. They include anger management, alcohol and drug counselling, employment skills, basic literacy, group therapy for children from abusive or violent families, and "life skills" like how to cook meals, budget and find an apartment.

The range is wide. Mr. Kragtwyk sees kids who just happened to be in the wrong place at the wrong time and probably won't re-offend, and surly toughs who punch holes in the walls and scream at staff.

But in many cases, there was poverty, neglect and abuse in their families. Mr. Kragtwyk opens a report he compiled on about 100 residents at the house in 1995-96. Half of them had been either physically or sexually abused at home. About a quarter had one or more family members with a criminal record. About half said at least one family member abused drugs or alcohol. About 45 percent were from single-parent families, and about half had trouble reading.

These youths just don't react to threats of boot-camp style discipline the same way a mature, responsible adult would, Mr. Kragtwyk says.

"A 'normal person' would probably say, 'I'm never going to that place again, I've learned my lesson.' But it's not that type of person getting involved in the youth justice system. They don't have those sound, logical frameworks built in."

The house uses a system where youths are given privileges, like passes to the outside, for good behaviour and for completing school and programs.

"If someone is going to sit down and teach me something, on sort of an equal level, I'm sort of receptive to it," Mr. Kragtwyk says. "I might even appreciate it. If someone is going to crack the whip and shout out drills, I don't know how appreciative I'm going to be, and how much I'm going to learn."

Source: *Ottawa Citizen* (September 14, 1997). Reprinted with permission.

JUSTICE MODELS[5]

How can we make sense of the data presented in this chapter? In this section, we will place these issues in the context of five "models" for understanding different criminal justice policy philosophies. Each of these is linked to philosophical and theoretical assumptions discussed in Chapter Three, but they are also useful ways of understanding the nature of contemporary youth justice in Canada.

The Crime Control Perspective:
Lock 'em up and throw away the key.

Those taking the crime control perspective contend that the proper role of criminal justice is to prevent crime through the judicious use of sanctions. It is argued that when the criminal justice system operates effectively, crime rates should go down because criminals are being deterred. Conversely, if the crime rates are going up, then the system should be punishing more "effectively" in order to ensure that all of us understand that "crime doesn't pay." As we pointed out in Chapter Three, those adhering to the principles of crime control highlight the importance of the victim, and emphasize that crime control measures should be sure and swift. Accordingly, this perspective is associated with the principles of classical and neoclassical criminology.

The Rehabilitative Perspective:
We can pay now or pay (more) later.

In the rehabilitative approach, it is argued that the justice system should be a means of caring for and treating people who cannot take care of themselves. Crime is thought to be an expression of frustration and anger created by a number of factors external to the individual, including social inequality. So, in contrast to the crime control perspective, which focuses on the offence, the rehabilitative perspective concentrates on the offender and the role that social conditions play in creating the offender. The assumption is that societal conditions breed new criminals, but the focus is on treating the individual.

Due Process Perspective:
A fair process for everyone.

The due process standpoint combines elements of the concern for the individual demonstrated in the rehabilitation perspective with the concept of legal fairness guaranteed by the Charter. The emphasis is on the ability of the system to provide fair and equitable treatment to those accused of crimes, which can only be achieved by monitoring justice officials' exercise of discretion. Here, the goal is to ensure that no one suffers racial, gender, ethnic, or other discrimination.

Nonintervention Perspective:
The system does more harm than good.

Proponents of this perspective on justice argue that we should limit the individual's involvement with the criminal justice system whenever possible. It is argued that the long-term effects of involvement, such as we would expect with incarceration, are harmful to the individual, as well as society because that individual will in all likelihood be released into the community someday.

Thus, noninterventionists support the decriminalization of "victimless crimes," the deinstitutionalization of nonviolent offenders, and diversion.

Justice Perspective:
Lock 'em up, but don't violate anyone's rights.

There are, of course, approaches that attempt to *combine* elements of the perspectives discussed above. For instance, in the justice model, the concern for due process is balanced with the notion that crime should be controlled. In addition, advocates of this point of view support limited discretion by officials of the criminal justice system, recommending instead that strict protocols and guidelines be developed regarding sentencing.

Conflict / Critical Perspective:
Justice is about power and control and wider social processes.

Critical perspectives emphasize differences in power and a concern for the underprivileged. Critical analyses recognize the social basis of crime, that law is a political tool, that the justice system is biased, and that criminal justice officials such as judges and police should be held accountable for their actions. Accordingly, critical models of justice concentrate on debunking mythologies about crime and criminal behaviour, and work toward creating a humane, fair, and rational criminal justice system, *in the context of a fair, humane, and just society.*

The final chapter of this book will emphasize some insights from this perspective because the data presented here, as in other chapters, suggest that current approaches to youth justice in Canada are woefully inadequate.

Summary

The Young Offenders Act is really an odd combination of the models of justice discussed above (with the exception of the critical model). For example, the Act's emphasis on due process and procedure fits within the concerns of the due process model. Furthermore, the existence of alternative measures meets a key requirement of the noninterventionist approach, although neither the frequency of use of diversion, nor its content, seems to have come anywhere near its potential in most parts of Canada. Still further, recent amendments to the act that were designed to "get tough" on youth crime fit within the basic ideological framework of the crime control perspective. Finally, although rehabilitation programs for youths do exist in the current system, the notion of rehabilitation itself seems to have taken a back seat to the idea of punishing, disciplining, and controlling youths (Schissel, 1997). Moreover, the rehabilitative ideal in today's system focuses on the individual, without reference to the role of social conditions and processes associated with "dehabilitation."

The data we have examined in this chapter illustrate that while there is a great deal of inconsistency in the application of the law, overall, Canada continues to emphasize the control and punishment of young offenders. Notwithstanding the judicious use of probation, we clearly continue to assume that incarceration is an appropriate response to youths in conflict with the law, despite evidence to the contrary. Canada's youth justice strategy also discriminates on the basis of gender and "race," and we seem convinced that prosecuting young people for petty offences is fruitful. Lastly, but just as central, current strategies seem more concerned with processing offenders *after* criminal offences have occurred while simultaneously ignoring, or paying lip service, to the social conditions that generate crime.

In summary, the "Canadian way" in relation to youth crime seems to be to continue to pursue dated and ineffectual policies and practices, despite evidence that the system is not achieving justice for all. As we will argue in the final chapter, there are other ways of achieving justice, should we choose to do so—if we are willing to challenge the ways in which criminal justice policy decisions are made and reconsider the goals of current policies.

Notes

[1] The statistics reported in Table 4.1 do not necessarily allow us to "predict" what is more likely to happen to offenders with particular characteristics. For a more detailed analysis of the data in the table, see Carrington, 1998.

[2] Not all victims agree to be involved in the process, but victim involvement is encouraged.

[3] In addition, evaluating success based on recidivism rates is problematic because any decision regarding the appropriate length of time without committing a crime is always arbitrary.

[4] For those offences for which the adult sentence would be life, the maximum youth sentence is three years; for first-degree murder, the maximum sentence is 10 years (Bala, 1997: 231).

[5] This section is a summary of Senna and Siegel, 1998.

DISCUSSION QUESTIONS AND PROBLEM-SOLVING SCENARIOS

1. Design what you would consider to be the ideal criminal justice system for youths. What principles regarding youth crime would you follow? What would your system look like?

2. What do you think would have happened if Julie had been non-native? What if David had murdered the man he scuffled with? What would likely have happened to John if he lived in Manitoba, or if he was poor?

3. What kinds of new alternative measures programs can you invent? How would you go about implementing them?

SUGGESTED READINGS

Schissel, B. (1993). *Social Dimensions of Canadian Youth Justice*. Toronto: Oxford University Press.

Lab, S. (1997). *Crime Prevention: Approaches, Practices and Evaluations*, 3rd ed. Cincinnati, OH: Anderson.

LaPrairie, C. (1996). *Examining Aboriginal Corrections in Canada*. Ministry of the Solicitor General Canada, Catalog Number: JS5-1/14-1996E.

A day care worker reads stories to children at a day care center run by a large corporation. Preventing youth crime in Canadian society demands social-structural change. One way to increase support for families and children is to encourage employers to help employees negotiate work and family obligations.

Chapter Five

From Youth Justice to Social Justice

INTRODUCTION

Although decades of research have shown unequivocally that crime is a complicated social problem that warrants complex solutions, Canada's approach to the problem of youth crime has been simplistic and ineffective. The numerous failures and shortcomings of the system leave many students feeling that nothing really works, nobody cares, and no one knows how to fix it.

In spite of the pessimism we might feel after reviewing the record of Canadian youth criminal justice policies, workable solutions to youth crime do exist. However, many of the solutions proposed in this final chapter will not be easy to implement because they are long-term, require fundamental changes in social structure and policy, and call for fundamental shifts in the way we think about youth and crime. Others are immediate, and attainable, but will also require political will.

We will briefly revisit some important arguments pertaining to the failures of youth justice policies in Canada. We will then examine the extent to which current policies and practices can be retained or modified, or discarded altogether to achieve a more equitable and effective youth justice system. Finally, we will review some potential solutions to the dilemmas and issues faced by young people and the criminal justice system they face today, through the lens of critical criminology.

IF IT DOESN'T WORK, DO IT AGAIN

A central theme of this book is that criminal justice policies for young Canadians have generally failed to reflect the fact that crime is a process that occurs in a social context. Crime is not just an "event" perpetrated by individuals against victims. Rather, all crime has a "dynamic history." As MacLean (1996: 3) argues:

> crime is not a an event or a "social fact," but a social process which includes a number of social events each of which is inextricably bound up with the other. If we conceptualize crime as being an event, the violation of law by an individual, then we run the risk of focusing on that individual at the expense of comprehending the entire process. We wonder what kind of person would violate the law and conclude that something is wrong with him or her.

Thus, one of the central obstacles to achieving effective youth justice policies in Canada stems from the tendency to individualize what are, in fact, *social* problems.

One of the central challenges facing progressive criminologists is combating the tendency to view crime as an individual act divorced from the social environment. Yet, as we have seen, the public's views on crime, fueled by media accounts, tend to place responsibility for crime squarely on the shoulders of perpetrators. Moreover, many Canadians believe that levels of both adult and youth crime are increasing, despite evidence to the contrary deriving from both victimization surveys and official data sources (NCPC, 1996).

Why do we continue to adhere to myths about crime and criminal justice? The first thing to consider in answering this question is the role of the media. As argued in Chapter One, media accounts exaggerate the reality of crime and are central to the creation and reproduction of "moral panics" about crime (Goode and Ben-Yehuda, 1994; Muncie, 1984; Schissel, 1997). Also problematic is that the media often know little about crime, criminal justice, or crime policy, and tend to be uncritical of political decisions made about crime (Lavrakas, 1997).

But does this mean that a sheep-like public simply believes what the media tells us to believe? Probably not. Indeed, people take an active role in creating their own belief systems about a host of social problems, including crime. For instance, Baron and Hartnagel (1996) have shown that a good portion of the public justifies their "confidence in" and demand for a punishment-oriented criminal justice system because they hold conservative or neoconservative values. As discussed in Chapter Three, those holding such values also tend to view youth crime as a calculated, rational choice, deserving calculated, "rational" responses such as punishment and (general and specific) deterrence. The trouble is, of course, that these strategies have never been shown to work (Lab, 1997).

Beliefs and values also exist in a social context. Currently, Canada is locked into a neoconservative stance regarding economic, political, and social issues. It is not surprising, therefore, that both the Young Offenders Act and proposed amendments to it (discussed in Chapter One) seem to favour punishment and "getting tough," in combination with "rehabilitation" strategies that pathologize the individual instead of the social system. Even more disturbing, in addition to cutting taxes that could be used to fund badly needed or decaying social programs, neoconservative governments in Canada have been elected and re-elected partially on their skill at encouraging public fear of a youth crime epidemic that does not exist, and trumpeting "get tough" solutions that do not work (DeKeseredy, 2000). (See Box 5.1 for a clear example of one government's incapacity to understand crime.)

Box 5.1

A Safer Ontario (Excerpted from Blueprint— Mike Harris' Plan to Keep Ontario on the Right Track, Ontario Progressive Conservative Party)

Everyone in Ontario has the right to be safe from crime. We should be able to walk in our neighbourhoods, use public transit, live in our homes and send our children to school free from the fear of criminals.

Too many Ontario families don't have that peace of mind. Some politicians will try to convince you that crime is not a major problem. They'll blame anyone but the criminals. Try telling that to the victims of crime and their families.

We've made it clear where we stand. Our government has done a great deal to turn things around. We are putting more police on the streets and increasing support for victims of crime while cracking down on criminals. But, there is still a lot more we can do.

Parole

When it comes to letting a convicted criminal back on to our streets, we think public safety and the rights of law-abiding people must come first.

That's why we've set **new and tougher standards** for members of parole boards and for the granting of early release. It's just common sense that parole should be treated as a privilege, not a right.

As a result of our reforms, more criminals are now being denied parole in Ontario than are being granted it—the first time that's ever happened! Not surprisingly, the number of crimes committed by parolees has dropped.

Box 5.1, *continued*

When criminals are released from jail, it's vital we do everything possible to ensure they don't commit more crimes. Crimes such as illegal drug use are also connected to a variety of other criminal activities. **We'll require parolees to take random drug tests** as a condition of their release. Those who fail will have their parole revoked.

There is still more work to do with Ottawa to help ensure public safety. For example, we will intensify our campaign against the federal government's 'discount law'. Under this law, **even the most serious offenders can get out of jail after serving only two-thirds of their sentences. That's simply wrong** and the discount law should be repealed.

It is also unacceptable that **Ottawa has set a target of increasing the number of convicts granted parole and reducing the frequency of parole being revoked.** We think public safety should come ahead of any quotas, and we'll let the federal government know that the people of Ontario want no part of federal plans to let more criminals out on our streets.

Sex Offenders

We're creating **Ontario's first registry of sex offenders** to strengthen our protection against these crimes. Our new law will require all pedophiles, rapists, molesters and other convicted sex offenders—as well as those found criminally insane—to register their locations with police and update them when they move. Police will be permitted to **notify communities about the presence of high-risk sex offenders** in their neighbourhoods.

Federal pardons allow convicted criminals to hide their pasts, allowing some to abuse more victims. We think it's far too dangerous to allow this privilege to sex offenders. Over the past 25 years, 704 convicted sex offenders pardoned by the federal government have committed new sex offences. Even worse, 458 of those new offences were against children. We will demand that Ottawa **stop giving pardons to convicted sex offenders, especially child molesters.**

Parental Responsibility

Respect for the law and the responsibilities of citizenship are something children must be taught, particularly by their parents. We think parents should get the credit when their children are good citizens but must also take some responsibility when their children break the law.

We'll bring in legislation **making parents financially responsible for property damage and other consequences of their children breaking the law.**

Young Offenders

Our government doesn't coddle young offenders. We've introduced strict discipline programs (including a 'boot camp') for serious offenders. Young people who break provincial laws get a sharp lesson in the consequences, and we're turning many lives around as a result.

Box 5.1, *continued*

Despite our successful example, the federal government still won't take youth crime seriously. To build on what we've done in Ontario, we need real, effective change to the federal law on young offenders, including **automatic adult consequences for crimes like murder, manslaughter, robbery, sexual assault and drug trafficking,** as well as **mandatory adult sentences for crimes involving weapons and repeat offences such as break and enter.**

We'll also demand changes to the federal rules on legal aid for young offenders. We want to be able to **refuse to pay for legal aid when a young person's parents can afford the cost of a lawyer,** rather than forcing law-abiding Ontario taxpayers to foot the bill.

Strengthening Victims' Rights

For too long, the criminal justice system treated victims of crime as an afterthought. **Our government has supported victims** through all stages of the legal process by creating the Victims' Bill of Rights, expanding victims' programs, making it easier to bring civil suits against offenders, and by launching an office for victims of crime staffed by crime victims and front-line justice professionals.

To help build on these accomplishments and provide even better support to all victims of crime, we will put all of the various programs and services for victims together under a single, focussed agency—**our Office for Victims of Crime.** The Office will be permanently established in legislation and have a new role in ensuring that the principles of the Victims' Bill of Rights are respected. It will also develop provincial standards for all victims' services.

All of this will be in addition to the vital network of shelters and sexual assault centres that work tirelessly on behalf of women victimized by crime. Our victims' rights initiatives will complement and strengthen that network in its current, independent, community-based form.

We'll also take **special action to address the needs of seniors who are victims of crime,** including creating 'elder shelters' for victims of assault, adding a seniors representative to the Office for Victims of Crime and pressing the federal government to make 'home invasion' a new category of offence under the Criminal Code.

Safer Schools

We have a detailed plan to make our schools safer, which you'll find here.

Domestic Violence

Domestic violence is wrong. Plain and simple. We don't tolerate it in Ontario. Our government has already taken important action by being the first government to create special courts dedicated to domestic violence cases. We've expanded assistance to domestic violence victims and domestic violence programs. We'll continue to maintain and improve those services, but there's more we can do.

The number of domestic violence courts will be doubled. They are an effective way of bringing these cases to justice quickly and better protecting victims and witnesses.

Box 5.1, *continued*

We'll issue a 'Zero Tolerance Directive' to all police agencies to make criminal charges automatic any time someone breaks a condition of bail, parole or a restraining order.

We will link all shelters and rape crisis centres to the cutting-edge information technology of our justice system. For example, this means that a worker in a women's shelter can take a victim impact statement or a record of a victim's concerns for her safety and send it, instantaneously, into the prosecutor's case file. It means victims and support workers can have instant access to information about court dates. And it means that, when bail conditions and restraining orders are imposed, every police force in Ontario will have those details on their computers.

Fighting Drugs

Drugs are not only illegal, they are linked to other crimes, destroy people's lives and undermine our communities. We must stamp out drug dealing in every neighbourhood in Ontario.

We'll start by **permanently revoking the liquor licenses or business permits of establishments** where it can be shown that drugs are habitually being used or sold.

We'll also amend the law to **streamline the eviction of people who allow their rental units to be used as bases for drug dealing,** and **kick out drug dealers who occupy a unit owned or leased by someone else.**

We'll **give municipalities the power to shut down crack houses** as public nuisances.

And, because of the link between organized crime and the drug trade, we'll increase funding for the special Organized Crime/Proceeds of Crime police task force.

Aggressive Panhandling

Whether you live in the city or are just visiting, you have the right to walk down the street or go to public places without being harassed or intimidated by aggressive panhandlers.

We'll **stop aggressive panhandling** by making threatening and harassing behaviour, such as blocking people on sidewalks, a provincial offence. We'll also give police the power to crack down on 'squeegee kids'.

Making Criminals Pay

Taxpayers know it costs money to investigate, prosecute and lock up criminals, but that public safety is worth the price.

At the same time, we're committed to exploring all reasonable ways of **making offenders accountable for their own actions,** and that includes making them contribute to the costs they have imposed on taxpayers. We'll take actions such as:

- Billing criminals for the cost of their custody in provincial jails and reformatories. This policy will be aimed at criminals who can afford to pay their own way and not at penalizing their already traumatized family members.

> **Box 5.1,** *continued*
>
> - Using the provincial licensing system to collect the millions of dollars outstanding in unpaid fines, bail forfeitures and restitution orders. Just as with deadbeat parents, those who don't pay will risk losing their licenses or permits until they live up to their obligations.
>
> - Getting offenders to reimburse the Criminal Injuries Compensation Board for the cost of awards to their victims.

Source: *http://www.mikeharrispc.com/scripts/ispage26.dll?Catalog=pcpo&File=4-0-ie.htm*

Predictably, when solutions requiring transformation of the social structure and current power relations are proposed, neoconservatives are quick to argue that "bleeding-heart" solutions can only make the problem worse, that the costs of a structural attack on crime outweigh those of building prisons, and that criminals should be dealt with via criminal justice policy rather than social policy (Walker, 1998). However, these assertions have been made without any good supporting data, and in spite of evidence that incarceration, punishment, and "getting tough" have been abject failures.

Some might presume that if so many people support neoconservative policies on crime, surely they must be right. From a scientific point of view, though, it is folly to pursue policies when the evidence supporting them is weak or nonexistent. From a moral point of view, conservatives are right only if it is true that social life consists *only* of freely chosen personal decisions and the responsibilities that go with them and that, ultimately, we have no obligations to others.

A related problem is that people generally look for simple solutions to complex problems, particularly if competing solutions tend to shake their world view. No wonder, then, that the public is so fascinated by the campaign to find "cures for crime" in well-established but narrowly focused professions such as medicine or psychology. As we have seen, when those seeking to understand crime assume that the answers lie *within* the individual (e.g., in "crime genes" or "dysfunctional personalities"), they presume that "treating" the individual will suffice to eliminate or reduce crime. In effect, this shifts our attention away from social issues toward individual ones.

There are bureaucratic issues at work here too. Criminal justice typically means processing individuals through a system that is highly structured, inflexible, and divorced from other institutions, a problem Currie (1985: 18) has identified as "compartmentalizing social problems along bureaucratic lines." Consider, for instance, that compared to the Young Offenders Act, the welfare model of justice that characterized the Juvenile Delinquents Act allowed for greater sensitivity to outside influences on the child and greater discretion and flexibility for criminal justice officials in dealing with young offenders. Under the current legislation, both the criminal act and the actor tend to be detached from their social circumstances in the name of due process and efficiency.

One of the paradoxes of Canadian youth criminal justice is that the Young Offenders Act does contain strategies that could, if implemented consistently and appropriately, reduce the *impact* of crime on victims and offenders, their families, and society. What this (or any other law) will *not* do is significantly reduce the *incidence* of crime, because law cannot address the original, pre-arrest causes of criminal behaviour. In short, because the law is limited in its ability to solve youth crime, we should be looking outside the law for solutions (Bala, 1997).

The position taken in this chapter is that neoconservatives are wrong, not only because their assumptions about the nature of society are flawed, but also because they assume that crime is a property of individuals not social conditions and policies. As you saw in earlier chapters, while people do make their own decisions, they do not make them under conditions they have necessarily chosen themselves. Many people's lives are structured by social processes and forces over which they have limited or no control. Accordingly, progressive solutions to crime and other social problems hinge on our ability to understand the interplay of individual lives and social conditions. What this suggests, then, is that a truly effective youth justice system requires rethinking criminal justice in terms of social justice, and then acting accordingly. Does this mean that current laws and the system in which they are embedded are completely useless? The answer is no. There are some redeeming aspects of the current legislation, while other components require serious reconsideration. In the next section, we will consider features of the youth criminal justice system in Canada that could be modified or retained to create a truly just approach to youth crime.

RETHINKING CURRENT POLICY

The Potential of Alternative Measures

The first component we will consider here is alternative measures. This important piece of the justice for youth legislation contains within it the seeds of a truly progressive—and potentially very effective— response to youths in conflict with the law. This is because the philosophy of removing youths from contact with the formal system as early as possible is essentially sound (except for those who believe in a strict punishment model). However, as we also saw in Chapter Four, problems such as net-widening, inconsistency in application across and within jurisdictions, and inadequate evaluation of programs still remain.

To make alternative measures work better, we require better data on how often they are being used, more program ideas, program evaluations that are theoretically and methodologically sound, and guidelines that are less vague (Bala, 1997).

You will recall that one of the central arguments in labeling and left-realist approaches to youth justice is that it is more effective (and much cheaper) to divert offenders than to process and adjudicate them in the formal system. Left realists also contend that young offenders need, among other things, to become more politicized. That is, they need to understand more clearly why their actions are crimes, the consequences of their actions, and the impact of their actions on victims. Moreover, given that the vast majority (57%) of referrals are for theft under $5,000, greater efforts must be made to utilize these programs to deal with offences, that in many provinces, are deemed ineligible for alternative measures (see Table 5.1).

At the same time, those designing and implementing alternative measures programs need to develop ways for offenders to cope and deal with the root causes of crime. Finally, care should be taken to ensure that these programs do not degenerate into the kind of adversarial and pointless processes evident in the formal justice system (Alvi, 1986).

Table 5.1
Youth Alternative Measures Cases, by Most Serious Offence, 1997-98

Offence	Percent of cases
Theft under $5000	57
Common Assault	7
Mischief	7
Other property	7
Other criminal code	7
Break and enter	5
Disturbing the peace	3
Other	3
Drugs	2
Theft over $5000	1

Source: Adapted from Kowalski, 1999: 8.

Youth Justice Committees

Although *Youth Justice Committees* are included as a component of the Young Offenders Act (under Section 69), they have received relatively little attention in the media and elsewhere as potentially a more progressive way of dealing with youth crime. These committees began in

First Nation's communities as an attempt to deal with high recidivism rates among aboriginal youth offenders. They are made up of volunteers working in concert with other components of the formal criminal justice system as well as community-based agencies to meet the needs of young offenders within their communities. They are often responsible for the administration of alternative measures programs (Paiment, 1996).

There is substantial variation (across and within provinces) in the activities of these committees but, generally, they hold the potential for restoring a sense of community responsibility for youth justice, reducing the destructive outcomes of the formal justice process, and providing communities with flexible ways of dealing with youths, thereby meeting the needs of the community.

There are, of course, dangers in using community members as the mechanism to deal with youth crime (Paiment, 1996). They include:

- Community members who bring an attitude of punishment and vigilantism to their work.

- The lack of resources to fund programs, and the out-of-pocket expenses incurred by committee members.

- Currently, eligibility is restricted to first-time, nonviolent offenders in most provinces.

- The lack of community-based programs for youth, and limited services and programs in remote areas.

- The lack of sound evaluations of this approach.

Sentencing Circles and Reintegrative Shaming

Sentencing circles include community members in decisions about sentencing. The basic ideas behind sentencing circles are healing, peacemaking, and reintegration of the offender into mainstream society (Braithwaite, 1989; Sharpe, 1998). This important alternative to formal processing and sentencing is actually very old, having its roots in the practices of many aboriginal communities (Braithwaite and Daly, 1994). More contemporary adaptations of this way of dealing with criminal behaviour also acknowledge that sanctions from the community are more effective in deterring criminal behaviour than the threat of prison (Currie, 1985).

As such, this perspective complements a "peacemaking" criminology framework (Fuller, 1998; Pepinsky and Quinney, 1991), which asks us to consider: ". . . . as fully as possible, the human potential for goodness, and . . . calls for us to recognize the commonalities and connections between ourselves and others" (Friedrichs, 1991: 105). In effect, this approach to dealing with crime requires us to act upon the idea that individuals as well as communities are responsible for crime (Sharpe, 1998) and that crime can be dealt with only by reconnecting community members with one another.

According to Braithwaite (1989), one of the central reasons for crime is the failure of communities to effectively "shame" their members into complying with norms. It is "social disapproval" that prevents individuals from committing crime, and communities in which individuals have lost their sense of interdependence and connection with one another are less able to exercise such forms of social control. The point is not just to shame individuals, but to shame them *and* "reintegrate" them into the community. Moreover, instead of focusing on the offender, *reintegrative shaming* strategies focus on the offence (Tomaszewski, 1997).

To what extent have these principles been put into action in the Canadian context and with respect to youth? Today, there are programs in place that are based on some variation of the philosophy discussed above. For instance, *sentencing circles* involve community members participating in decisionmaking about offender sentences in conjunction with victims. Other approaches within this philosophy include *healing circles*, which attempt to resolve criminal behaviour before it occurs by bringing community members together, and *community circles*, which attempt to involve community members at all stages of the formal criminal justice process (Sharpe, 1998).

This innovative and decidedly radical (in comparison with the traditional western model of justice) step has received some attention from policymakers in Canada (Bell, 1999). It remains to be seen, however, whether this framework can or will be applied to all offenders (native as well as non-native) and to what extent it might eventually be "contaminated" by elements of the existing justice model.

Changes in the mandates and operations of alternative measures programs and youth justice communities, as well as the implementation of strategies based on reintegrating offenders could potentially go a long way to reduce the harmful effects of formal processing. Ultimately, however, such programs are post-hoc. In other words, they do not allow us to address the *causes* of youth crime. A central argument of this book is that we cannot deal with youth crime appropriately if we deal with it *only* after it has happened, no matter how progressively we do so. Accordingly, it is to an examination of preventative approaches that we turn next.

FROM YOUTH JUSTICE TO SOCIAL JUSTICE

There will always be a role for the criminal justice system in dealing with crime, but it is no secret that preventing youth crime in society demands social-structural change, and according to at least one report, recent trends in the status of Canada's children indicate that we have a long way to go (see Table 5.2). Many pages could be written about social structural change and its relationship to crime, and we do not have space here to cover all possibilities. Accordingly, in what follows, we will examine only a few dimensions of change necessary for revitalizing and rebuilding appropriate, effective and preemptive responses to youth crime.

Table 5.2
Trends Emerging from *The Progress of Canada's Children 1998*

Area	Trend Assessment	Evidence
Economic Security	Negative	• Child and youth poverty rates rising • Higher poverty rates among the rapidly growing Aboriginal and immigrant youth populations • Increasing gap between rich and poor families with children • Stagnating average family incomes
Community Resources	Negative	• Increasing number of children in care of welfare agencies in five provinces • Decrease in child care funding • 100% increase in food bank use since 1989 • Increasing housing affordability problems • Increasing post-secondary education costs • Reduced access to recreation for low-income kids
Family Life	Negative	• Divorce and separation rates tripled in last 20 years • One third of kids in separated families lack assured financial support from non-custodial parent • Increase in runaway kids
Labour Force Participation	Negative	• Declining youth summer employment rates • Declining employment and wage rates for young parents
Health	Mixed	• Majority of children and teens are in good physical condition • Teen smoking rates rising significantly • Increasing rates of teen pregnancy • Significant minority of teens report depression • Low income families spend less than half as much as higher income families on health • Poor kids face serious environmental hazards to their health
Civic Vitality	Positive	• Increase in volunteering rates among youth • Increase in number of "child-friendly" municipal initiatives
Social Engagement	Positive	• Criminal charges against youth declining • Most kids report having someone they can confide in
Learning	Positive	• Math and sciences skills improved compared to other countries • High rate of youth literacy • Record number of young women enrolled in post-secondary education
Physical Safety	Positive	• General crime rate dropping • Use of bike helmets increasing • Use of seat belts increased significantly since 1989 • Rate of injury-related deaths of children and youth falling

Source: Canadian Council on Social Development, 1999, at *http://www.ccsd.ca/pcc98/pcctrend.htm*. Reprinted with permission.

Tailoring Policies to Reflect Realities

First and foremost, we must understand that if crime is committed disproportionately by poor, disenfranchised young men, then we need to make a close examination of the social conditions in which they live if we are to create useful alternatives to the current system. Similarly, we need to examine the social conditions and circumstances in which young girls in conflict with the law find themselves, and take into account that there are clearly "racial" differences in the administration of youth criminal justice policies. Certainly, we must tailor our policies to reflect the needs of individuals and communities. To do this, however, the public must become aware of the realities of crime, and they must be given the opportunity to participate meaningfully in political decisions about crime.

One way to raise awareness is to engage in a strategy to overcome biases and inaccuracies about youth crime that are shaped and regurgitated by the media. To do this, criminologists must become more credible spokespeople about crime (Barak, 1988), and engage in "newsmaking criminology," a strategy that involves "actively challenging silences, identifying omissions, and resurrecting the eliminated through participating in the making of news stories" (Henry and Milovanovic, 1996: 216).

If people are better informed about crime, they will be more likely to demand policies that reflect realities. At the same time, politicians are less likely to prey upon public fears of youth (or adult) crime if they know that an informed electorate is reluctant to listen to misleading claims about the causes of crime and what is to be done about it.

Better Support for Families and Children

We have seen throughout this book that youth crime is very much an outcome of the intersection of social structural and familial factors. We know, for instance, that poverty, unemployment, welfare dependency, lack of opportunities and community resources, and racism all combine to create "criminogenic" conditions. Moreover, mental, physical, and sexual abuse; inadequate supervision; excessively harsh, lax, or inconsistent discipline; family violence; and poor school performance, among other factors, all contribute to youth crime. What is to be done about these issues?

This is a difficult question to answer because it entails examining the complex ways in which such factors work together to create the conditions under which some youths may commit crime. For example, while it is true that inadequate parental attention is correlated with delinquency, this does not mean that, as neoconservatives suggest, the solution to youth crime is to focus only on training "better parents." It certainly does not require that parents should be punished for the actions of their children. Parenting in modern Canadian society, like many other post-industrial societies, involves managing competing demands, high levels of stress, decreasing time for meaningful family interaction, and declining resources for families in general. Hence, if we are to expect to improve the quality of parenting in our society, we will need to address the social conditions in which modern families find themselves (Schaffner, 1997).

Two of the most important things we can do to create a better experience for children now, and in the future, is to implement a nationally funded child care system in Canada, and to encourage employers to help their employees negotiate competing work and family obligations. This two-pronged approach would do the following:

- Many women cannot work at all, or are restricted to low-paying, dead-end jobs because they do not have access to affordable, high-quality child care. A nationally funded child care system would increase the chances that these women, many of whom are single parents, could enter the paid labour force and thereby improve the economic conditions of their families.

- A nationally funded, universal child care program would be more able to deliver high-quality services to a larger proportion of the Canadian population than existing child care models. As the Ontario Ministry of Community and Social Services (1990: 20) points out, "quality child care programs act as a preventative measure against poor school performance and emotional and behavioural problems, particularly for poor children, regardless of whether their parents are working."

Although adequate child care is important, it is only part of the problem facing families. Increasingly, scholars are urging us to look at the larger economic context in which children and families exist. When we do so, it is clear that changing work conditions, the "disappearance" and reconfiguration of work, declines in real wages, and disappearing or diminishing social programs are all contributing to major stresses faced by contemporary families. When we look at why these conditions have come to pass, it is clear that they are outcomes of a society that values its members only insofar as they can compete (on the "global stage," to use a current cliché) as individuals, and without complaining when they "fail to make the grade."

In a nutshell, for many youths the new realities of parent-family interaction are the outcomes of larger global economic processes about which they can do nothing. On the other hand, it is certainly within the power of adults (particularly powerful ones) to take responsibility for managing the impact of rapid economic change on children and families. Doing so, though, will require adults to recognize that the emotional, physical, and psychological care of children should take precedence over enhanced corporate profits.

What about schooling? As one of the primary socialization agents, schools play a very important role in preparing children for life in the adult world. Moreover, as Chapter One argued, the lack of meaningful school experiences affects a child's life chances, and his or her participation in risk-taking behaviours. Clearly, changes in the nature of schooling and education must be made. In particular, we need to make the schools more responsive to the needs of contemporary children, but this is unlikely to happen in today's environment where teachers are demoralized, pupil-teacher ratios are high, funding for "special needs" is being cut, and curricula are revised to reflect the cult of competitive individualism (Alvi et.al., in press).

Rethinking Criminal Justice Spending

Spending public money on social problems such as crime should reflect both our understanding of the problem and the priorities we value in solving them. As you might suspect, though, criminal justice spending in Canada reflects exactly the opposite of what we know about youth crime. Indeed, as Table 5.3 shows, after spending on legal aid, the highest category of growth in criminal justice spending between 1991-92 and 1994-95 was on youth incarceration.

How much money *should* we be spending on youth justice, and how should we spend it? This is a question that can be answered only after an honest evaluation of our priorities. Consider, for example, that although incarceration is an inadequate response to youth crime, we continue to spend money on jails when that money could be diverted to community development and assisting families and children experiencing difficulty managing everyday life.

Compare, for instance, levels of spending on "justice" components such as policing and corrections (Table 5.3), compared with federal spending on transfer payments such as social assistance and family and youth allowances (Table 5.4). Clearly, Canadian governments seem content to spend nearly as much (and, in some categories of spending, more) on post hoc "solutions" to crime as they do on programs that could prevent the occurrence of criminal behaviour in the first place.

Table 5.3
**Levels of Federal Spending on Criminal Justice in Canada,
and Percent Change by Category, 1991-92 to 1994-95**

	1991-1992	1992-1993	1993-1994	1994-1995	Percent Change 91-92 to 94-95
	Thousands of Dollars				
Justice spending[1]	9,101,107	9,554,864	9,623,161	9,942,423	+9
Police[2]	5,426,887	5,716,833	5,790,165	5,783,656	+7
Courts[3]	*	867,006	*	835,404	−4
Prosecutions	*	*	*	257,855	
Legal aid	513,953	602,128	594,939	646,433	+26
Youth corrections	471,211	489,078	507,960	525,545	+12
Adult corrections	1,872,371	1,879,819	1,878,892	1,893,530	+1

* no data

[1] In order to allow annual comparisons, court expenditures for 1989/90, 1991/92 and 1993/94 are estimated, based on the average between the reporting years immediately preceding and following the reference period. These estimates are included in the total. Note that prosecution expenditures are included in the total for 1994-1995 only.

[2] Most municipal police forces report on a calendar year, all other data represent fiscal year reporting.

[3] Figures for courts are collected every second year.

Source: Adapted from Statistics Canada, Catalogue no. 85002 XPE at *http://www.statcan.ca/english/ Pgdb/State/Justice/legal13.htm*

Table 5.4
Selected Government Transfer Payments to Persons in Millions of Dollars, 1992-1996

	Year				
	1992	1993	1994	1995	1996
	Millions of dollars				
Federal					
Family and youth allowances	2,870	37	37	38	39
Unemployment Insurance benefits	18,648	17,592	15,012	12,889	12,324
Scholarships and research grants	726	727	779	687	686
Other transfer payments	1,868	1,659	1,652	1,632	1,735
Provincial					
Social assistance, income maintenance	9,371	10,059	10,224	10,370	9,868
Social assistance, other	1,213	856	1,936	1,934	2,065
Workers Compensation benefits	4,091	3,980	3,815	3,900	4,140
Grants to benevolent associations	6,848	6,975	5,879	6,695	6,713
Other transfer payments	2,487	2,589	3,700	3,777	3,757

Source: Adapted from Statistics Canada, CANSIM, Matrix 9164 at *http://www.statcan.ca/english/Pgdb/ State/Government/govt05.htma*

Reducing Poverty and Inequality

Perhaps the most challenging strategy considered here is the reduction of poverty and all forms of inequality. Reducing poverty is the most important crime-fighting strategy because the level of poverty directly or indirectly shapes criminogenic factors such as access to education, the quality of education, diminished parental authority, and communities that lack cohesion (Hackler, 1994; Reiman, 1998). Among the approaches that could be pursued in this regard are:

- Job creation and training programs that meet the needs of individuals and fit with the new reality that the nature and type of work available in our society has changed dramatically. More specifically, we should be focusing on the possibilities offered by the creation of a "social economy"— one that allows people to contribute to their communities by emphasizing paid and volunteer community service for which governments pay a "shadow" wage. (For a detailed discussion, see Rifkin, 1996.)

- Higher minimum wage levels, and a guaranteed minimum income.

- More housing assistance.

- Nationally funded, universal child care.

- Giving youth a better stake in the adult world by introducing entrepreneurial skills into the high school curriculum, and making the school-to-work transition a more realistic and meaningful experience.

- Creating better linkages between schools, private business, and government agencies.

These and similar initiatives would help to improve social conditions while reducing gender, class, and ethnic inequality in our society. One other related area in which great improvements could be made is community cohesion. Many youth crimes are related to boredom, lack of opportunities, poor role models, and lack of social cohesion in local communities. Recent research by Robert J. Sampson and his colleagues (1997) has shown that neighbourhoods with high levels of *collective efficacy* tend to have lower rates of crime than those with lower levels. Here, collective efficacy is defined as "mutual trust among neighbors combined with a willingness to intervene on behalf of the common good, specifically to supervise children and maintain public order" (Sampson et al., 1998: 1). What this suggests, then, is that in communities in which people are willing to converse with, support, help, and otherwise "look out for" their neighbours and their children, youth crime could be greatly reduced.

SUMMARY

This chapter has focused on solutions to youth crime from the standpoint of "critical criminology." It has emphasized that much of the youth crime problem stems from public and political misunderstanding of the realities of crime, at the very least, and quite likely, from deliberate manipulation of "the facts" for political or other gain.

We examined a few policies and practices that could be modified to create a more equitable and effective youth justice system and identified some key social-structural transformations that must be taken seriously if we are to create a realistic response to crime. The main argument of this book is we have not made a genuine effort to understand youth crime in terms of the lives of youths themselves. Moreover, we have failed to act upon the truth that our society is criminogenic and continues to be so, choosing instead to blame children for adult failures (Schissel, 1997). Current law-and-order approaches to youth crime in Canada serve to pathologize and individualize children. Unless we honestly rethink crime, its context, and the policies and practices that *should* emerge from this knowledge, we are doomed to repeat the mistakes of the past.

DISCUSSION QUESTIONS AND PROBLEM-SOLVING SCENARIOS

1. Provide a critical analysis of the arguments made in Box 5.1. What kinds of errors of fact and assumption do the authors make? Is there anything compelling about their arguments?

2. What do you see as the main obstacles to creating a more humane, equal, and just society? How can these hurdles be overcome?

3. Discuss some strategies that could be used to politicize youth.

4. Brainstorm some ways in which crime myths perpetuated by the media can be debunked. How could Internet resources be harnessed to achieve a clearer understanding of crime among the general public?

SUGGESTED READINGS

Reiman, J. (1998). *The Rich get Richer and the Poor Get Prison: Ideology, Class, and Criminal Justice*. Boston: Allyn & Bacon.

Currie, E. (1998). *Crime and Punishment in America: Why the Solutions to America's Most Stubborn Social Crisis Have Not Worked—and What Will*. New York: Metropolitan Books.

Braithwaite, J. (1989). *Crime, Shame and Reintegration*. New York: Cambridge University Press.

References

Adlaf, E.M., Ivis, F.J., Smart, R.G., & Walsh, G.W. (1995). *The Ontario Student Drug Use Survey: 1977-1995*. Toronto: Addiction Research Foundation.

Adler, F. (1975). *Sisters in Crime*. New York: McGraw-Hill.

Agnew, R. (1985). "A Revised Strain Theory of Delinquency." *Social Forces, 64,* 151-167.

Akers, R.L. (1998). *Social Learning and Social Structure: A General Theory of Crime and Deviance*. Boston: Northeastern University Press.

Alvi, S. (1986). "Realistic Crime Prevention Strategies Through Alternative Measures for Youth." In D. Currie & B.D. MacLean (eds.) *The Administration of Justice* (pp. 112-127). Saskatoon: Social Research Unit, Department of Sociology, University of Saskatchewan.

Alvi, S., DeKeseredy, W., & Ellis, D. (In press). *Social Problems in North American Society*. Toronto: Prentice Hall.

Andrews, D., & Bonta, J. (1998). *The Psychology of Criminal Conduct* (2nd ed.). Cincinnati, OH: Anderson.

Bala, N. (1996). "The Politics of Responding to Youth Crime: Myths and Realities." In *Canada's Children: Promising Approaches to Issues of Child and Youth Violence* at *http://www.cwlc.ca/crccy/eng/indexe.htm*

Bala, N. (1997). *Young Offenders Law*. Concord, Ontario: Irwin Law.

Barak, G. (1988). "News-Making Criminology: Reflections on the Media, Intellectuals, and Crime." *Justice Quarterly, 5,* 565-588.

Barak, G. (1998). *Integrating Criminologies*. Boston: Allyn & Bacon.

Baron, S.W. (1997). "Canadian Male Street Skinheads: Street Gang or Street Terrorists?" *Canadian Review of Sociology and Anthropology, 34,* 125-155.

Baron, S.W., & Kennedy, L.W. (1998). "Deterrence and Homeless Male Street Youths." *Canadian Journal of Criminology, 40,* 27-60.

Baron, S.W., & Hartnagel, T.F. (1996). "'Lock 'em up': Attitudes Toward Punishing Juvenile Offenders. *Canadian Journal of Criminology, 38,* 191-212.

Barrett, M., & McIntosh, M. (1982). *The Anti-Social Family.* London: Verso.

Bartollas, C. (1997). *Juvenile Delinquency* (4th ed.). Boston: Allyn & Bacon.

Becker, G. (1968). "Crime and Punishment: An Economic Approach." *Journal of Political Economy, 76,* 169-217.

Becker, H. (1973). *Outsiders: Studies in the Sociological Study of Deviance.* New York: Free Press.

Beirne, P., & Messerschmidt, J.W. (1991). *Criminology.* Toronto: Harcourt Brace.

Beirne, P., & Messerschmidt, J.W. (1995). *Criminology* (2nd ed.). Toronto: Harcourt Brace.

Bell, S. (1999). *Young Offenders and Juvenile Justice: A Century After the Fact.* Toronto: ITP Nelson.

Berg, B. (1995). *Qualitative Research Methods for the Social Sciences* (2nd ed.). Boston: Allyn & Bacon.

Bograd, M. (1988). "Feminist Perspectives on Wife Abuse: An Introduction." In K.A. Yllo & M. Bograd (eds.) *Feminist Perspectives on Wife Abuse* (pp. 11-27). Beverly Hills: Sage.

Bohm, R. (1986). "Crime, Criminals and Crime Control Policy Myths." *Justice Quarterly, 3,* 193-214.

Bohm, R. (1997). *A Primer on Crime and Delinquency.* Belmont, CA: Wadsworth.

Bonger, W. (1916). *Criminality and Economic Conditions.* Boston: Little, Brown.

Bordua, D. (1967). "Recent Trends: Deviant Behavior and Social Control." *Annals of the Academy of Political and Social Science, 369,* 149-163.

Boritch, H. (1997). *Fallen Women: Female Crime and Criminal Justice in Canada.* Cambridge, UK: Cambridge University Press.

Box, S. (1971). *Deviance, Reality and Society.* London: Holt, Rinehart and Winston.

Braithwaite, J. (1989). *Crime, Shame and Reintegration.* New York: Cambridge University Press.

Braithwaite, J., & Daly, K. (1994). "Masculinities, Violence and Communitarian Control." In T. Newburn & E. Stanko (eds.) *Just Boys Doing Business? Men, Masculinities and Crime* (pp. 189-213). London: Routledge.

Britt, C.L. (1994). "Crime and Unemployment Among Youth in the United States, 1957-1990: A Time Series Analysis." *The American Journal of Economics and Sociology, 53,* 99-110.

Brockman, J., & Rose, V.G. (1996). *An Introduction to Canadian Criminal Procedure and Evidence for the Social Sciences.* Toronto: Nelson Canada.

Bynum, J., & Thompson, W. (1996). *Juvenile Delinquency: A Sociological Approach* (3rd ed.). Needham Heights, MA: Allyn & Bacon.

Canada, H.R.D.C. and S.C. (1996). *Growing Up in Canada: National Longitudinal Survey of Youth.* Ottawa: Minister of Industry.

Canadian Centre for Justice Statistics (1994). *A Review of the Alternative Measures Survey, 1991-92.* Ottawa: Statistics Canada.

Canadian Centre for Justice Statistics (1998). *A Profile of Youth Justice in Canada.* Ottawa: Statistics Canada.

Canadian Council on Social Development (1996). *The Progress of Canada's Children.* Ottawa: Canadian Council on Social Development.

Canadian Council on Social Development (1997). *The Progress of Canada's Children.* Ottawa: Canadian Council on Social Development.

Canadian Council on Social Development (1999). *Youth at Work in Canada: A Research Report.* Ottawa: Canadian Council on Social Development.

Caputo, T., & Goldenberg, S. (1986). "Young People and the Law: A Consideration of Luddite and Utopian Responses." In B.D. MacLean & D. Currie (eds.) *The Administration of Justice* (pp. 91-111). Saskatoon: Social Research Unit, University of Saskatchewan.

Carrigan, D.O. (1998). *Juvenile Delinquency in Canada: A History.* Concord: Irwin.

Carrington, P. (1995). "Has Violent Youth Crime Increased? Comment on Corrado and Markwart." *Canadian Journal of Criminology, 37,* 61-93.

Carrington, P. (1998). *Factors Affecting Police Diversion of Young Offenders: A Statistical Analysis.* Report to the Solicitor General Canada, February.

Carrington, P. (1999). "Trends in Youth Crime in Canada, 1977-1996." *Canadian Journal of Criminology, 41,* 1-32.

Carrington, P., & Moyer, S. (1994). "Trends in Youth Crime and Police Response, Pre- and Post-YOA." *Canadian Journal of Criminology, 36,* 1-28.

Casper, L.M., McLanahan, S.S., & Garfinkel, I. (1994). "The Gender Poverty Gap: What We Can Learn From Other Countries." *American Sociological Review, 59,* 594-605.

Caston, R.J. (1998). *Life in a Business-Oriented Society: A Sociological Perspective.* Boston: Allyn & Bacon.

Cernkovich, S., & Giordano, P. (1979). "A Comparative Analysis of Male and Female Delinquency." *Sociological Quarterly, 20,* 131-145.

Chesney-Lind, M. (1986). "Women and Crime: The Female Offender." *Signs: Journal of Women in Culture and Society, 12,* 78-96.

Chesney-Lind, M. (1995). "Girls, Delinquency, and Juvenile Justice: Toward a Feminist Theory of Young Women's Crime." In B.R. Price & N.J. Sokoloff (eds.) *The Criminal Justice System and Women: Offenders, Victims and Workers* (2nd ed., pp. 71-88). New York: McGraw-Hill.

Chesney-Lind, M., & Sheldon, M. (1992). *Girls, Delinquency and Juvenile Justice.* Belmont, CA: Brooks/Cole.

Church Council on Justice and Corrections. (1996). *Satisfying Justice: A Compendium of Initiatives, Programs and Legislative Measures.* Ottawa: Church Council on Justice and Corrections.

Cloward, R., & Ohlin, L. (1960). *Delinquency and Opportunity: A Theory of Delinquent Gangs.* New York: Free Press.

Cohen, A. (1955). *Delinquent Boys.* New York: Free Press.

Cohen, L.E. (1981). "Modeling Crime Trends: A Criminal Opportunity Perspective." *Journal of Research in Crime and Delinquency, 18,* 138-164.

Cohen, L., & Felson, M. (1979). "Social Change and Crime Rate Trends: A Routine Activities Approach." *American Sociological Review, 44,* 588-608.

Cohen, L.E., Kluegel, J.R., & Land, K.C. (1981). "Social Inequality and Predatory Criminal Victimization: An Exposition and Test of a Formal Theory." *American Sociological Review, 46,* 505-524.

Cohen, S. (1980). *Folk Devils and Moral Panics* (2nd ed.). Oxford: Basil Blackwell.

Collins, R. (1994). *Four Sociological Traditions.* New York: Oxford University Press.

Colvin, M. (1996). "Crime and Social Reproduction." In J.E. Conklin (ed.) *New Perspectives in Criminology* (pp. 60-70). Boston: Allyn & Bacon.

Colvin, M., & Pauly, J. (1983). "A Critique of Criminology: Toward an Integrated Structural-Marxist Theory of Delinquency Production." *American Journal of Sociology, 89,* 513-551.

Conly, D. (1978). *Patterns of Delinquency and Police Action in the Major Metropolitan Areas of Canada During the Month of December, 1976.* Ottawa, Solicitor General Canada.

Corrado, R.R., & Bala, N. (1992). "The Evolution and Implementation of a New Era of Juvenile Justice in Canada." In R.R. Corrado, N. Bala, R. Linden, & M. Leblanc (eds.) *Juvenile Justice in Canada: A Theoretical and Analytical Assessment.* Toronto: Butterworths.

Corrado, R.R., & Markwart, A.E. (1992). "The Evaluation and Implementation of a New Era of Juvenile Justice in Canada." In R.R. Corrado, N. Bala, R. Linden, & M. LeBlance (eds.) *Juvenile Justice in Canada* (pp. 35-50). Toronto: Butterworths.

Crutchfield, R.D., & Pitchford, S.R. (1997). "Work and Crime: The Effects of Labor Stratification." *Social Forces, 76,* 93-118.

Curran, D.J., & Renzetti, C.M. (1994). *Theories of Crime.* Boston: Allyn & Bacon.

Currie, E. (1985). *Confronting Crime: An American Challenge.* New York: Pantheon.

Currie, E. (1986). "The Transformation of Juvenile Justice in Canada." In B.D. MacLean (ed.) *The Political Economy of Crime* (pp. 56-72). Toronto: Prentice Hall.

Currie, E. (1993). *Reckoning: Drugs, the Cities and the American Future.* New York: Hill and Wang.

Currie, E. (1998). *Crime and Punishment in America: Why the Solutions to America's Most Stubborn Social Crisis Have Not Worked—and What Will.* New York: Metropolitan Books.

Daly, K., & Chesney-Lind, M. (1988). "Feminism and Criminology." *Justice Quarterly, 5,* 497-538.

Davis, N.J. (1975). *Sociological Constructions of Deviance.* Dubuque, IA: Brown.

DeKeseredy, W.S. (2000). *Women, Crime and the Canadian Criminal Justice System.* Cincinnati, OH: Anderson.

DeKeseredy, W.S., & MacLeod, L. (1997). *Woman Abuse: A Sociological Story.* Toronto: Harcourt Brace.

DeKeseredy, W.S., Saunders, D.G., Schwartz, M.D., & Alvi, S. (1997). "The Contexts, Meanings and Motives of Women's Use of Violence in Canadian University/College Dating Relationships: Results from a National Survey." *Sociological Spectrum, 17,* 199-222.

DeKeseredy, W.S., & Schwartz, M.D. (1996). *Contemporary Criminology.* Belmont, CA: Wadsworth.

DeKeseredy, W.S., & Schwartz, M.D. (1998). *Woman Abuse on Campus: Results from the Canadian National Survey.* Thousand Oaks, CA: Sage.

Dell, C. (1998). *Summary and Analysis of the Youth Justice Strategy.* Unpublished paper.

Doob, A.N., & Chan, J. (1982). "Factors Affecting Police Decisions to Take Juveniles to Court." *Canadian Journal of Criminology, 24,* 25-37.

Doob, A.N., Marinos, V., & Varma, K.N. (1998). *Youth Crime and the Youth Justice System in Canada.* Toronto: University of Toronto Centre of Criminology.

Duffy, A. (1996). "Bad Girls in Hard Times: Canadian Female Juvenile Offenders." In G. O'Birek (ed.) *Not a Kid Anymore.* Scarborough, ON: ITP Nelson.

Einstadter, W., & Henry, S. (1995). *Criminological Theory: An Analysis of its Underlying Assumptions.* Fort Worth, TX: Harcourt Brace.

Elias, R. (1986). *The Politics of Victimization: Victims, Victimology and Human Rights.* New York: Oxford University Press.

Elliot, D., & Ageton, S. (1980). "Reconciling Race and Class Differences in Self-Reported and Official Estimates of Delinquency." *American Sociological Review, 45,* 95-110.

Elliot, D., Ageton, S., & Canter, R. (1979). "An Integrated Theoretical Perspective on Delinquent Behavior." *Journal of Research in Crime and Delinquency, 16,* 3-27.

Esbensen, F., & Winfree, L.T. (1998). "Race and Gender Differences Between Gang and Non-gang Youths: Results From a Multi-site Survey." *Justice Quarterly, 15,* 505-525.

Eshleman, J.R. (1997). *The Family* (8th ed.). Boston: Allyn & Bacon.

Faith, K. (1993). *Unruly Women: The Politics of Confinement and Resistance.* Vancouver: Press Gang.

Farnworth, M., Thornberry, T. P., Krohn, M. D., & Lizotte, A. J. (1994). "Measurement in the Study of Class and Delinquency: Integrating Theory with Research." *Journal of Research in Crime and Delinquency, 31,* 32-61.

Finnie, R. (1993). "Women, Men and the Economic Consequences of Divorce: Evidence from Canadian Longitudinal Data." *Canadian Review of Sociology and Anthropology, 30,* 205-241.

Fisher, L., & Janetti, H. (1996). "Aboriginal Youth in the Criminal Justice System." In J. Winterdyk (ed.) *Issues and Perspectives on Young Offenders in Canada* (pp. 237-255). Toronto: Harcourt Brace.

Frank, N., & Lynch, M.J. (1992). *Corporate Crime, Corporate Violence: A Primer.* New York: Harrow and Heston.

Fraser, N. (1989). *Unruly Practices: Power, Discourse, and Gender in Contemporary Social Theory.* Minnesota: University of Minnesota Press.

Friedrichs, D.O. (1991). "Peacemaking Criminology in World Filled with Conflict." In B. D. MacLean & D. Milovanovic (eds.) *New Directions in Critical Criminology* (pp. 101-106). Vancouver, BC: Collective Press.

Fuller, J.R. (1998). *Criminal Justice: A Peacemaking Perspective.* Boston: Allyn & Bacon.

Gabor, T. (1994). "The Suppression of Crime Statistics on Race and Ethnicity: The Price of Political Correctness." *Canadian Journal of Criminology, 36,* 153-163.

Gagnon, D. (1984). *History of the Law for Juvenile Delinquents.* Ministry of the Solicitor General of Canada, Government Working Paper No. 1984-56.

Gartner, R., & Doob, A.N. (1994). *Trends in Criminal Victimization: 1988-1993.* Ottawa: Canadian Centre for Justice Statistics.

Gibbs, J.J., Giever, D., & Martin, J.S. (1998). "Parental Management and Self-control: An Empirical Test of Gottfredson and Hirschi's General Theory. *Journal of Research in Crime and Delinquency, 35,* 40-70.

Gilmore, G.A. (1994). *Hate-Motivated Violence.* Research Section Department of Justice Canada, Unpublished working document, at *ftp://ftp2.ca.nizkor.org/pub/nizkor/ orgs/canadian/canada/justice/hate-motivated-violence/hmv-000-00*

Glueck, S., & Glueck, E.T. (1950). *Unraveling Juvenile Delinquency.* New York: Commonwealth Fund.

Gomme, I., Morton, M., & West, G. (1984). "Rates, Types and Patterns of Male and Female Delinquency in an Ontario County." *Canadian Journal of Criminology, 26,* 313-324.

Goode, E. (1994). *Deviant Behavior* (4th ed.). Englewood Cliffs, NJ: Prentice Hall.

Goode, E., & Ben-Yehuda, N. (1994). "Moral Panics: Culture, Politics and Social Construction." *Annual Review of Sociology, 20,* 149-171.

Goodey, J.O. (1997). "Boys Don't Cry: Masculinities, Fear of Crime and Fearlessness." *British Journal of Criminology, 37,* 401-419.

Gordon, D.M. (1973). "Capitalism, Class and Crime in America." *Crime & Delinquency, 19,* 163-186.

Gottfredson, M.R., & Hirschi, T. (1990). *A General Theory of Crime.* Stanford, CA: Stanford University Press.

Greenberg, D. (ed.). (1981). *Crime and Capitalism: Readings in Marxist Criminology.* Palo Alto, CA: Mayfield.

Hackler, J. (1994). *Crime and Canadian Public Policy.* Scarborough, ON: Prentice Hall.

Hagan, F. (1997). *Research Methods in Criminal Justice and Criminology* (4th ed.). Boston: Allyn & Bacon.

Hagan, J. (1989). *Structural Criminology.* New Brunswick, NJ: Rutgers University Press.

Hagan, J., & Kay, F. (1990). "Gender and Delinquency in White Collar Families: A Power-Control Perspective." *Crime & Delinquency, 36*(3), 391-407.

Hagan, J., & McCarthy, B. (1997). *Mean Streets: Youth Crime and Homelessness.* Cambridge, UK: Cambridge University Press.

Hagan, J., Simpson, J., & Gillis, A.R. (1987). "Class in the Household: A Power Control Theory of Gender and Delinquency." *American Journal of Sociology, 92,* 788-816.

Hall, S., Critcher, C., Jefferson, T., Clarke, J., & Roberts, B. (1978). *Policing the Crisis: Mugging, the State and Law and Order.* London: Macmillan.

Hawkins, D., Von Cleve, E., & Catalano, R.F. (1991). "Reducing Early Childhood Aggression: Results of a Primary Prevention Program." *Journal of the Academy of Child and Adolescent Psychiatry, 30,* 208-217.

Heidensohn, F. (1985). *Women and Crime.* London: Macmillan.

Henry, F., Tator, C., Mattis, W., & Rees, T. (1995). *The Colour of Democracy: Racism in Canadian Society.* Toronto: Harcourt Brace.

Henry, S., & Milovanovic, D. (1996). *Constitutive Criminology: Beyond Postmodernism.* London: Sage.

Herrnstein, R.J., & Murray, C. (1994). *The Bell Curve: Intelligence and Class Structure in American Life.* New York: Free Press.

Hirschi, T. (1969). *Causes of Delinquency.* Berkeley, CA: University of California Press.

Hirschi, T., & Gottfredson, M. (1983). "Age and the Explanation of Crime." *American Journal of Sociology, 89,* 552-584.

Hylton, J.H. (1994). "Get Tough or Get Smart? Options for Canada's Youth Justice System in the Twenty-First Century." *Canadian Journal of Criminology, 36,* 229-246.

Jaggar, A. (1983). *Feminist Politics and Human Nature.* Totowa, NJ: Roman and Littlefield.

Jensen, G., & Thompson, K. (1990). "What's Class Got to Do With It? A Further Examination of Power-Control Theory." *American Journal of Sociology, 95,* 1009-1023.

Jenson, J.M., & Howard, M.O. (1998). "Youth Crime, Public Policy, and Practice in the Juvenile Justice System—Recent Trends and Needed Reforms." *Social Work, 43,* 324-334.

Juristat (1994). *Canadian Crime Statistics.* Canadian Centre for Justice Statistics; Ottawa; Cat. No. 85-205

Juristat (1997). *Canadian Crime Statistics.* Canadian Centre for Justice Statistics, Ottawa; Cat. No. 85-002-XPE, Vol 18, No. 11.

Juristat (1999). *Youth Court Statistics 1997-98 Highlights.* Vol2, No. 19 85-002 XIE.

Justice Canada (1998). "General Overview." *http://canada.justice.gc.ca/publications/prevention/english/02.html#return1*

Kappeler, V.E., Blumberg, M., & Potter, G.W. (1996). *The Mythology of Crime and Criminal Justice* (2nd ed.). Prospect Heights, IL: Waveland Press.

Kasarda, J. (1992). "The Severely Distressed in Economically Transforming Cities." In G. Peterson & A. Harrell (eds.) *Drugs, Crime, and Social Isolation: Barriers to Urban Opportunity* (pp. 45-98). Washington, DC: Urban Institute Press.

Katz, J. (1988). *Seductions of Crime: Moral and Sensual Attractions in Doing Evil.* New York: Basic Books.

Kelly, D. (1996). "Rehabilitating Social Systems and Institutions." In D. Kelly (ed.) *Deviant Behaviour* (5th ed., pp. 646-658). New York: St. Martins Press.

Kelly, L. (1988). *Surviving Sexual Violence*. Minneapolis: University of Minnesota Press.

Kenewell, J., Bala, N., & Colfer, P. (1991). "Young Offenders." In R. Barnhorst & L. C. Johnson (eds.) *The State of the Child in Ontario*. Toronto: Oxford University Press.

Kornhauser, R. (1978). *Social Sources of Delinquency: An Appraisal of Analytical Models*. Chicago: University of Chicago Press.

Kowalski, M. (1999). *Alternative Measures for Youth in Canada*. Statistics Canada, Catalogue No. 85-002-XIE, Vol. 19, no. 8.

Lab, S. (1997). *Crime Prevention: Approaches, Practices and Evaluations* (3rd ed.). Cincinnati, OH: Anderson.

LaPrairie, C. (1983). "Native Juveniles in Court: Some Preliminary Observations." In T. Fleming (ed.) *Deviant Designations* (pp. 337-50). Toronto: Butterworths.

LaPrairie, C. (1996). *Examining Aboriginal Corrections in Canada*. Ministry of the Solicitor General Canada, Catalog Number: JS5-1/14-1996E.

LaPrairie, C., & Griffiths, C. T. (1984). "Native Juvenile Delinquency: A Review of Recent Findings." *Canadian Legal Aid Bulletin, 5*, 39-46.

Larzelere, R.E., & Patterson, G.R. (1990). "Parental Management: Mediator of the Effect of Socioeconomic Status on Early Delinquency." *Criminology, 28*, 301-324.

Lavrakas, P.J. (1997). "Politicians, Journalists, and the Rhetoric of the 'Crime Prevention' Public Policy Debate." In S.P. Lab (ed.) *Crime Prevention at a Crossroads*. Cincinnati, OH: Anderson.

Lea, J., & Young, J. (1984). *What Is to Be Done About Law and Order. New York: Penguin*. New York: Penguin.

LeBlanc, M. (1983). "Delinquency as an Epiphenomenon of Adolescence." In R. Corrado, M. LeBlanc, & J. Trepanier (eds.) *Current Issues in Juvenile Justice*. Toronto: Butterworths.

Leiber, M.J, Nalla, M.K, & Farnworth, M. (1998). "Explaining Juveniles' Attitudes Toward the Police." *Justice Quarterly, 15*, 151-173.

LeMarquand, D., Pihl, R.O., & Benkelfat, C. (1994). "Serotonin and Alcohol Intake, Abuse and Dependence." *Clinical Evidence in Biological Psychiatry, 36*, 326-337.

Lemert, E. (1951). *Social Pathology: A Systematic Approach to the Theory of Sociopathic Behavior*. New York: McGraw-Hill.

Leschied, A.W., & Gendreau, P. (1994). "Doing Justice in Canada: YOA Policies that can Promote Community Safety." *Canadian Journal of Criminology, 36*, 291-303.

Levine, D.N. (1995). *Visions of the Sociological Tradition*. Chicago: University of Chicago Press.

Lowman, J. (1986). "Street Prostitution in Vancouver: Notes on the Genesis of a Social Problem." *Canadian Journal of Criminology, 28*, 1-16.

Lyman, M.D., & Potter, G.W. (eds.). (1996). *Drugs in Society: Causes, Concepts and Control* (2nd ed.). Cincinnati, OH: Anderson.

MacKenzie, D.L., & Shaw, J.W. (1993). "The Impact of Shock Incarceration on Technical Violations and New Criminal Activities." *Justice Quarterly, 10*, 463-487.

MacLean, B.D. (ed.). (1986). *The Political Economy of Crime: Readings for a Critical Criminology*. Toronto: Prentice Hall Canada Ltd.

MacLean, B.D. (1994). "Gender Inequality in Dispositions Under the Young Offenders Act." *Humanity & Society, 18*, 64-81.

MacLean, B.D. (1996). *Crime and Society: Readings in Critical Criminology*. Toronto: Copp Clark.

Mathews, F. (1994). *Youth Gangs on Youth Gangs*. Ottawa: Solicitor General Canada.

Matsueda, R. (1988). "The Current State of Differential Association Theory." *Crime and Delinquency, 34*, 277-306.

Matthews, R. (1979). "Decarceration and the Fiscal Crisis." In B. Fine (ed.) *Capitalism and the Rule of Law* (pp. 100-117). London: Hutchinson.

Matza, D. (1964). *Delinquency and Drift*. New York: John Wiley and Sons.

McGuire, M. (1997). "C.19: An Act to Amend the Young Offenders Act and the Criminal Code—Getting Tougher?" (Canada). *Canadian Journal of Criminology, 39*, 185-214.

Mears, D.P., Ploeger, M., & Warr, M. (1998). "Explaining the Gender Gap in Delinquency: Peer Influence and Moral Evaluations of Behavior." *Journal of Research in Crime and Delinquency, 35*, 251-266.

Merton, R. (1938). "Social Structure and Anomie." *American Sociological Review, 3*, 672-682.

Messerschmidt, J.W. (1986). *Capitalism, Patriarchy, and Crime: Toward a Socialist Feminist Criminology*. Totowa, NJ: Roman and Littlefield.

Messerschmidt, J.W. (1993). *Masculinities and Crime: Critique and Reconceptualization of Theory*. Lanham, MD: Roman and Littlefield.

Michalowski, R. J. (1991). "'Niggers, Welfare Scum and Homeless Assholes': The Problems of Idealism, Consciousness and Context in Left Realism." In B.D. MacLean & D. Milovanovic (eds.) *New Directions in Critical Criminology* (pp. 31-38). Vancouver: Collective Press.

Miller, J. (1996). "An Examination of Disposition Decision-making for Delinquent Girls." In M. Schwartz & D. Milovanovic (eds.) *Race, Gender and Class in Criminology: The Intersection* (pp. 219-245). New York: Garland.

Miller, W. (1958). "Lower Class Culture as a Generating Milieu of Gang Delinquency." *Journal of Social Issues, 14*, 5-19.

Morash, M., & Chesney-Lind, M. (1991). "A Re-formulation and Partial Test of the Power-Control Theory of Delinquency." *Justice Quarterly, 8*, 347-377.

Morin, B. (1990). "Native Youth and the Young Offenders Act." *Legal Perspectives, 14*, 13-15.

Morse, S.J. (1998). "Immaturity and Irresponsibility." *Journal of Criminal Law & Criminology, 88*, 15-67.

Mosher, C. (1996). "Minorities and Misdemeanours: The Treatment of Black Public Order Offenders in Ontario's Criminal Justice System—1892-1930." *Canadian Journal of Criminology, 38*, 413-438.

Muncie, J. (1984). *The Trouble with Kids Today*. Dover, NH: Hutchinson.

National Crime Prevention Council (NCPC) (1996). *Incarceration in Canada*. Ottawa: National Crime Prevention Council.

National Crime Prevention Council (NCPC) (1998). *Bullying and Victimization: The Problems and Solutions for School-aged children*. National Crime Prevention Council at: *http://www.crime-prevention.org/ncpc/*

Nettler, G. (1974). *Explaining Crime*. New York: McGraw-Hill.

Neugebauer-Visano, R. (1996). "Kids, Cops and Colour: The Social Organization of Police-Minority Youth Relations." In G. O'Birek (ed.) *Not a Kid Anymore: Canadian Youth Crime and Subcultures* (pp. 283-308). Toronto: Nelson.

Ontario (1995). *Report of the Commission on Systemic Racism in the Ontario Criminal Justice System*. Toronto: Queen's Printer.

Ontario Ministry of Community and Social Services (1990). *Ontario Child Health Study: Children at Risk*. Toronto: Queen's Printer.

Paiment, R. (1996). *An Exploratory Study of Youth Justice Committees*. Technical Report, Department of Justice Canada, Research, Statistics and Evaluation Directorate, Policy Sector, TR1996-8e.

Parker, H. (1996). "Young Adult Offenders, Alcohol and Criminological Cul-de-sacs." *British Journal of Criminology, 36*, 282-298.

Pepinsky, H., & Quinney, R. (1991). *Criminology as Peacemaking*. Bloomington, IN: Indiana University Press.

Petersen, A.C., & Mortimer, J.T. (eds.). (1994). *Youth Unemployment and Society*. Cambridge: Cambridge University Press.

Peterson-Badali, M., Abramovitch, R., & Duda, J. (1997). "Young Children's Legal Knowledge and Reasoning Ability." *Canadian Journal of Criminology*, 145-170.

Pollock, O. (1950). *The Criminality of Women*. New York: Barnes.

Raine, A. (1997). *The Psychopathology of Crime: Criminal Behavior as a Clinical Disorder*. London: Academic Press.

Reckless, W. (1961). "A New Theory of Delinquency and Crime." *Federal Probation, 25*, 42-46.

Rehnby, N., & McBride, S. (1997). *Help Wanted—Economic Security for Youth*. Vancouver: Canadian Centre for Policy Alternatives.

Reiman, J. (1998). *The Rich Get Richer and the Poor Get Prison: Ideology, Class, and Criminal Justice*. Boston: Allyn & Bacon.

Reitsma-Street, M. (1993). "Canadian Youth Court Charges and Dispositions for Females Before and After Implementation of the Young Offenders Act." *Canadian Journal of Criminology, 35*, 437-458.

Renzetti, C.M. (1993). "On the Margins of the Malestream (Or, They Still Don't Get It, Do They?): Feminist Analyses in Criminal Justice Education." *Journal of Criminal Justice Education, 4*, 219-234.

Rex, J. (1983). *Race Relations in Sociological Theory*. London: Routledge and Keegan Paul.

Rifkin, J. (1996). *The End of Work: The Decline of the Global Labor Force and the Dawn of the Post-market Era*. New York: Tarcher/Putnam.

Rigakos, G. (1999). "Risk Society and Actuarial Criminology: Prospects for a Critical Discourse." *Canadian Journal of Criminology, 41*, 137-147.

Roberts, J. (1995). *Disproportionate Harm: Hate Crime in Canada*. Department of Justice Canada, unpublished working document, at *ftp://ftp2.ca.nizkor.org/pub/nizkor/orgs/canadian/canada/justice/disproportionate-harm/*

Robins, L.N. (1975). "Alcoholism and Labelling Theory." In W.R. Gove (ed.) *The Labelling of Deviance* (pp. 21-33). Beverly Hills, CA: Sage.

Rosenblum, K. (1980). "Female Deviance and the Female Sex Role: A Preliminary Investigation." In S. Datesman & F. Scarpitti (eds.) *Women, Crime and Justice*. New York: Oxford University Press.

Rothenberg, J., & Heinz, A. (1998). "Meddling with Monkey Metaphors—Capitalism and the Threat of Impulsive Desires." *Social Justice, 25*(2), 44-63.

Sampson, R.J., & Groves, W.B. (1989). "Community Structure and Crime: Testing Social Disorganization Theory." *American Journal of Sociology, 94*, 774-802.

Sampson, R.J., & Lauritsen, J. (1994). "Violent Victimization and Offending: Individual, Situational and Community-level Risk Factors." In A. Reiss & J. Roth (eds.) *Understanding and Preventing Violence* (Vol. 3, pp. 1-114). Washington, DC: National Academy Press.

Sampson, R., Raudenbush, S., & Earls, F. (1997). "Neighborhoods and Violent Crime: A Multilevel Study of Collective Efficacy." *Science, 277*, 918-924.

Sampson, R.J., Raudenbush, S.W., & Earls, F. (1998). *Neighbourhood Collective Efficacy: Does it Help Reduce Violence?* Washington, DC: U.S. Department of Justice.

Schaffner, L. (1997). "Families on Probation: Court Ordered Parenting Skills Classes for Parents of Juvenile Offenders." *Crime & Delinquency, 43*, 412-437.

Schissel, B. (1993). *Social Dimensions of Canadian Youth Justice*. Toronto: Oxford University Press.

Schissel, B. (1997). *Blaming Children: Youth Crime, Moral Panics and the Politics of Hate*. Halifax: Fernwood.

Schneider, A. (1990). *Deterrence and Juvenile Crime*. New York: Springer-Verlag.

Schur, E.M. (1973). *Radical Nonintervention*. Englewood Cliffs, NJ: Prentice Hall.

Schwartz, M.D. (1991). "The Future of Critical Criminology." In B.D. MacLean & D. Milovanovic (eds.) *New Directions in Critical Criminology* (pp. 119-124). Vancouver: Collective Press.

Schwartz, M.D., & Friedrichs, D.O. (1994). "Postmodern Thought and Criminological Discontent: New Metaphors for Understanding Violence." *Criminology, 32*, 221-246.

Schwartz, M.D., & Milovanovic, D. (1996). *Race, Gender, and Class in Criminology: The Intersection*. New York: Garland.

Schwendinger, H., & Schwendinger, J. (1975). "Defenders of Order or Guardians of Human Rights?" In I. Taylor, P. Walton, & J. Young (eds.) *Critical Criminology* (pp. 113-146). London: Routledge and Kegan Paul.

Schwendinger, J., & Schwendinger, H. (1983). *Rape and Inequality*. Newbury Park, CA: Sage.

Sealock, M.D, & Simpson, S.S. (1998). "Unraveling Bias in Arrest Decisions: The Role of Juvenile Offender Type-scripts." *Justice Quarterly, 15*, 427-457.

Senna, J., & Siegel, L. (1998). *Essentials of Criminal Justice* (2nd ed.). Belmont, CA: Wadsworth.

Sharpe, S. (1998). *Restorative Justice: A Vision for Healing and Change*. Edmonton: Edmonton Victim-Offender Mediation Society.

Shaw, C., & McKay, H.D. (1931). *Social Factors in Juvenile Delinquency*. Chicago: University of Chicago Press.

Shaw, C., & McKay, H.D. (1942). *Juvenile Delinquency and Urban Areas*. Chicago: University of Chicago Press.

Short, J.F. (1997). *Poverty, Ethnicity and Violent Crime*. Boulder, CO: Westview Press.

Simon, D.R. (1996). *Elite Deviance*. Boston: Allyn & Bacon.

Simon, J. (1995). "They Died with Their Boots On: The Boot Camp and the Limits of Modern Penality." *Social Justice, 22*, 25-49.

Simon, R. (1981). "American Women and Crime." In L. Bowker (ed.) *Women and Crime in America* (pp. 18-39). New York: Macmillan.

Simourd, D.J., Hoge, R.D., Andrews, D.A., & Leschied, A.W. (1994). "An Empirically-Based Typology of Male Young Offenders." *Canadian Journal of Criminology*, 447-461.

Simpson, S.S., & Elis, L. (1994). "Is Gender Subordinate to Class? An Empirical Assessment of Colvin and Pauly's Structural Marxist Theory of Delinquency." *Journal of Criminal Law & Criminology, 85*, 453-480.

Smith, D.A., & Paternoster, R. (1987). "The Gender Gap in Theories of Deviance: Issues and Evidence." *Journal of Research in Crime and Delinquency, 24*, 140-172.

Smock, P.J. (1993). "The Economic Costs of Marital Disruption for Young Women Over the Past Two Decades." *Demography, 30*, 353-371.

Smock, P.J. (1994). "Gender and the Short-Run Economic Consequences of Marital Disruption." *Social Forces, 73*, 243-262.

Solicitor General Canada (1997). *Police Perceptions of Current Responses to Youth Crime* at *http://www.sgc.gc.ca/epub/pol/e199731/e199731.htm* (June 10).

Solicitor General of Canada (1994). *Youth Violence and Youth Gangs: Responding to Community Concerns*. Ottawa: Ministry of Solicitor General of Canada.

Sprott, J. (1996). "Understanding Public Views of Youth Crime and the Youth Justice System." *Canadian Journal of Criminology, 38*, 271-290.

Stanko, B. (1998). "Making the Invisible Visible in Criminology: a Personal Journey." In S. Holdaway & P. Rock (eds.) *Thinking About Criminology* (pp. 35-54). Toronto: University of Toronto Press.

Sullivan, R., & Wilson, M.F. (1995). "New Directions for Research in Prevention and Treatment of Delinquency: A Review and Proposal." *Adolescence, 30*, 1-18.

Sutherland, E.H. (1947). *Principles of Criminology* (4th ed.). Philadelphia: J.B. Lipincott.

Sykes, G.M., & Matza, D. (1957). "Techniques of Neutralization: A Theory of Deliquency." *American Sociological Review, 22*, 664-670.

Tanner, J. (1996). *Teenage Troubles: Youth and Deviance in Canada*. Scarborough: Nelson.

Thornberry, G. (1987). "Toward an Interactional Theory of Delinquency." *Criminology, 25*, 863-891.

Thrasher, F. (1927). *The Gang: A Study of 1,313 Gangs in Chicago*. Chicago: University of Chicago Press.

Tittle, C., & Meier, R. (1990). "Specifying the SES/Delinquency Relationship." *Criminology, 28*, 271-99.

Tomaszewski, A. (1997). "'AlterNative' Approaches to Criminal Justice: John Braithwaite's Theory of Reintegrative Shaming Revisited." *Critical Criminology, 8*, 105-118.

Tong, R. (1989). *Feminist Thought*. Boulder, CO: Westview.

Trojanowicz, R. (1978). *Juvenile Delinquency: Concepts and Control*. Englewood Cliffs, NJ: Prentice Hall.

Tunnell, K. (1992a). "Film at Eleven: Recent Developments in the Commodification of Crime." *Sociological Spectrum, 12*, 293-313.

Tunnell, K. (1992b). *Choosing Crime: The Criminal Calculus of Property Offenders*. Chicago: Nelson-Hall.

Vanier Institute of the Family. (1994). *Profiling Canada's Families*. Ottawa: Vanier Institute of the Family.

Vold, G.B., Bernard, T.J. & Snipes, J.B. (1998). *Theoretical Criminology* (4th ed.). New York: Oxford University Press.

Walker, S. (1998). *Sense and Nonsense About Crime and Drugs: A Policy Guide* (4th ed.). Belmont, CA: West/Wadsworth.

Wardell, B. (1986). "The Young Offenders Act: A Report Card, 1984-1986." In D. Currie & B. Maclean (eds.) *The Administration of Justice* (pp. 128-158). Saskatoon: Social Research Unit, University of Saskatchewan.

Weis, J., & Hawkins, D. (1981). *Preventing Delinquency*. Washington, DC: U.S. Government Printing Office.

Wells, L. E., & Rankin, J. H. (1991). "Families and Delinquency: A Meta-Analysis of the Impact of Broken Homes." *Social Problems, 38*, 71-93.

West, W.G. (1984). *Young Offenders and the State: A Canadian Perspective on Delinquency*. Toronto: Butterworths.

Williams, F.P., & McShane, M.D. (1994). *Criminological Theory* (2nd ed.). Englewood Cliffs, NJ: Prentice Hall.

Williams, K., & Hawkins, R. (1986). "Perceptual Research on General Deterrence: A Critical Review." *Law and Society Review, 20*, 545-572.

Wilson, J.Q., & Herrnstein, R. (1985). *Crime and Human Nature: The Definitive Study of the Causes of Crime*. New York: Simon and Schuster.

Wilson, W.J. (1987). *The Truly Disadvantaged: The Inner City, The Underclass and Public Policy.* Chicago: University of Chicago Press.

Wilson, W.J. (1996). *When Work Disappears: The World of the New Urban Poor.* New York: Knopf.

Yllö, K.A. (1993). "Through a Feminist Lens: Gender, Power, and Violence." In R.J. Gelles & D.R. Loseke (eds.) *Current Controversies in Family Violence* (pp. 47-62). Newbury Park, CA: Sage.

Young, J. (1992). "Ten Points of Realism." In J. Young & R. Matthews (eds.) *Rethinking Criminology: The Realist Debate* (pp. 24-68). London: Sage.

Young, K., & Criag, L. (1997). "Beyond White Pride: Identity, Meaning and Contradiction in the Canadian Skinhead Subculture." *Canadian Review of Sociology and Anthropology, 34,* 175-207.

Subject Index

Name Index

About the Author

Shahid Alvi is Assistant Professor of Sociology in the Department of Sociology at the University of St. Thomas in St. Paul, Minnesota, where he teaches criminology, criminal justice policy, and introductory sociology. He received his bachelor's and master's degrees in Sociology from the University of Saskatchewan, and a Ph.D. in Sociology from Carleton University in Ottawa, Canada. He is a coauthor of *Contemporary Social Problems in North American Society* (Prentice Hall) and the forthcoming *Under Siege: Joblessness, Drugs, and Predatory Street Crimes in a Vulnerable Canadian Urban Community* (University of Toronto Press). Alvi has published on violence against women, youth crime, alcohol and drugs, work and family conflict, and concentrated urban disadvantage. His current research interests include critical criminology, workplace violence, crime and public housing issues, and violence against women.